Duncan Redford is Senior Research Fellow in Modern Naval History at the National Museum of the Royal Navy (NMRN). He previously held a Leverhulme Early Career Research Fellowship at the Centre for Maritime Historical Studies, University of Exeter, and is the author of *The Submarine: A Cultural History from the Great War to Nuclear Combat* (I.B.Tauris).

A History of the Royal Navy: The Age of Sail
Andrew Baines (ISBN: 978 1 78076 992 9)

A History of the Royal Navy: Air Power and British Naval Aviation
Ben Jones (ISBN: 978 1 78076 993 6)

A History of the Royal Navy: The American Revolutionary War
Martin Robson (ISBN: 978 1 78076 994 3)

A History of the Royal Navy: Empire and Imperialism
Daniel Owen Spence (ISBN: 978 1 78076 543 3)

A History of the Royal Navy: The Napoleonic Wars
Martin Robson (ISBN 978 1 78076 544 0)

A History of the Royal Navy: The Nuclear Age
Philip D. Grove (ISBN: 978 1 78076 995 0)

A History of the Royal Navy: The Royal Marines
Britt Zerbe (ISBN: 978 1 78076 765 9)

A History of the Royal Navy: The Seven Years' War
Martin Robson (ISBN: 978 1 78076 545 7)

A History of the Royal Navy: The Submarine
Duncan Redford (ISBN: 978 1 78076 546 4)

A History of the Royal Navy: The Victorian Age
Andrew Baines (ISBN: 978 1 78076 749 9)

A History of the Royal Navy: Women and the Royal Navy
Jo Stanley (ISBN: 978 1 78076 756 7)

A History of the Royal Navy: World War I
Mike Farquharson-Roberts (ISBN: 978 1 78076 838 0)

A History of the Royal Navy: World War II
Duncan Redford (ISBN: 978 1 78076 546 4)

The Royal Navy: A History Since 1900
Duncan Redford and Philip D. Grove (ISBN: 978 1 78076 782 6)

A HISTORY OF THE

ROYAL NAVY

World War II

Duncan Redford

in association with

Published in 2014 by
I.B.Tauris & Co. Ltd
London • New York
Reprinted 2016
www.ibtauris.com

References to websites were correct at the time of writing.

ISBN:	978 1 78076 546 4
eISBN:	978 0 85773 505 8
ePDF:	978 0 85772 345 1

A full CIP record for this book is available from the British Library
A full CIP record is available from the Library of Congress

Library of Congress Catalog Card Number: available

Typeset in Perpetua by A. & D. Worthington, Newmarket, Suffolk
Printed and bound by CPI Group (UK) Ltd, Croydon, CR0 4YY

Contents

Tables and Figures

Colour Plates

Series Foreword

The Royal Navy has for centuries played a vital if sometimes misunderstood or even at times unsung part in Britain's history. Often it has been the principal, sometimes the only, means of defending British interests around the world. In peacetime the Royal Navy carries out a multitude of tasks as part of government policy – showing the flag, or naval diplomacy as it is now often called. In wartime, as the senior service of Britain's armed forces, the Navy has taken the war to the enemy, by battle, by economic blockade or by attacking hostile territory from the sea. Adversaries have changed over the centuries. Old rivals have become today's alliance partners; the types of ship, the weapons within them and the technology – the 'how' of naval combat – have also changed. But fundamentally what the Navy does has not changed. It exists to serve Britain's government and its people, to protect them and their interests wherever they might be threatened in the world.

This series, through the numerous individual books within it, throws new light on almost every aspect of Britain's Royal Navy: its ships, its people, the technology, the wars and peacetime operations too, from the birth of the modern navy following the restoration of Charles II to the throne in the late seventeenth century to the war on terror in the early twenty-first century.

The series consists of three chronologically themed books covering the sailing navy from the 1660s until 1815, the Navy in the nineteenth century from the end of the Napoleonic Wars, and the Navy since 1900. These are complemented by a number of slightly shorter books which examine the Navy's part in particular wars, such as the Seven Years' War, the American Revolution, the Napoleonic Wars, World War I, World War II and the Cold War, or particular aspects of the service: the Navy and empire, the Women's Royal Naval Service, the Royal Marines, naval aviation and the submarine service. The books are standalone works in their own right, but when taken as a series present the most comprehensive and readable history of the Royal Navy.

Duncan Redford
National Museum of the Royal Navy

'The role in Britain's history of the Royal Navy is all too easily and too often overlooked; this series will go a long way to redressing the balance. Anyone with an interest in British history in general or the Royal Navy in particular will find this series an invaluable and enjoyable resource.'

Tim Benbow
Defence Studies Department,
King's College London at the
Defence Academy of the UK

Acknowledgements

Producing this book has been a considerable undertaking, with tight deadlines. However, writing a book is very much a team effort and more people are involved than just those named on the cover. My sincerest thanks go to the Leverhulme Trust, who between 2008 and 2011 funded my research and provided me with the support I needed to immerse myself in naval history in its widest sense; the fruits of their generosity underpin this book. I should also like to record my deep thanks to Matthew Sheldon, the Head of NMRN Portsmouth's curatorial team, and Dominic Tweddle, the NMRN's Director General, whose fantastic support made this book and the accompanying series on the history of the Royal Navy a possibility. I should also like to thank Nick Hewitt, who read the entire manuscript and made some very helpful suggestions, and the many other NMRN staff at all its various museums, especially Stephen Courtney, who assisted me by supplying many wonderful pictures from which to chose the illustrations for this book. Thanks also go to the NMRN's library staff, Allison, Heather and Maggie, for giving excellent support in obtaining obscure books and journals at very short notice; Jenny Wraight at the Naval Historical Branch was also a tower of strength. Gratitude is also due to the nameless archival staff in museums, archives and universities dotted around the UK who promptly supplied me with documents to further my research. Finally, and above all, I want to thank my partner Katie for her unswerving support and encouragement – this book could not have been written without her.

Duncan Redford

Introduction

In late August 1939, without any fanfare, the ships of the Royal Navy quietly slipped out of their base ports at Plymouth, Portsmouth and Chatham and on the 31st they were all at their war stations. That day a significant part of the Home Fleet – Britain's main naval strength around the British Isles – under Admiral Sir Charles Forbes, was at sea, patrolling the northern waters between the United Kingdom and Norway in order to block Germany's only effective access to the world's oceans. The move to the war stations was almost the final step in a long chain of events and decisions that had been set in motion much earlier in the year. When the last of the naval reserves were called up on 1 September, the Royal Navy was ready for war.

World War II was above all a maritime war. It was a war that the Allies fought from the sea. It was a war by which the Allies supported each other by sea. It was a war where the sea proved to be a barrier; sometimes for Britain, sometimes for the Allies, and sometimes for Britain's enemies – Germany, Italy and Japan. At other times the sea – and the ability to use the sea – was a powerful tool and a means of striking at an enemy who could not respond on a comparable level.

For Britain, who controlled the sea was of vital importance; it was the single factor on which rested the United Kingdom's entire war effort. Pre-war plans foresaw the Royal Navy exploiting Britain's geographical position to bottle up and isolate Germany from the world, allowing the slow, cold pressure of economic warfare to strangle the Nazi war machine. After the fall of France and the entry of Italy into the war, the sea was even more important to Britain. It was the only way of communicating with Britain's remaining allies – the British Empire and its Dominions – and benevolent neutrals such as the United States of America. It was also now the most effective barrier the British had against invasion. With the widening of the war in 1942 the sea was the only way Britain and her allies could effectively take the fight to the enemy by using it to maintain armies in North Africa and India as well as landing military forces in raids or eventually invasions to liberate occupied countries. The Royal Navy was therefore the service on which Britain depended for survival and for victory.

Yet the Royal Navy struggled to cope with the evolving war. Quite simply it was too small to face the combination of Germany and Italy, let alone the naval might of Japan. The fact that the Royal Navy from the mid-1930s onwards was too small to deal with the increasing number of hostile or potentially hostile states was one of the reasons behind the British government's dalliance with appeasement. By trying to appease potential aggressors the government was not just putting off the outbreak of war, or giving Britain time to rearm, but also increasing the chance that when war came Britain and the Royal Navy would be able to win it. But why was Britain forced into this abject policy of conceding to aggression? Why was the Royal Navy too small to fight those enemy states that some politicians claimed were lining up against Britain? Why was the Royal Navy unable to be the sword and shield that Britain needed in the late 1930s?

The simple answer is that Britain could not, or would not, spend enough money on its navy. But within such a simple, bland answer lays a complex series of issues. First there was the corrosive legacy of World War I. This war was – and remains – a trauma for the British who were used to fighting their wars at a distance, with relatively few casualties, negligible civilian involvement and, for preference, using proxies and allies to do the bulk of the bloody work. Instead, World War I exposed Britain, arguably for the first time, to the shock of war, a shock that continental countries had experienced many times over many years. Part of the reaction was the perception that the proliferation of armaments had caused World

War I. When in 1925 Viscount Grey, who as Foreign Secretary in 1914 had taken Britain into the Great War, commented 'that great armaments lead inevitably to war' he was endorsing a view that was already widespread. By the 1930s the British had completely embraced naval arms limitations and in 1930, as part of the London Naval Treaty, the Labour government overturned the Navy's advice and cut the number of British cruisers from 70 to 50. This created a gap between commitments and resources – one of many – that the Royal Navy found difficult to close when rearmament got under way or even once the British economy mobilized for war after the outbreak of fighting in 1939.[1]

The second issue was the attitude to the Navy and its role in British defence. For centuries the Royal Navy had been Britain's first and indeed only line of defence for the home islands and that maritime empire which was the envy of many of her rivals. While Britain was an island and while it had a navy it was safe. But by the late 1930s this was no longer seen as being true. Aircraft and the unproven theories of strategic bombing had captured the imagination of the public and politicians. For them, no matter how unrealistic their viewpoint, no matter how much it ignored technological realities and the limitations of airpower, Britain was no longer an island. The bomber was the interwar British bogeyman. In November 1932 Stanley Baldwin, the prime minister, gave voice to all these concerns declaring that 'the bomber will always get through'.[2]

Britain's obsession with the bomber adversely affected the rearmament plans for the Royal Navy. When in late 1933 Britain decided to start putting right the defence deficiencies that had accumulated since 1928 – the year Winston Churchill, then Chancellor of the Exchequer, made the ten-year rule self-repeating so that it would be reset after each year to year zero – the Defence Requirements Committee (DRC) overseeing the process decided that putting right the naval shortages was the key issue. The Cabinet, however, had other ideas. Neville Chamberlain, as the current Chancellor, led the opposition to the report. The DRC plans were too expensive; Britain could not afford to prepare for war against both Japan *and*

Germany – only Germany should be the issue. The plans were also
spending money on the wrong things. Chamberlain and his supporters wanted priority to be given to the RAF, *not* the Navy, in order to
build up a bomber force, despite the fact that strategic bombing was
almost totally unproven in theory and in practice. Airpower won
and the DRC was ordered to think again.[3]

Even when rearmament proper started in 1935–36, it proved
impossible to meet the requirements of all three services. The Navy
had by 1936 successfully argued for a fleet that could take on Japan
and Germany – the 'DRC Standard Fleet' of 15 battleships and
battlecruisers (although most would be new, replacing older Great
War veterans), eight aircraft carriers, 70 cruisers, 16 destroyer
flotillas and 55 submarines – to be achieved by 1942 at a cost of £88
million. By the late 1930s the argument was over a bigger fleet – the
'new standard fleet'. However, the pace of rearmament of all three
services, not just the Navy, was being challenged by the Treasury,
which thought that the spending on defence would damage the
economy on which rearmament, of course, rested.[4]

In many respects, the debate about the level of naval spending
was academic. There was not the economic capacity to build the
'new standard' fleet. As part of the 1922 Washington Naval Treaty
and the 1930 London Naval Treaty Britain had enjoyed a battleship-
building holiday – only two had been built during the early 1920s.
The battleship-building holiday since 1922, the generally low levels
of spending on the Navy after 1928 and the massive economic
contraction in the depression of the 1930s had ensured that Britain's
ability to quickly produce machines of the complexity of modern
warships had been drastically reduced. Skilled labour, steel and
other materials were also in short supply as money, materials and
workers were thrown at combating the airpower bogeyman by the
British.

Despite the problems and wrangles over rearmament, the materiel state of the Royal Navy in August 1939 was much better than
in 1932. Radar sets suitable for warships were close to production.
Older battleships like HMS *Warspite* had received massive recon-
structions, others more limited refits. Five new *King George V* class

battleships had been laid down and two larger *Lion* class battleships had been started. Seven new aircraft carriers were under construction or had entered service including five 'Armoured Fleet Carriers', with more planned and 19 new cruisers completed. The Fleet Air Arm, control of which had been split between the RAF and Royal Navy for much of the interwar period, had been handed back to the Admiralty in its entirety.

During the spring of 1939 the Navy's intelligence analysis organization – the Operational Intelligence Centre (OIC) – was slowly refined and expanded, and the Director of Naval Intelligence advised consular reporting officers and Lloyds agents what their preparations for war should look like. In July the naval reserves were called up and told to report for duty at the end of the month. In August, Germany and the USSR signed a non-aggression pact (and secretly agreed to carve up Poland between them when Germany fabricated an excuse to invade). The Navy responded by mobilizing the OIC and preparing for war. The Admiralty informed all commands what it thought the dispositions of the fleet would be if Japan intervened on the side of Germany following the outbreak of war. On 24 August the Admiralty, following discussions between the chiefs of staff, recognized that the situation with Germany was critical. Naval preparations for war would be complete by 1 September. That very morning Germany invaded Poland and the Admiralty sent a war warning signal to all commands. At 11:17 on 3 September the Admiralty signalled all its ships and units 'Total Germany'. The war at sea had begun.

CHAPTER 1

A 'Phoney' War?

After the message 'Total Germany' flashed around the world to
every ship and naval base in the Royal Navy signalling the start of the
war, it was followed a few hours later by another more prosaic one
– 'Winston is back'. For some, this message was one of inspiration.
An aggressive leader who had championed the need for rearmament
during his years in the wilderness, one who was always looking to
take the offensive against an enemy, and one who had previously
served as the political head of the Navy had been appointed to lead
them. For others, it was a warning. Winston Churchill, First Lord of
the Admiralty between 1911 and 1915, architect of the Dardanelles
fiasco, the man who had whipped the Admiralty into line and cut
its budget while he was chancellor of the Exchequer in the 1920s,
a man notorious for interfering in operational matters and who
would brook no opposition, had his hand back on the Navy's tiller.
Whichever view of the new First Lord of the Admiralty was correct,
it was certain that the Navy would find itself closing with the enemy
far sooner than its sister services.

There was not long to wait before the first blow fell.

At just after 19:30 on the very day war was declared, the first
'SSS' message was transmitted – a merchant ship had been torpedoed by a German U-boat: 'SSS SSS SSS SSS ATHENIA GFDM
torpedoed position 5644 1405.'[1]

The ship was the Donaldson liner SS *Athenia* (13,580 tons),
outbound for Montreal on her normal route, having left Glasgow
on 1 September and called at Liverpool and Belfast on the way with
1,418 passengers and crew aboard, including 311 Americans. At

the time the torpedo from *U-30* hit, the *Athenia* was at 54°42'N, 14°05'W – about 250 miles north-west of Ireland and about 60 miles south of that bleak, sheer, 70-foot-high volcanic plug jutting out of the Atlantic – Rockall.

Fortunately the Atlantic was calm that evening and the *Athenia* died slowly. Merchant vessels and British warships raced to the scene to help rescue survivors as the *Athenia* reluctantly settled by the stern. In all, only 112 lives were lost, but this included 28 neutral Americans, and at 10:40 on 4 September the *Athenia* finally slipped below the waves. International – especially neutral – opprobrium was heaped on Germany over its breach of the international rules covering the treatment of merchant vessels. The fact that *U-30* had misidentified the *Athenia* as an auxiliary merchant cruiser – a passenger liner that had been 'taken up from trade' and converted to a warship by adding a number of medium-calibre guns (normally 6-inch guns in the British case) – was rather irrelevant. When *U-30* got back from its patrol, its log was altered to expunge any mention of the *Athenia* or an attack on a large vessel on that day and the crew were sworn to secrecy. Certainly the Germans refused to admit an error, claiming that no U-boats were in the area and that the *Athenia* had been sunk by the British, possibly by a British mine. The Admiralty instituted convoys for merchant ships in the Atlantic on 7 September, starting a system that would continue to run until the end of the war.[2]

The early months of the war

That Germany appeared to have immediately embarked on an unrestricted campaign against British, Allied and possibly even neutral vessels was not unexpected. The Admiralty had considered this possibility in their war plans and dispositions months earlier.

The Admiralty had three broad priorities. First was the defence of the waters surrounding Britain and Northern Europe. Only through establishing control of these waters could a number of tasks be met: the protection of trade on which the import and export of war materials and food supplies depended, and indeed on which

Britain's ability to wage war rested; the protection of military deployments and their seaborne supply lines such as the move of the army's British Expeditionary Force and the RAF's Advanced Air Striking Force to France; and finally the imposition of an economic blockade on Germany to slowly starve it of the raw materials it needed to prosecute a war.

The second priority was the protection of supply lines through the Mediterranean, in particular the movement of oil tankers from the Persian Gulf to the United Kingdom. It was felt that if Italy followed Germany into the war, the Mediterranean might be closed to British shipping until such point that the Italian Navy was neutralized by the British Mediterranean Fleet and Italian airpower destroyed. If Italy did not enter the war, this problem was vastly reduced, but the possibility that German U-boats might move to the area could not be discounted.

The third priority was the Far East and facing any possible Japanese aggression. This third priority was the most problematic. While the British had vital interests in China and in Imperial possessions throughout the Far East, and it was acknowledged that Japan's outlook was undoubtedly hostile, there were not the ships to protect seaborne trade or military supplies lines and take on the Imperial Japanese Navy unless the Mediterranean was stripped bare.

These priorities exposed a problem that was to dog the Royal Navy throughout the war – not enough ships, men or resources to fight a widening global war against three strong or extremely strong navies. The new ships built under the rearmament plans during the late 1930s had vastly increased the fighting potential of the Navy, and the war-emergency construction plans approved from 1939 onwards would also add hugely to its strength, but it wasn't going to be enough to take on Germany, Italy and Japan at the same time. Fortunately, in September 1939 the Navy only had to worry about beating the Germans while keeping a close watch on Italy and a weather eye on Japanese movements. The Navy's focus was therefore very clear: Germany, wherever her warships and merchant vessels could be found, and the waters around the British Isles and the Atlantic in particular. But Germany, like Britain, had taken steps to ensure her navy was ready for war during August.

Intelligence estimates suggested that there were several U-boats stationed in British waters. With the attack on the *Athenia* and other merchant vessels, it seemed clear to the British that the Germans were embarking on an unrestricted submarine campaign from the outset of hostilities. As a result, the British introduced convoys more quickly and over a wider area than their pre-war plans had suggested. Rather than only introducing mercantile convoys for the shipping route that ran along Britain's east coast where the possibility of attack by U-boats, aircraft and even surface ships was highest, within days of the *Athenia* being sunk, ocean convoys for merchant ship heading in and out of the western approaches to the UK were started.

However, convoys on such a large scale would take time to set up, and there was still a large number of British, Allied and neutral ships that needed protection, as they were already at sea when war was declared. On any one day it was estimated that there could be up to 2,500 British flagged merchant vessels at sea. This mass of British shipping moving either towards or away from Britain were each given routes to follow by the Admiralty as a stop-gap measure, or were told to avoid the normal shipping lanes. Additionally, destroyers were formed into anti-submarine hunting groups to cover the move of British vessels though the south-western and north-western approaches to the United Kingdom. Churchill, as First Lord of the Admiralty, was very much in favour of this, likening these hunting groups to a fast cavalry division able to reinforce a dangerous area. Aircraft carriers – HMS *Ark Royal* and HMS *Courageous* – were also used to support these hunting groups and their air groups flew protective sweeps looking for signs of German U-boats.

Unfortunately, while the use of aircraft as an anti-submarine weapon was known to be very effective from the experiences gained during World War I, the use of hunting groups, although promising a great deal of activity, had been demonstrated to be a far less effective countermeasure – even if it was only to cover the mass of shipping that had been at sea on the outbreak of war and that was being shepherded to safety in British and Allied ports. More importantly, it also provided the Germans with an opportunity to strike at the very forces that were expending so much energy trying to find them – especially as the Royal Navy only had four large 'fleet' aircraft carriers available to it – *Ark Royal*, *Furious*, *Glorious* and *Courageous*.

On 14 September the *Ark Royal* was attacked by *U-39* west of the Hebrides but the German torpedoes were faulty and exploded early, alerting the carrier and its escort, which succeeded in sinking the U-boat. On the 17 September it was the turn of *U-29* to have a crack at another British aircraft carrier, HMS *Courageous*, which was patrolling south-west of Ireland. This time, however, the German torpedoes worked correctly and *U-29* scored two hits from the three torpedoes she fired. *Courageous* was fatally damaged and in less than 15 minutes had rolled on to her port side and sank with the loss of 518 of her crew. In a sad repetition of the naval losses at the very start of World War I, it was found that not all of *Courageous*'s company had been issued with lifejackets. It was enough to deter the Admiralty from risking any more major warships in ASW hunting groups.[3]

Fig. 1.1. HMS *Courageous* sinking after being torpedoed by *U-29*.

Then there was the *Royal Oak* disaster.

Just before 01:00 on 15 October, there was an apparently minor explosion right in the bows of HMS *Royal Oak* as she lay at her moorings in the Home Fleet's main base at Scapa Flow. The *Royal Oak*'s captain and officers who investigated the explosion concluded that it was an internal explosion – the paint store was the likely culprit. At 01:16, as the ship's company got down to the business of dealing with this small incident, three massive explosions tore open the old battleship's starboard side between A turret and X turret. The *Royal Oak* started listing to starboard with increasing rapidity until she capsized at around 01:29, killing 833 of her crew.

The cause of the explosions and sinking was now clear. The German *U-47* commanded by Günther Prien had managed to find a way through to the British fleet's anchorage between the islands that sheltered Scapa Flow, despite the passage she was using being nominally closed by blockships. Once there, Prien fired three torpedoes at what he thought were two battleships but actually were the seaplane carrier HMS *Pegasus* and the *Royal Oak*. Only one of this first salvo of torpedoes hit its mark – the strike in the bows of the *Royal Oak* which her crew thought was an internal explosion. Prien then calmly reloaded his torpedo tubes and fired a second salvo which destroyed the old battleship. *U-47* then slipped away in the darkness and escaped the way it had come. With Scapa Flow vulnerable to U-boat attack as well as having weak air defences, the Home Fleet decamped to Loch Ewe on the west coast of Scotland until the holes in Scapa Flow's defences were fixed.

Despite the loss of HMS *Courageous*, HMS *Royal Oak* and the unescorted shipping that did not have the protection of convoy, the German U-boats at the outbreak of the war and for months afterwards were singularly ineffective. The Germans sank only 215 merchant ships up to the end of December 1939 and U-boats only accounted for 103 of these. Conversely, 201 ocean trade convoys arrived or were dispatched from Britain, convoying 3,552 ships. Indeed, more Allied merchant ships were lost to normal 'marine' causes between 3 September and 31 December 1939 (shipwreck, collision, fire, foundered at sea, or just unknown) – a total of 108 –

than were sunk by German U-boats, while the Royal Navy managed to sink nine U-boats out of the total German force of at most 38. Nor did the first half of 1940 bring any serious U-boat attack on Britain's life-line across the Atlantic. So low were the numbers of U-boats available to the Germans that they could rarely keep more than eight at sea at any one time – but this would change in late 1940 and 1941.

The surface raider threat was in many ways harder to deal with than the small number of U-boats the Germans were able to put into combat against British merchant vessels. The Royal Navy's anti-surface raider policy was simple: patrol focal areas with cruisers, use ocean convoys with an anti-surface raider escort in especially dangerous waters and, most importantly, rely on routing shipping away from dangerous areas – evasive routing. If a surface raider was suspected or confirmed to be at sea, then hunting groups would be formed. The Admiralty was told that there was a pocket battleship operating in the South Atlantic when the survivors of the British SS *Clement*, sunk off the coast of Brazil, were landed on 1 October, but the first confirmation the British had that German surface raiders were at large in the North Atlantic was not until later that month, when the Norwegian tanker *Kongsdal* entered Kirkwall in the Orkneys with survivors from another Norwegian vessel, the *Lorentz W. Hansen*, and the news that she had been searched by a German pocket battleship who had transferred the survivors of the *Hansen* to her. Just before midnight, the Admiralty alerted all the British warships and merchant vessels that one, possibly two, pocket battleships were at sea in the Atlantic.[4]

The Admiralty's guess was correct. Two German warships, the *Admiral Graf Spee* and the *Deutschland*, had sailed from Germany and hidden themselves in the vast Atlantic. The *Graf Spee* had been ordered to wait off Pernambuco, while the *Deutschland* loitered off Greenland. In late September, once it seemed clear to the Germans that any hope of an early peace had fizzled out, both ships were ordered to start preying on ships – British and Allied merchant ships as well as any neutral vessels with cargoes bound for British ports.

The British reacted very promptly to the first indication

of a pocket battleship being at large in the South Atlantic and in conjunction with the French formed eight powerful hunting groups on 5 October which covered both the North and South Atlantic. Furthermore, the battleships *Resolution* and *Revenge*, together with two *E* class cruisers (HMS *Enterprise* and *Emerald*), were sent to Halifax to escort ocean convoys back to the UK – and they were soon joined by the battleship HMS *Warspite*, the aircraft carrier *Furious* and the battlecruiser *Repulse*, while the *Warspite*'s sister ship HMS *Malaya* and the aircraft carrier HMS *Glorious* were sent to cover the Indian Ocean. When confirmation was received that the *Deutschland* was also raiding shipping in the North Atlantic towards the end of October, one of the hunting groups, Force F, was disbanded before it could even start operations in order to provide reinforcements to strengthen the ocean escort of the homeward-bound North Atlantic convoys.

All in all, the hunt for the *Graf Spee* and the *Deutschland* and the protection of UK-bound convoys absorbed a massive number of British and French warships. Four British battleships out of 12, all the aircraft carriers, two battlecruisers out of three, eight heavy and four light cruisers from a total of 54 were involved, while the French navy contributed two battlecruisers, their solitary aircraft carrier and four cruisers to the search and the enhanced protection of convoys.

Fortunately for the Allies and the Royal Navy in particular, the *Deutschland* achieved very little during her raiding cruise in the North Atlantic. Ordered to concentrate on independently routed merchant ships, and avoid enemy warships, the *Deutschland* only sank two merchant ships and captured a third, before being ordered to return to Germany, arriving at Kiel on 15 November, having slipped past the hunting groups and Royal Navy's Home Fleet via the Denmark Strait. Despite the lack of material success the *Deutschland* helped stretch the Royal Navy and demonstrate, if demonstration were needed, how short of cruisers, fast battleships and aircraft carriers as well as effective land-based air support the Royal Navy actually was.[5]

Table 1.1. Surface raider hunting groups, October 1939.

Force	Composition	Area of operations
F	The heavy cruisers HMS *Berwick* and *York*	North America and the West Indies
G	The heavy cruisers HMS *Exeter* and *Cumberland* (later joined by the light cruisers HMS *Ajax* and *Achilles*)	South-east coast of America
H	The heavy cruisers HMS *Sussex* and *Shropshire*	Cape of Good Hope
I	The heavy cruisers HMS *Cornwall* and *Dorsetshire*, the aircraft carrier HMS *Eagle*	Ceylon
K	The battlecruiser HMS *Renown* and the aircraft carrier *Ark Royal*	Pernambuco
L	The French battlecruiser *Dunkerque*, the French aircraft carrier *Bearn* and three French light cruisers	Brest
M	Two French heavy cruisers	Dakar
N	The French battlecruiser *Strasbourg* and the British aircraft carrier *Hermes*	West Indies

Just to complicate the Royal Navy's picture of what the German surface ships intended to do while it was still unsure of where the pocket battleships were, in late November 1939 the German battlecruisers *Scharnhorst* and *Gneisenau* raided the British patrol lines between the United Kingdom, Iceland and Greenland. Their object was to destroy any patrolling cruisers they could surprise and cause the British to fear that they had broken out into the North Atlantic. On 23 November, they surprised the British merchant cruiser HMS *Rawalpindi* armed with eight 6-inch guns north of the Faroes. The *Rawalpindi*'s captain, E.C. Kennedy, sent two signals to the Commander in Chief Home Fleet at 15:45 GMT: 'One battle cruiser 280° four miles, course 135°, position 63°41'N, 11°55'W' and then 'Chased by battle cruiser. My position is 63°38'N, 11°55'W, course S.E. "*Deutschland*"' [6]

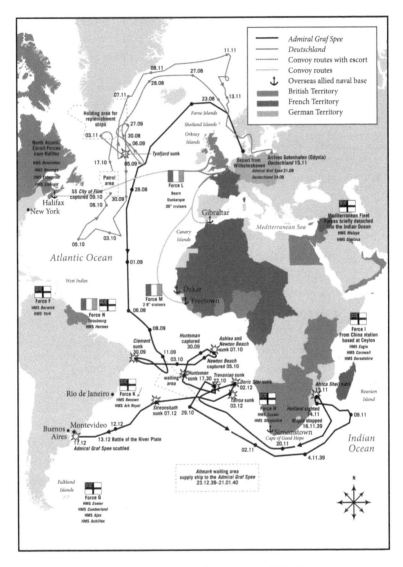

Fig. 1.2. The commerce-raiding cruises of the German
pocket battleships *Deutschland* and *Graf Spee*.

At 16:04 the *Scharnhorst* opened fire at a range of around 8,000 yards, and a couple of minutes later the *Rawalpindi* returned fire. It was no contest, but despite being hopelessly out-gunned and out-ranged by the faster German battlecruisers, the *Rawalpindi* fought in the gathering dusk until she was crippled and ablaze. After less than ten minutes the battle was over and the *Rawalpindi*'s survivors abandoned ship. The *Gneisenau* and *Scharnhorst* picked up survivors in the thickening darkness until they feared that they had sighted another British ship and broke off contact. As they left, the *Rawalpindi* was burning furiously until around 19:20 when, after two further explosions, all signs of the ship disappeared.[7]

The Germans were right to worry that they had been sighted by another warship. HMS *Newcastle*, the next ship north in the patrol line, had closed the *Rawalpindi*'s position and in the darkness sighted two darkened ships to the east at a range of 13,000 yards at just after 18:15, but a heavy rain squall swept across the ship reducing visibility to a few hundred yards, allowing the German ships to escape into the night. Having avoided the Home Fleet, which lacking an aircraft carrier and effective land-based reconnaissance support from the RAF, was somewhat limited in its ability to find the German ships, the *Gneisenau* and *Scharnhorst* returned to Wilhelmshaven on 27 November. The question now was whether the Royal Navy could catch the remaining German pocket battleship that was preying on British and Allied shipping or would it too escape destruction.[8]

The *Graf Spee*, unlike the *Deutschland*, was having a successful cruise in the South Atlantic and Indian Ocean. After the *Graf Spee* announced herself by sinking SS *Clement* she sank another three ships that were plying the Cape–Freetown route between 5 and 10 October, before claiming her fourth victim on the 22nd. The *Graf Spee* then passed round the Cape of Good Hope and entered the Indian Ocean with the clear intention of causing as much disruption and confusion over her movements as possible, sinking an oil tanker off the East African coast in the southern approaches to the Mozambique channel between East Africa and Madagascar on 15 November. Having drawn attention to her presence in the Indian Ocean, the *Graf Spee* turned round and headed back into the South

Atlantic and again preyed on the Cape–Freetown route, sinking her seventh and largest victim, the *Doric Star*, on 2 December and the *Tairoa* the next day. The German pocket battleship now moved west towards the South American coast, there to meet her supply ship the *Altmark* in order to refuel on 6 December. The next day the *Graf Spee* sank her ninth and final victim before heading south-west towards the River Plate estuary, an area dense with British and Allied shipping. As she approached the River Plate on 13 December she sighted smoke to the south-west and soon her lookouts reported a British cruiser and two destroyers. Faced with such a small British force the *Graf Spee*'s captain, Hans Langsdorff, decided to attack – only it wasn't a single British cruiser and two destroyers, it was the heavy cruiser HMS *Exeter* and two light cruisers, HMS *Ajax* and the New Zealand manned HMS *Achilles*.

Commodore Henry Harwood, the commander of the British force which was part of the net that had been spread to catch the *Graf Spee*, had suspected that the German pocket battleship would sooner or later turn up off the River Plate and had ordered his ships to concentrate there. Harwood's plan to deal with a pocket battleship was simple – attack at once, day or night. As soon as the *Graf Spee* was sighted, Harwood's ships charged into action: *Ajax* and *Achilles* as one division which aimed to work around to the north-west of the German ship, while the *Exeter* attacked from the south-west, splitting the pocket battleship's fire. Gone was the rigid battle-line of Jutland; instead came a flexible and aggressive attack that harried the *Graf Spee* as she attempted to flee.

No matter how effective Harwood's appreciation of the *Graf Spee*'s likely movements, or his tactics for dealing with a pocket battleship, it did not prevent the German gunnery being accurate. Battle was joined at 06:14. HMS *Exeter* was quickly hit by an 11-inch shell that knocked out B turret, swept the bridge with shell splinters and put her steering gear out of action, forcing her to be steered from the secondary position aft, with orders passed by a chain of messengers for a while. Having attempted to hit the *Graf Spee* with torpedoes, *Exeter* was again hit by 11-inch shells which disabled another gun turret, started fires and left her listing to starboard while her remaining turret continued to engage the enemy, until she was forced to limp to the south. It was not, however, a one-sided battle; the *Exeter* repeatedly hit the German ship, but her 8-inch shells were not heavy enough to inflict serious damage.

Meanwhile, *Ajax* and *Achilles* were also engaging the *Graf Spee*, which was firing at them with her 5.9-inch secondary armament as the range decreased from 19,000 yards to 13,000. Like the *Exeter*, the gunnery of *Ajax* and *Achilles* was accurate, but again their 6-inch shells were too light to inflict critical damage. In order to take the pressure off the *Exeter* the two light cruisers continued to close the range. At 07:25 *Ajax* was hit by an 11-inch shell that knocked out X and Y turrets aft, and 5.9-inch shells from the *Graf Spee*'s secondary armament hit her bridge. With the range down to 8,000 yards, at 07:38 and still unable to inflict fatal damage in return for the hits they had received, it looked like the British cruisers might be destroyed. Harwood decided that the only course open to him was to break off the action, shadow the pocket battleship during the day and then attack her under the cover of darkness. But as the British cruisers turned away in a smoke screen, so too did the *Graf Spee*. Soon it was clear that the German ship was heading to the safety of a neutral port – Montevideo in Uruguay, where international law would allow her to stay for 24 hours before having to leave or face internment.

With the *Graf Spee* in a neutral port it was vital for the British to keep her there while they rushed reinforcements to Harwood's battered force; the cruisers *Dorsetshire, Shropshire, Cumberland* and *Neptune*, the battlecruiser *Renown* and the aircraft carrier *Ark Royal* were converging on the Plate. Yet these ships would not be in position until 19 December. Ironically the Germans too wished to delay their departure, but the Uruguayan government were adamant that the *Graf Spee* would sail in 72 hours. With a mix of diplomacy and subterfuge the British succeeded in keeping the pocket battleship in harbour; they sailed merchant vessels at intervals and asked the Uruguayans to give each ship a day's start before allowing the *Graf Spee* to leave. The British also leaked false reports that *Renown* and *Ark Royal* were heading a massive naval concentration off the Plate, just

Fig. 1.3. HMS *Achilles* entering Auckland harbour in February 1940.
Damage to her bow can be clearly seen.

waiting to destroy the German ship, when in fact the British heavy
ships were still over 1,000 miles away. Convinced that an overwhelming force awaited him, when his 72 hours expired, Langsdorff
decided to scuttle his ship on the evening of 17 December rather
than be interned or give the British a victory. Three days later,
Langsdorff shot himself.

For the British it was a massive propaganda victory: a small force
of cruisers, aggressively led, had fought a bigger and more powerful ship to a standstill – the Royal Navy had clearly recovered its
Nelsonian verve and panache after the disappointments of World
War I. The reception HMS *Exeter* received when she returned to
her home port of Plymouth for badly needed repairs was raptur-
ous. More importantly, with the end, for the moment, of a German
surface raider at large, the Royal Navy could re-deploy its forces
and return to one of its main priorities – tightening the noose
around Germany, with its economic blockade interdicting neutral
and German ships attempting to get raw materials and goods to the
Fatherland.

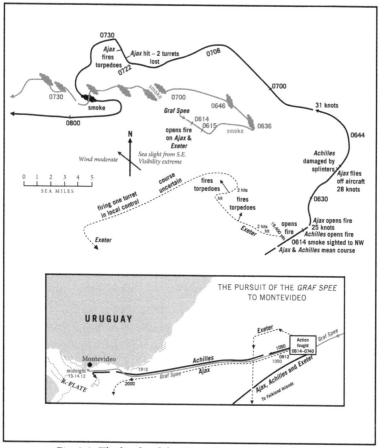

Fig. 1.4. The battle of the River Plate and the *Graf Spee*'s
retreat to a neutral port.

The blockade and the Norwegian campaign

From the moment war was declared the Navy was involved
in attempting to strangle Germany's trade by intercepting her
merchant ships as they tried to reach Germany or take refuge
in a neutral port; thus a blockade of Germany was immediately
declared. 'Examination Stations' to search for and seize contraband
from neutral ships were established at the Orkneys, the Downs (an
anchorage off Deal, Kent), Gibraltar, Malta, Haifa and Aden. To
search for German and neutral blockade runners, the Navy had a

number of cruisers which were vital for this task; fortunately, as part of the preparations for war, older cruisers had been brought forward from the reserve fleet and were ideal for the job. Within days of the war starting, steps were taken to seal off the northern approaches to Germany via the North Sea, Norwegian Sea and Atlantic, and to watch for any attempt by German warships and surface raiders to break out into the wider Atlantic. In the first six weeks of the war over 338,000 tons of contraband heading for Germany was seized. But the regular interception of neutral and even German steamers could not disguise the Navy's shortage of cruisers. Pre-war, it had been estimated that the Royal Navy needed 70 cruisers for trade defence, blockade work and for work within the main fleets such as the Home Fleet or Mediterranean Fleet. At the outbreak of the war the Navy had just 58.

To supplement these few cruisers, the Admiralty took up from trade a number of fast cargo liners to be converted into 'Armed Merchant Cruisers' (AMCs). These ships would be fitted with a number of medium-calibre guns (typically 6-inch guns in British service) and commissioned as warships flying the white ensign. But the conversion process took time and for the first few months of the war, the Royal Navy was reliant on its pre-war cruiser strength.

As the number of cruisers, AMCs and ocean boarding vessels increased, together with diplomatic pressure on neutrals, the blockade of Germany grew tighter. There was one area that the British did not exploit – unrestricted submarine warfare. The use of unrestricted submarine warfare had been examined during the late 1930s, but it had been decided not to pursue such a policy. As a result, British submarines would have to operate in accordance with prize rules – stopping a suspect vessel, searching it for contraband and, if any was found, placing a prize crew aboard to take the ship to a friendly port – a significant handicap for a submarine. The submariners persevered but could not safely operate in such a manner close to enemy-held territory where the risk of air attack and encountering anti-submarine forces was high. In December 1939 news leaked out that a British submarine had sighted the German liner *Bremen* but had not attacked her as it had not been possible to act in accordance with the prize rules. The *Daily Mirror* gave a highly sarcastic report of the event and ran a large cartoon that suggested Nelson would have disapproved strongly of the inaction of his successors. The *Daily Express* ran the headline 'The question all Britain is asking today WHY DIDN'T WE SINK THE BREMEN?' The Royal Navy was condemned as being 'too chivalrous'. The *Daily Mail* took a more ambivalent view but still thought many would ask 'Are we at war or not?' The press opinion, however, was divided over the *Bremen* affair; the 'quality' broadsheets took a different, more sophisticated view to that of the tabloids as the tabloids were advocating the very behaviour they were condemning.[9]

There were, however, areas where the seaborne blockade could not be enforced. Resources could reach Germany from the USSR or from those neutrals that, like Russia, shared a land border with Germany or occupied Poland. One of the more significant areas, at least as far as the Allies were concerned, was the perceived German reliance on imported iron ore from Scandinavia. In the summer the trade was seaborne, but in winter the main Swedish port associated with the trade was blocked by sea ice and instead the ore was moved by train to the Norwegian port of Narvik where it was loaded into ships. Thanks to the nature of Norway's North Sea coast these ore carriers could effectively travel down to the entrance to the Baltic while remaining in neutral Norway's territorial waters and thus immune, thanks to the British observance of international law, from being stopped by the Royal Navy.

Soon after his appointment as First Lord of the Admiralty, Churchill was agitating for action against the Scandinavia–Germany iron ore trade. His first suggestion was to lay a number of declared minefields in Norwegian territorial waters in order to force the German and neutral ships out into international waters where they could be searched and seized. The Cabinet, however, demurred. At the same time as the mining issue was raised, Churchill also dreamed up Operation *Catherine* as a means of getting a naval surface force into the Baltic to sever Germany's iron ore trade with Scandinavia while at the same time using the presence of a powerful naval force to help pressure Sweden and Norway to join the war on the Allied

side. Based on the idea of a small fleet of ships centred on four heavily modified old *R* class battleships with thousands of tons of extra
armour to withstand the expected savage German air attacks on the
British ships as they forced their way into the Baltic, the scheme
was at best hare-brained. Yet Churchill persisted with the idea in
the face of determined opposition from the Naval Staff who were
frankly horrified by the suggestion. With only 12 battleships to play
with, a plan that wrote off up to four of them was lunacy.

With Operation *Catherine* eventually scotched by the Navy's
opposition, attention returned to mining Norwegian territorial
waters, and from November 1939 increasing attention was paid
to this plan. It was thought that if the mining took place, it might
provoke a reaction from Germany which could threaten Norway.
Therefore, in concert with the mining proposal, a plan to land
British army units in order to forestall a German occupation of
Norway was developed – Plan R4 – but any intervention in Norway
could not be ready before the end of March 1940. After much
order and counter-order during March 1940, as evidence mounted
that Germany too was considering some sort of operation against
Norway, the Allies decided to lay several minefields in Norwegian
waters on 5 April while holding a contingency force ready to land
and seize Trondheim and Bergen. The mining operation – Operation
Wilfred – was then postponed to 8 April. Late on 7 April it seemed
that a major German force was at sea that was either preparing to
invade Norway or raid the North Atlantic convoy routes. The Naval
Staff favoured the first option, whereas the First Sea Lord, Admiral
Sir Dudley Pound, his deputy, Rear Admiral Tom Phillips, and
Churchill thought the latter scenario more likely. Unsurprisingly
Churchill's view won out and Admiral Forbes and his Home Fleet
were told to assume that the Germans were looking to break out
into the Atlantic. Thus the combined operation Plan R4 to forestall
a German invasion by landing army units in Norway was abandoned,
and the cruisers that were to have carried the landing force diverted
to trying to stop a breakout into the Atlantic. Operation *Wilfred*
went ahead and a minefield was laid on 8 April. On 9 April the true
German intentions were revealed: they were not planning a raid on

the convoy routes; instead they invaded Norway and Denmark. The initiative had passed to the Germans, and the Allies were trying to catch up.

First blood at sea went to the Germans. The British destroyer HMS *Glowworm* had lost contact with the *Wilfred* force while trying to find a crewman who had been lost overboard. At around 08:00 on 8 April the *Glowworm* encountered some destroyers and then the German heavy cruiser *Hipper* which avoided the torpedoes the British ship fired at her. Heavily damaged by German shells, the *Glowworm* laid a smokescreen and as the *Hipper* followed, managed to ram the German cruiser, causing serious damage. A few minutes later, the *Glowworm*, fatally damaged and listing, blew up and sank. When the circumstances of her loss were discovered the *Glowworm*'s captain was awarded the first Victoria Cross of World War II – in part on the recommendation of the captain of the *Hipper*, who wrote to the Admiralty via the Red Cross, expressing his admiration for the bravery shown by the *Glowworm* in attacking a vastly superior force.

Events moved extremely quickly on 9 April. Denmark was overrun in a matter of hours and German forces were landed at Oslo, Bergen, Trondheim, Narvik, Kristiansand and Arendal. The betrayed Norwegians fought back as well as they could, sinking the heavy cruiser *Blucher* in Olsofijord and damaging the light cruiser *Konigsberg*. Early on 9 April the battlecruiser HMS *Renown*, part of the Operation *Wilfred* force, managed to establish contact with the German battlecruisers *Scharnhorst* and *Gneisenau*, and a brief running battle in dreadful conditions ensued as the Germans turned and ran, escaping in heavy rain which drastically limited visibility. HMS *Truant*, a *T* class submarine, sank the light cruiser *Karlsruhe* off Kristiansand. The Home Fleet, closing the Norwegian coast off Bergen, was heavily attacked by German aircraft and although only the destroyer HMS *Gurhka* was sunk, some ships had fired off significant amounts of anti-aircraft ammunition. Admiral Forbes realized that any attempt to interdict German movements and supply ships off southern Norway must be left to submarines. The same day, at a War Cabinet, the First Sea Lord asked for 'the approval of the

War Cabinet to draft instructions to our submarine commanders to attack without warning all shipping in the Skagerrak' – in short carry out unrestricted submarine warfare – assuring the politicians that 'Normal mercantile shipping had been held up' and 'that any other ships were ships of war or transports'. It was also resolved that Allied land forces should be dispatched as soon as possible to Norway to support the Norwegians in their fight and attempt to throw out the Germans, but any such forces could not leave until 12 April at the earliest.[10]

On 10 April, the Royal Navy went over to the attack. Fleet Air Arm Skua dive-bombers flying from the Orkneys sank the already damaged *Konigsberg* in Bergen harbour, while a force of five destroyers under Captain Bernard Warburton-Lee penetrated the Vestfjord and attacked Narvik, sinking two German destroyers, crippling three more, sinking six merchant ships plus an ammunition ship, and damaging two more destroyers as the British force fought its way clear, losing HMS *Hardy*, and HMS *Hunter*, while *Hotspur* was disabled. The force commander, Warburton-Lee, was killed and later awarded the second Victoria Cross of the war. That night, the British submarine *Spearfish* managed to put a torpedo into the pocket battleship *Lutzow* (formerly the *Deutschland*), wrecking her stern. For a time it looked like she might sink, but the Germans managed to get her back to Kiel where it took a year to repair the damage.

British attempts to regain the initiative continued on 12 April; the Home Fleet's solitary aircraft carrier, HMS *Furious*, carried out an air strike on Narvik and Admiral William Whitworth, the commander of Operation *Wilfred* and nominally the commander of the Home Fleet's battlecruiser squadron, was readying another attack on Narvik by surface ships, only this time in overwhelming force using the newly arrived battleship HMS *Warspite*. The second battle of Narvik (13 April) saw eight German destroyers and a U-boat sunk and left the German garrison isolated. But there were no land forces available to the British to follow up this success, nor did the Royal Navy have any specialist amphibious assault shipping available or even mechanized landing craft. When the British army arrived, it would have to get ashore via gangways

Fig. 1.5. HMS *Warspite* and her escorting destroyers during the second battle of Narvik. *Warspite* can be seen on the left with two destroyers ahead of her and closer to the camera.

from transports or by small boats rowed by sailors.

The first landings took place around Namsos, Aandalsnes, Aalesund and Molde in central Norway on 17 April and on the night of 19/20 April French forces joined the British at Namsos. The battle to hold the Namsos and central Norway region was futile, hampered by deep snow that the British troops had not been trained to cope with and by heavy air attack from the outset. On 28 April the decision was taken to abandon central Norway and concentrate on Narvik; the evacuation started on 30 April and was completed by 2 May. Allied hopes for achieving something in Norway would now rely on their ability to take and hold Narvik.

Attempts had been made to get army units into Narvik to capitalize on the Navy's successes there at the second battle of Narvik. Only after 19 April did troops start landing in the region around Narvik in order to slowly prepare for an attack on the strong German defences there. Allied forces gradually built up in the area and the next major event was not until 12/13 May when a new landing was made about seven miles away from Narvik, thanks to the Royal Navy's almost total command of the sea approaches to the area. But air supremacy was another matter. While the aircraft carriers did what they could, the Fleet Air Arm was outnumbered from the start and furthermore the RAF was unable to match the German effort. Before the main land attack on Narvik the British and French governments informed their commanders on 24/25 May of the decision to evacuate their forces from Norway. However, the Narvik attack was to go ahead, as the operation of the port and destruction of German forces would make the evacuation easier. The attack went in on 28 May and was a success; by the end of the month the Germans had been pushed back and were in a desperate situation. On 7 June the evacuation of the Allied forces from Narvik started and was completed on the 8th. Unfortunately, after the evacuation the aircraft carrier *Glorious* and her two escorting destroyers were surprised by the *Scharnhorst* and *Gneisenau* on 8 June and all three British ships were sunk with exceptionally heavy loss of life. For reasons that have never been satisfactorily explained, *Glorious* had not had any of her aircraft airborne since she parted company with the Home Fleet covering the Narvik evacuation; the result was ignorance of the approach of the German ships until it was too late to escape them – a terrible end to a sorry campaign, which showed that much still needed to be learned about amphibious operations, especially their command and control. Indeed the only silver lining was that while the Royal Navy had lost ships trying to prevent the German invasion, then land the army and finally evacuate it, the German navy's loses were far worse.

The defeat of France and the Low Countries

On 10 May an event occurred that would in a matter of weeks – and to British shock and German surprise – overturn the strategic situation: Germany invaded France and the Low Countries. Britain's 'phoney war' – not that it had ever existed for the Royal Navy – was over. It was the deteriorating situation in France that caused the Allied decision to abandon Norway. The Allied armies' plans swung into action, with the British Expeditionary Force (BEF) and the French 7th and 1st Armies advancing into Belgium to hold the line of the River Dyle and then south-east along the Wavre–Namur line to link up with the French 9th Army in the Ardennes. By the 12 May the BEF and the French 1st and 7th Armies were in position and awaiting the advancing Germans. However, the main German thrust was not through the Low Counties, in a repeat of the 1914 Schlieffen Plan that the Allies were anticipating. Instead the main weight of 'Plan Yellow' was against the Allied centre though terrain that the Allies thought was impassable to tanks and modern mechanized forces – in the Ardennes. Before the Germans managed to crush all Dutch resistance, the Royal Navy had succeeded in getting back to Britain the Dutch gold reserves, 26 merchant ships, 50 tugs and 600 barges and dredgers, as well as carrying out limited demolitions of Dutch ports such as Flushing and IJmuiden, while attempts were made to block Zeebrugge and wreck Antwerp's port facilities.[11]

By 12 May the German forces advancing through the Ardennes had reached the line of the River Meuse, along the west bank of which was the main French line of resistance. But by 12 May, the Germans had managed to throw three bridgeheads across the Meuse at Sedan, near the boundary between the French 9th and 2nd Armies, at Monthermé, near the centre of the French 9th Army's line, and at Dinant, to the north near where the French 9th and 1st Armies met. The French forces at Sedan collapsed as the Germans attacked, and panic spread along the French line. With the French line breaking between Sedan and Dinant, the seven German armoured divisions and two motorized divisions surged out of their bridgeheads on the Meuse and struck out towards the Channel coast. On 19 May the German Panzer forces cut the supply lines to the BEF at Abbeville and on 20 May German tanks were overlooking the Channel, cutting off the BEF, together with the French 1st, 7th and elements of the 9th Armies and the Belgian army, in a massive pocket with its base on the coast. As the Germans charged across France, it was realized on 19 May by the British that an evacuation of the northern Allied armies, including the BEF, might be needed.

The naval preparations to evacuate the BEF and French forces started to take shape after 20 May, under the command of Vice

Admiral Bertram Ramsey, the flag officer responsible for the Navy's Dover Command, with steps being taken to call up small boats and suitable merchant vessels and arrange crews for them, including Dutch coasters – *schuyts* or *skoots* – that had escaped from Holland as it was being overrun by the Germans. As these preparations took place the Navy also had to transfer its effort to keep the BEF supplied from Le Havre to ports such as Boulogne, Calais and, above all, Dunkirk.

Events were moving quickly and by 23 May both Boulogne and Calais were cut off. A naval demolition party under Lt Cdr Welman, protected by two platoons of Royal Marines and four platoons of sailors commanded by Major Holford, Royal Marines, and the destroyer HMS *Vimy*, was dispatched to Boulogne to destroy the port. By mid-afternoon the Germans had occupied most of the town, but naval reinforcements arrived throughout the afternoon and night until nine destroyers were off the port. Just before 6 o'clock in the evening, the Navy received orders to evacuate all the surviving British forces in Boulogne.

As the demolition party was preparing to fire the last of its charges at around 20:00, German tanks and guns appeared on the hills overlooking the harbour, just as the first three destroyers were coming in to evacuate the demolition teams and surviving British forces. A violent fight started between the German guns and the British destroyers, which used every weapon they had while embarking the British soldiers. By around 22:30 about 3,000 troops had been brought off, with the destroyer *Windsor* entering the harbour once darkness fell to take off another 600 soldiers. The news that the *Windsor* had got in and out without meeting any resistance led HMS *Vimiera* to be ordered to go in; she found over 1,000 troops waiting on the jetty and managed to evacuate all but about 200, who had to be left behind. In all just short of 4,400 personnel were brought off from Boulogne.

At Calais, however, it was a different story. Throughout 24 and 25 May the Navy kept the cut-off garrison at Calais supplied and even landed army reinforcements. Late on 25 May a mixed force of warships, fishing vessels and small craft were readied to evacuate the army from Calais, but the army decided that the garrison must stay in place and fight until overrun by the Germans. As communications with the garrison had failed, the Navy was sent to ensure that the order was delivered by hand. On 27 May Calais fell.

With evacuation the only way of saving the BEF and French forces trapped against Dunkirk, Operation *Dynamo* was launched at 19:00 on 26 May. It was hoped that 45,000 men from the BEF could be lifted in two days. In the end *Dynamo* lasted nine days, and over 338,000 British, French and Belgian soldiers were eventually evacuated.

The image of Dunkirk is of the 'little ships' lifting the BEF off the beaches. It is indeed a powerful image for the British. In 2010 – the 70th anniversary of the evacuation – the emphasis was still very much on the little ships and their civilian crews plucking troops from sandy beaches. The Dunkirk myth makes much of civilian involvement, of the amateur, of the improvisation, of the success – if not victory – of Britain alone but undefeated, of Britain as an island nation, fending off the onrushing Nazi war machine.[12]

As with so much of the imagery associated with Britain in 1940, Churchill's speeches made a significant contribution to the way Dunkirk was understood and assimilated. But as he pointed out: 'We must be very careful not to assign to this deliverance the attributes of a victory. Wars are not won by evacuations.'[13]

The reality of Operation *Dynamo* (26 May to 4 June) was that it was made possible by four factors: relatively calm weather; British and French warships – mainly destroyers; personnel ships which in peacetime had been cross-channel passenger ferries or similar that had been taken up from trade and were manned by their peacetime merchant navy crews; and the use of the moles and breakwaters in Dunkirk's outer harbour to facilitate embarkation of large number of troops. In all 338,226 men (366,162 if troops evacuated before the start of the operation are included), British and French, were brought back to Britain during the operation. Only on one day – 30 May – were more troops evacuated from the beaches than from the outer harbour. The 'little ships', particularly the civilian-manned pleasure craft that have 'become one of the most famous features of the operation', only arrived in strength between 30 and 31 May, but by late on 31 May La Panne beach had been abandoned, and as the perimeter contracted over the remaining days of the operation the ability to lift troops off of the beaches reduced; worse still, the surf increased, making use of the remaining beaches even more difficult.[14]

Table 1.2. Operation *Dynamo*. Total of British and French troops rescued on each day of the operation.

Date	Evacuated from the harbour	Evacuated from the beaches	Total
27 May			7,669 (nearly all from the harbour)
28 May	11,874	5,930	17,804
29 May	33,558	13,752	47,310
30 May	24,311	29,512	53,823
31 May	45,072	22,942	68,014
1 June	47,081	17,348	64,429
2 June	19,561	6,695	26,256
3 June	24,876	1,870	26,746
4 June	25,553	622	26,175

The Royal Navy suffered greatly as it saved the British army from destruction. Six destroyers and five minesweepers were sunk; the anti-aircraft cruiser HMS *Calcutta*, 19 destroyers and seven minesweepers were damaged. However, the end of Operation *Dynamo* did not mean the end of the evacuation of British forces from France – there were still 140,000 troops, mostly from support units, scattered along the army's former lines of communication south of the River Somme and the German-held areas, together with large numbers of British civilians. It was decided that the remaining British land forces would be evacuated from Cherbourg, St Malo, Brest, St Nazaire and La Pallice. The final evacuation of the remaining BEF units was given the code name Operation *Aerial*. It lasted 11 days, from 15 to 25 June. Over 60,000 were rescued from

Fig. 1.6. Destroyers alongside in Dover harbour with rescued
BEF troops waiting to disembark.

Cherbourg and St Malo by 18 June, but large amounts of stores and
equipment had to be left behind – just as had happened at Dunkirk.
The evacuation from Brest started on 16 June and finished the next
day after 31,500 soldiers and civilians had been brought off with no
interference from the Luftwaffe. The 16th of June also saw the start
of the evacuation from St Nazaire, which resulted in 42,000 troops
and civilians being brought home, but it also saw one of the single
heaviest naval losses of the war – the sinking of the liner *Lancastria*
which was crammed with thousands of troops and civilians; the
number killed is unknown but is estimated to be at least 3,000. By
18 June the evacuation from St Nazaire was over and the focus of
operations moved ever further south as the military situation deteriorated and then France capitulated, with 4,000 being rescued from
La Pallice and another 10,000 at least from the Gironde region.

Nor did the end of Operation *Dynamo* mean the end of the
Royal Navy's other activities to deny port facilities to the advancing

Germans. On 10 June three blockships were successfully used to block Dieppe harbour. And then there was the emotive decision over whether to fight for the Channel Islands or evacuate them. Churchill wanted the islands to be defended, but it was impractical to do so, and on 17 June the evacuation of 3,500 service personnel started, followed by 22,000 civilians on the 19th. On 23 June the islands were abandoned and on the 30th the Germans landed on the Channel Islands and 'for the first time since 1066 a portion of the British Isles passed under the yoke of a foreign invader'.[15]

What happened next would in no small part be down to the Royal Navy and Britain's seapower.

CHAPTER 2

The War Against the U-boat
The Battle of the Atlantic from the Fall of
France to America Entering the War

Until the summer of 1940, the Battle of the Atlantic had been a campaign that the British were containing, if not actively winning. Yes, there had been some significant setbacks, such as the loss of one of the Royal Navy's four large aircraft carriers, HMS *Courageous*, in September 1939 as it carried out offensive anti-submarine patrols in the south-western approaches. There had, on the other hand, been some significant achievements too: losses had been relatively light and British anti-submarine forces had managed to inflict significant damage to the rather small German U-boat arm. The German anti-shipping campaign was constrained by both its lack of numbers and the geographical barriers which prevented the U-boats having easy access to the Atlantic. The fall first of Norway and then France fundamentally changed Britain's maritime war at sea.

The Germans were not slow to exploit their strategic windfall. Karl Dönitz, the commander of the German U-boat force, and his staff had watched the progress of the German Panzers across France and prepared a special train carrying key personnel, spares and weapons which was dispatched to the French Biscay ports the day after the armistice was signed; the first U-boat – *U-30* – entered Lorient for refuelling and rearming on 7 July.[1]

Before the fall of France and Norway, Britain had been astride German links to the wider world; now Germany had effectively bypassed the British stranglehold on the North Sea and English Channel and had gained bases on the Biscay coast of France and in

35

Norway that would allow U-boats and surface ships almost unfet-
tered access to British convoy routes in the Atlantic and beyond,
while aircraft could range across the south-western and north-
western approaches to the United Kingdom. No longer would
German U-boats and surface ships face a long and dangerous jour-
ney up the North Sea and round the northern coast of Scotland
to try to gain access to the Atlantic through one of the channels
between Britain, the Shetland and Faroe Islands, Iceland and
Greenland. Worried about a possible German descent on the Faroes
and Iceland, Britain seized both these Danish territories in April
and May 1940 respectively. At the same time, due to the proximity
of German forces in France, the British had to shift convoy routes
away from the south-western approaches and ports along the English
Channel to the north-western approaches to the United Kingdom
centred on the ports of Glasgow and Liverpool. By February 1941
the move – and the new command system – was complete. But with
so many destroyers and escort vessels held in readiness to defeat
a German seaborne invasion, convoys of merchant vessels were
weakly defended and easy targets for German U-boats and aircraft.
The German U-boat crews called the period from July to October
1940 their 'Happy Time'.

This was the time of the U-boat 'ace'. Commanding officers such
as Günther Prien, Joachim Schepke and Otto Kretschmer racked up
considerable tonnages of ships sunk by picking off individual vessels
after convoys had dispersed, ships which had straggled from a convoy,
or ships which were proceeding alone 'independently routed'. Their
preferred tactic was running in on the surface at night into the heart
of a convoy and torpedoing the ships around them. By the start of the
autumn the U-boats had sufficient strength to try 'pack attacks' –
massed attacks on convoys by night and on the surface, making them
almost impossible to locate with sonar. Once a U-boat, or better still
a roaming reconnaissance aircraft, had come across a convoy it would
signal the position, course and speed to U-boat headquarters, which
would then assemble a line of submarines across the convoy's path
and overwhelm the escorts. The peacetime training of the German
U-boat arm by Dönitz was reaping dividends.

The battle for the convoys

The first pack attack fell on SC 2, a UK-bound convoy from Canada, during the second week of September. Two ships out of 53 were sunk as the convoy and U-boats battled a Force 8 Atlantic storm in a running fight that lasted four days and nights. To lose only two ships out of 53 might be seen as a minor event, but it was a harbinger of what was to come. The next major pack operation was against another UK-bound slow convoy, SC 7. This had sailed from Sydney, Nova Scotia, on 5 October with 34 merchant ships, some of which (notably four Great Lakes steamers that were designed to operate on inland waterways, not the open ocean) really had no business being out in the Atlantic. The weather – a factor that should never be forgotten in the grinding attrition of the Atlantic campaign – struck first. On 9 October a southerly gale blew up and the four Great Lakes steamers fell out of the convoy, while the rest of the ships were badly disorganized. Three of the steamers were sunk by U-boats, whose commanders always enjoyed scooping up stragglers away from a convoy's escorts. Fortunately the U-boats initially failed to find SC 7, especially as for the first 11 days that the convoy was at sea there was only one escort, the pre-war sloop *Scarborough*. However, on 16 October, the *Scarborough* was reinforced by another *Hastings* class sloop, HMS *Fowey*, and a *Flower* class corvette, HMS *Bluebell*. The additions to SC 7's escort arrived not a moment too soon. That night, *U-48* sighted the convoy and reported its course, speed and position to U-boat headquarters, which then ordered six more submarines to join the attack.

The first attack on the main body of SC 7 fell on 17 October. *U-48* torpedoed two ships: the tanker *Languedoc* (9,512 gross registered tons) with a cargo of 13,700 tons of fuel oil, and the *Scoresby* (3,843 GRT) carrying pit props. *U-48* was unsuccessfully hunted by the *Scarborough* – in fact the *Scarborough* never rejoined the escort – while the corvette *Bluebell* picked up survivors – all of which meant that the convoy's escort was reduced. Having avoided the escorts, *U-48* was forced to dive by a long-range Sunderland flying boat of the RAF's Coastal Command and lost contact with the convoy.

Meanwhile, another sloop, HMS *Leith*, and a second corvette, HMS *Heartsease*, joined the escort, but two sloops and two corvettes with a third sloop off somewhere on a fruitless U-boat hunt was still not much of an escort.

U-38 was the next to find and attack the convoy, although it only managed to damage one freighter in two attacks and sank nothing. However, the location reports sent by *U-38* allowed Dönitz to finalize the positions for his pack attack, and on 18 October *U-46*, *U-99* and *U-101* managed to sink six members of SC 7, while the next night *U-99*, *U-100*, *U-101* and *U-123* sank another seven. The total losses were 15 freighters sunk out of 34. Nor was this the end of the pack attacks for October. HX 79 was savaged by *U-36*, *U-46*, *U-47*, *U-48* and *U-100* on the 19th and 20th, sinking ten out of 49 merchant vessels – a huge loss, but not quite as bad as the mauling SC 7 had received.[2]

The problems facing the Royal Navy's escort forces at this stage of the Battle of the Atlantic were acute. Yes, they had sonar, but that was only effective against dived U-boats and the U-boats were avoiding submerged attacks, preferring to attack on the surface at night where the only method of locating them was the human eye. The retention of convoy escorts on anti-invasion duties until November 1940 also had a serious impact on the cohesiveness of a convoy's defence; there were simply not enough escorts to form permanent escort groups that could learn to work together and appreciate each ship's strengths and weaknesses. The shortage of ships also meant that it was hard to develop any coherent navy-wide response to U-boat tactics, as ships could not be spared from their duties for training. At the same, it was only possible to provide an anti-submarine escort to convoys out as far as at first 17° west and, by October, 19° west, when the escort would leave to meet an incoming convoy.[3]

The politicians also made things harder for the Royal Navy in November 1940 by mistakenly insisting that dropping the upper speed limit for inclusion in a convoy from 15 to 13 knots would help the situation. It may be, given the appearance of a demand from Churchill to look at reducing the upper speed limit to 12 knots in

March 1941, that some prime-ministerial nagging was behind this Cabinet error in judgement. The impact is clear in the statistics. Ships whose speeds were between 13 and 15 knots were liberated from convoy under this Cabinet instruction and made to sail independently. Their losses on the Halifax and Freetown routes were 7.3 per cent between 15 November 1940 and 5 May 1941; the loss rate in convoys was just 2.8 per cent. Yet the loss rate for independently routed ships whose speed was greater than 15 knots was similar to that of the convoys.[4]

Nor was the support given by the RAF of much help during 1940. The Coastal Command of the RAF, which was responsible for providing land-based air support to the Navy, was very much the 'Cinderella' command of the RAF. Coastal Command lacked modern aircraft or an effective anti-submarine weapon, as the anti-submarine bombs used by the RAF proved to be more dangerous to the aircraft dropping them than to a U-boat, and the crews had no bomb sight with which to aim them. Above all, Coastal Command lacked long-range aircraft to provide support as the battle slowly moved further out into the Atlantic and away from British coastal waters. Part of the problem faced by Coastal Command was that specialist aircraft ordered before the war, such as the Lerwick flying boat or the Botha reconnaissance and torpedo bomber, proved to be utterly useless. This forced Coastal Command to use aircraft purchased from the USA, which took time to be delivered, or converted bombers – and the RAF and Air Ministry begrudged every bomber aircraft allocated to it, as these could be used to carry out a strategic bombing campaign against Germany.[5]

With the release of vessels from anti-invasion duties, the escort shortage eased. Permanent escort groups were formed. More ships also entered service, including *Hunt* class destroyers and more *Flower* class corvettes. These ships had been ordered for a very different war, one where Britain and France had Germany bottled up in the North Sea and the U-boat attack on British and Allied trade was confined to coastal waters, rather like the experience of World War I. This was exactly how the Navy had foreseen the new war at sea developing in its pre-war planning, until the collapse of

France and the German army's conquest of Europe from the Arctic Circle to the Spanish border.

The *Hunt* class escort destroyers were not a success on the North Atlantic convoy routes. Originally the *Hunts* had been designed very much with the North Sea and coastal waters in mind. They had a heavy anti-aircraft armament, ideal for convoy work in the North Sea, Channel and south-western approaches, and a limited endurance. It was found that the early ships – the Type 1s – were much less stable than originally intended and as a result the armament had to be reduced. Also they were not good sea-boats and had difficulty coping with the Atlantic weather, while their limited endurance was unhelpful in the new anti-submarine war that was moving further out into the Atlantic.[6]

The other pre-war design, ordered in numbers during July and August 1939 as well as during the war, was the *Flower* class corvette. Based on a design for a deep-ocean whale catcher, these were again envisaged as being used for convoy work in coastal waters. Fortunately they turned out to be excellent sea-boats, able to withstand far more of a pounding than perhaps their reservist and 'Hostilities Only' crews could. The habitability was improved in later ships too, with a better and longer forecastle reducing much of the wetness experienced by the crew. The ships were quick and cheap to build, the fastest average building time being less than six and a half months (the worst shipyard took on average 19 months). But the *Flowers* were cursed with a slow speed – just 16 knots, slower than the speed of a German Type VII U-boat on the surface.[7]

A different solution to the escort problem came about as a result of Churchill's personal intervention. Churchill negotiated the transfer of 50 mothballed World War I vintage destroyers from the US Navy to the Royal Navy in exchange for basing rights in Bermuda and the Caribbean. The deal was struck on 1 September 1940, but so much work was needed to bring these *Town* class destroyers – named after towns that could be found in both the UK and America – up to modern sonar and radar standards that only nine were in service with the Royal Navy by the end of 1940. Nor were the ships very popular; their large turning circle made them less

Fig. 2.1. The *Flower* class corvette HMS *Campanula*. One of the ship's officers
was the writer Nicholas Monsarrat, who wrote a fictional account of
life in a *Flower* class corvette in his bestselling book *The Cruel Sea*.

agile in hunting U-boats and they certainly were not good sea-boats
with their flush decks and narrow hulls which rolled viciously. But
they were hulls and also the first indication that attitudes in the USA
were softening from a strict attitude of neutrality.

The Royal Navy's expanded escort force was manned mostly
by reservists rather than pre-war regulars. Initially the reservists
were professional merchant seamen who were also members of the
longstanding Royal Naval Reserve, supported by the Royal Navy's
volunteer reserves – nicknamed the 'Wavy Navy', thanks to the
officers' distinctive rank markings – whose experience of the sea
tended to derive from the halcyon days of peacetime yachting. The
reservists were soon joined by wartime volunteers and conscripts –
a 'Hostilities Only' Navy.

The 'Wavy Navy' was far from homogenous, having two main
groups: those who had been volunteer reservists in the pre-war
period, the Royal Naval Volunteer Reserve (RNVR); or those
who had put themselves down for the Royal Naval Volunteer

Supplementary Reserve (RNV(S)R). The RNVR consisted of both officers and ratings who had carried out training during evenings and weekends at one of eight 'Divisions'. All but one of its vessels were old warships converted for the purpose at major port cities around the UK, like HMS *Caroline*, a World War I C class cruiser, home of the Ulster RNVR division in Belfast. The RNVR was actually quite small, numbering only 809 officers and 5,371 ratings in 1939. The RNV(S)R had been formed in 1936 and was aimed at amateur yachtsmen who had some experience in seamanship and navigation. It was hoped that on the outbreak of war this cadre could be trained as officers to meet the manpower demands of a rapidly expanding navy. The other group were those who were 'Hostilities Only' – conscripts called up to fight for the duration of the war or those who had volunteered after its outbreak and, in order to avoid manning problems at the end of the war, would not automatically serve in the demobilized, peacetime Navy. These ratings were given a crash course in seamanship and the Navy – about 12 weeks in all – in converted coastal holiday camps before being sent to one of three drafting centres at the naval barracks in Portsmouth, Devonport and Chatham as ordinary seamen. From the barracks these sailors – some volunteers and others reluctant conscripts – were sent to seagoing warships or assigned to other duties.[8]

One problem facing the Navy and its force of reservists and conscripts was quite simply that there was a limited supply of potential officers of the right age and with the right experience and training to warrant a direct entry as an officer in the RNVR or RNV(S)R. The solution was to end direct officer recruiting for volunteer reserve commissions. Instead, all 'temporary' commissions would be given to ratings, be they RNVR or 'Hostilities Only', who had served a minimum period at sea and been recommended for officer training by their commanding officers. As soon as December 1940 the first escort commanded and officered entirely by volunteer reservists or 'temporary' officers was commissioned – HMS *Verbena*.[9]

Despite the increasing numbers of ships coming into service and the resources being poured into training new personnel and devel-

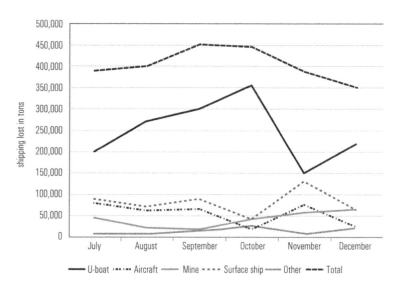

Fig. 2.2. British and Allied merchant vessel losses by cause,
July–December 1940.

oping new equipment, the merchant ship losses in this period (July–October) to U-boats, mines and surface attack were immense: 1,675,748 tons of shipping sunk by all types of enemy action, 216 ships sunk by U-boats, another 69 by aircraft, 50 by mines, but only 50 by surface ships – and most of these were sunk by disguised merchant raiders, not normal warships. Of the 216 ships sunk by U-boats in this four-month period, 47 had straggled from a convoy and 96 had been sailed independently. But ominously, compared to the opening nine months of the war when only 48 British, Allied and neutral merchant vessels had been sunk while in convoy (25 by U-boats), 127 had been sunk while in convoy in just three months. Seventy-three of these had been destroyed by U-boats, and there had been fewer than ten submarines at sea at any one time. However, the British had only managed to sink six U-boats in exchange. Fortunately for the British, the low numbers of U-boats and the very poor weather gave some respite in November and December. The U-boat situation was therefore not too bad for the Royal Navy at the end of 1940. Moreover, invasion had been deterred, releasing more ships for escort work; merchant shipping losses, although worrying, had fallen in November and December; and more escort vessels were entering service, as were new surface search radars. The question was: what would happen in 1941?[10]

The first crisis in the battle

The lull in activity in the Atlantic, especially by the U-boats, soon came to an end. In January 1941 U-boats sank 21 ships of 126,782 tons; in February they sank another 39 ships of 196,783 tons; and in March 41 ships of 243,020 tons. The trend remained high until July. The U-boats were joined by German warships. In February the *Hipper*, which had sailed from Brest, as well as the *Scharnhorst* and the *Gneisenau*, were at large in the Atlantic. Fortunately for the Royal Navy, only the *Hipper* did any appreciable damage, sinking seven ships from convoy SLS 64. After replenishing in Brest in late February, the *Hipper* put to sea again in mid-March in order to return to Germany via the Denmark Strait, while by the end of March the *Scharnhorst* and the *Gneisenau* had reached Brest after their disappointing foray. The *Hipper* never again operated against convoys in the Atlantic. At the same time, enemy aircraft suddenly became a significant problem for the British, sinking 88 merchant ships between the start of January and the end of March 1941. German aircraft sank few ships in convoy, the eight merchant ships sunk by aircraft from convoy OB 290 which had sailed from Liverpool with 41 vessels in late February 1941 being one of the exceptions rather than the rule. Rather, just like the U-boats during their earlier 'Happy Time' throughout much of 1940, the German Luftwaffe's long-range Focke-Wulf Condors and Heinkel 111 bombers did their best work attacking independently routed merchant vessels. The situation in the western approaches to the UK appeared to be deteriorating rapidly.

Indeed, in the opening months of 1941 the combination of air and U-boat attacks inflicted very heavy losses. In January 1941 U-boats sank 126,782 tons (21 ships) of British, Allied or neutral shipping; German aircraft sank a further 78,597 tons (20 ships). The next month U-boats sank 196,783 tons while aircraft contributed another 89,305 tons – all told 66 merchant ships were sunk. The impact of German submarines and aircraft individually was severe, but when combined in cooperative operations they had the potential to make the Atlantic impassable.

The greatest problem the U-boats had was locating convoys. The British made great use of evasive routing to move convoys around areas of U-boats who had advertised their position through radio transmissions to their French bases. The U-boat also had a relatively small search area and could only move relatively slowly while on the surface and was even slower – virtually stationary – while submerged. An aircraft could search thousands of square miles of the Atlantic in the same time that a U-boat, or even a pack strung out in a search line, could search hundreds of square miles. If the Germans were smart they would use their aircraft not just to attack shipping as it approached Britain, but also to guide U-boats to the convoys: the German Focke-Wulf Condor aircraft with its long range, great enough to fly from Brittany in France, out into the Atlantic west of Ireland and then to a base in occupied Norway, was perfect for such a role. On 22 February a Condor accurately reported the position of convoy OB 288 to *U-73*, which led to a pack attack by seven U-boats, sinking ten ships of 52,875 tons.[11]

Fortunately for the Allies and the Royal Navy especially, the level of cooperation between the German navy and air force was poor. The location of and assault on OB 288, for example, was the exception rather than the rule. The cause of the poor German cooperation between naval and air forces was found at the highest levels: Hermann Goering, the commander of the Luftwaffe, objected to any cooperation with the navy and did everything he could to make sure that German maritime airpower was starved of resources and support.

**Table 2.1. British, Allied and neutral merchant ships sunk by
German U-boats and aircraft, January–June 1941.**[12]

Month	Tonnage sunk by U-boats	Ships sunk by U-boats	Tonnage sunk by aircraft	Ships sunk by aircraft	Total tonnage sunk	Total ships sunk
Jan	126,792	21	78,597	20	205,389	41
Feb	196,783	39	89,305	27	286,088	66
Mar	243,020	41	113,314	41	356,334	82
Apr	249,375	43	323,454	116	572,829	159
May	310,143	58	146,302	65	456,445	123
Jun	94,209	61	61,414	25	155,623	86
Total	1,220,322	263	750,972	294	1,971,294	557

Despite these German divisions, Allied merchant ship losses
continued to mount as March got under way, and the deteriorating
situation led Winston Churchill to make his 'Battle of the Atlantic'
declaration on 6 March 1941, in which he called for an all-out offensive effort against:

> the U-boat and the Focke-Wulf wherever and whenever we can.
> The U-boat at sea must be hunted, the U-Boat in the building yard
> or in dock must be bombed. The Focke-Wulf and other bombers
> employed against our shipping must be attacked in the air and in
> their nests.[13]

It was thought that four months of effort would see Britain through
the crisis in the Atlantic. Indeed much of the first half of the declaration emphasized the need for the air defence of shipping, including the development of catapult-equipped ships to provide fighter
defence beyond the range of the RAF's land-based aircraft. The
directive also emphasized the need for the non-military aspects of
the battle to get full attention and be effectively coordinated: the
repair of shipping, port congestion and degaussing – the neutrali-
zation of a ship's magnetic field – were all singled out. To ensure
that ministries, including the Admiralty and Air, as well as the
civil departments, gave the battle the appropriate consideration,

Churchill established a 'Battle of the Atlantic Committee'.[14]

One of the most important aspects of the Battle of the Atlantic directive was its emphasis on the use of airpower. However, the impact on the RAF's Bomber Command was quickly emasculated by the Air Staff. In his covering letter to the resulting bombing policy document, Air Chief Marshall Sir Wilfred Freeman (vice chief of the Air Staff) pointed out to the commander in chief of Bomber Command that 'this does not entirely exclude attacks on the primary objectives; given in the directive issued in A. M. letter dated 15th January' (before the Battle of the Atlantic Directive was issued). Furthermore, Freeman went on to say that 'Priority of selection should be given to those [targets] in Germany which lie in congested areas where the greatest moral[e] effect is likely to result.' That Bomber Command obeyed these instructions is borne out by the weight of attack delivered against targets in Germany as compared to those in occupied France. During 1941 the submarine base at Lorient sustained just five attacks (with a total of 200 tons of high explosive (HE) dropped); St Nazaire suffered six attacks (with 120 tons of HE dropped), while Brest attracted 1,092 tons of bombs. In contrast, attacks on German naval bases and construction yards at Hamburg, Kiel, Bremen, Emden, Wilhelmshaven, Stettin, Rostock and Warenemunde involved the dropping of 6,751 tons of HE and 592,100 incendiary bombs.[15]

In among the increasing losses inflicted on Britain's merchant shipping by U-boats and aircraft in March, there was perhaps a small success for the British to savour. Convoy OB 293 was sighted by Günther Prien in *U-47* on the evening of 6 March, four days after it sailed from Liverpool. His signals brought several U-boats to the scene, including Otto Kretschmer's *U-99*. The convoy's escort was distinctly spirited and well drilled; *U-70* was heavily depth-charged by the corvettes HMS *Camellia* and *Arbutus* and forced to the surface where the crew abandoned their submarine just before it sank. On 7 March the pack returned to the attack, and this time *U-47* was spotted by the World War I destroyer *Wolverine*. After a five-hour hunt, *U-47* was again sighted on the surface as she attempted to escape. The *Wolverine* attempted to ram the U-boat, but *U-47* crash dived.

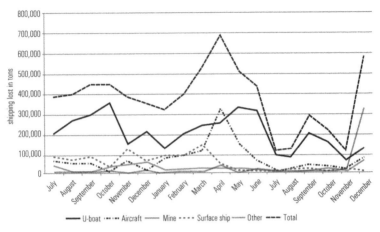

Fig. 2.3. British and Allied merchant vessel losses by cause,
July 1940–December 1941.

Following her down was a pattern of depth-charges. After the
explosions, all that remained of Prien's U-boat were small amounts
of floating debris, clearly from a submarine that had been torn apart
by the hammer blows of a highly accurate depth-charge attack.
Worse was to follow for the Germans a few days later. Another pack
attack, this time on HX 112, saw HMS *Vanoc* sink *U-100*, which was
commanded by another U-boat ace, Joachim Schepke, while in the
same battle Kretschmer and some of his crew were lucky enough
to be picked up after *U-99* was blown to the surface in a sinking
condition after a depth-charge attack. In less than two weeks four
U-boats had been sunk with the loss of two U-boat aces, while a
third ace was a prisoner.[16]

The British, however, failed to see this as much to celebrate.
Britain's position worsened in April, despite the high-level political attention afforded to the battle. The UK-bound convoy SC 26
was mauled by a pack attack at the start of that month, losing six
merchant ships sunk and two damaged, while HX 121 was found at
the end of the month by a U-boat pack and lost four ships. But again,
the bulk of the losses were from independently routed ships that did
not have the protection of convoy: 59 in April plus four more that
had straggled from a convoy.

Where the British did have cause to celebrate was the passing in the USA on 11 March 1941 of the Lend-Lease Act, which included the transfer of ten US Coastguard cutters to the Royal Navy. More importantly as far as the Battle of the Atlantic was concerned, the USA decided to take a more assertive role and introduced more overtly aggressive anti-U-boat measures as part of its well-established neutrality patrols. At the same time, the area claimed by the USA in order to protect its neutrality was moved hundreds of miles closer to Britain, from 60°W to 26°W, and US Navy warships and aircraft helped escort convoys within this zone as well as carrying out patrols to deter U-boats. It also meant that the USN and German U-boats were increasingly likely to come to blows, and soon they did. On 4 September 1941 USS *Greer* was attacked by *U-652* and replied with depth-charges, on 4 October the USS *Kearney* was torpedoed but remained afloat, and on 31 October the USS *Reuben James* was sunk by a U-boat. But this was not enough to bring the USA into the war. The Royal Navy and Royal Canadian Navy would have to continue their lonely fight in the Atlantic for a while.

Stemming the tide?

Yet for all the British concerns in the late spring of 1941, the Germans' ability to inflict losses on British, Allied and neutral merchant ships decreased significantly from the levels of March and April. Only the minor panic caused by the brief appearance of the German battleship *Bismarck* (see Chapter 5) near the convoy routes threatened the by now well-established routine of the convoy cycle. The weight of German air attacks steadily diminished, although heavy attacks were made in May on Liverpool and Glasgow docks. At sea the British had improvised with great rapidity rocket-assisted catapults for converted naval auxiliaries, to create 'Fighter Catapult Ships'. The first of these ships, HMS *Pegasus*, was a converted seaplane carrier, which entered service in December 1940 and carried three Fairey Fulmar fighters. In April 1941 *Pegasus* was joined by another three ships, each armed with a single fighter, either a Fulmar or a Hurricane. These four ships were deployed to support convoys on the Gibraltar convoy route, where the threat of air attack was often greatest, and on 3 August 1941 a German Condor was surprised 400 miles from the Iberian peninsula and shot down by a Hurricane launched by HMS *Maplin* and flown by a Royal Naval Volunteer Reserve pilot, Lt R. Everett. The rocket-assisted catapults were also fitted to merchant ships from April 1941 onwards; these 'Catapult Aircraft Merchantmen' or 'CAM ships' carried one fighter and remained cargo vessels. However, the main reason for the decline in German air raids on British port cities (and elsewhere) and the collapse of merchant ship losses due to aircraft attacks at sea was the German invasion of first the Balkans and then Russia.

There were other improvements in the air war against the U-boats. Most importantly, Coastal Command was placed under the operational control of the Admiralty in February 1941, but it remained under the administrative control of the RAF and the Air Ministry. This meant that the Admiralty could tell Coastal Command what it wanted it to do, but the RAF's Air Staff and the Air Ministry would decide what resources Coastal Command got in order to carry out its role, a clear area for future arguments between the maritime airpower supporters and the strategic bombing lobby. In practice the operational control of Coastal Command was exercised at a relatively low level. The commanders in chief of naval commands gave their requirements directly to their opposite numbers at the relevant Coastal Command group HQs. As far as the U-boat war was concerned the most important of these was the Western Approaches Command which had just moved to a new HQ in Liverpool; working for it would now be Coastal Command 15 Group. Indeed Western Approaches Command and 15 Group shared the same headquarters building. There were also extremely close links between Coastal Command and the Operational Intelligence Centre's (OIC) submarine tracking room.

This was not, however, the first time that the relationship between the Royal Navy, Coastal Command and the wider RAF had surfaced. The control of land-based maritime airpower had been an unresolved issue since the 1937 decision to hand back the

Fig. 2.4. HMS *Springbank*, a fighter catapult ship. A Fairey
Fulmar fighter can be seen amidships.

Fleet Air Arm — ship-borne maritime airpower — to the Royal
Navy. In November 1940 the Minster of Aircraft Production,
Lord Beaverbrook, during a meeting about improving Coastal
Command's resources suggested that Coastal Command should be
handed over in its entirety to the Royal Navy. The rather surprised
meeting discussed the issue briefly before getting back to the matter
in hand, but not before Churchill decided to form a sub-committee
to consider Beaverbrook's suggestion. The sub-committee rejected
the proposal to give Coastal Command to the Royal Navy, but it
did agree a new short- and medium-term expansion programme
between the Navy and the RAF which included more long-range
fighters, Wellington aircraft fitted with ASV II radar and new
torpedo-bombers. But the real difference for Coastal Command
was in the imminent arrival of 57 new Catalina flying boats from
the USA. These long-range aircraft would represent a significant
increase in Coastal Command's strength and capability.[17]

The reasons for the reduction in Allied and neutral shipping losses to U-boats, however, were more complex, involving the operational use of intelligence, better tactics and better technology. The result was that while February, March, April and May had seen 18, 28, 13 and 29 per cent of all convoys arriving or departing from the UK losing one or more merchant ship, June, July, August and September saw 3, 13, 8 and 17 per cent of convoys losing one of more merchant ship.

The problems the U-boats were facing in the summer of 1941 become even clearer when the tonnage sunk per U-boat day at sea is considered, as this removes fluctuations in U-boat numbers as a possible cause for changes in the amount of shipping sunk. In May 1941, 39 U-boats spent 708 days on war patrols in the Atlantic and UK home waters, sinking 325,492 tons of Allied and neutral merchant ships. By July, 49 U-boats that spent 770 days at sea in the month only managed to sink 94,209 tons of merchant shipping. August was even better for the Royal Navy: 63 U-boats spending 1,154 days on war patrols only managed to sink 80,310 tons. The British were winning.

This sudden reduction in the ability of U-boats to find and sink merchant ships was baffling for the Germans, as it seemed that suddenly there were no convoys. The British were routing convoys around the positions of the U-boats even as they moved further out into the Atlantic to find their prey. How the British had suddenly found a way to emasculate the U-boats became one of the most precious secrets of the entire war. It was signals intelligence: the British had broken the 'unbreakable' German radio codes.

Table 2.2. Numbers of convoys arriving/departing the UK
and the percentage losing one or more merchant ships.

Month	Number of convoys arriving or departing the UK	Number losing one or more merchant ship	Percentage
June 1940	60	6	10
July 1940	49	8	17
August 1940	48	10	21
September 1940	48	10	21
October 1940	48	6	13
November 1940	35	7	20
December 1940	36	3	8
January 1941	34	3	9
February 1941	33	6	18
March 1941	29	8	28
April 1941	31	4	13
May 1941	31	9	29
June 1941	31	1	3
July 1941	30	4	13
August 1941	40	3	8
September 1941	30	5	17
October 1941	33	5	15
November 1941	29	4	14
December 1941	28	2	7

The intelligence war in the Atlantic 1940–41

The Admiralty and its Naval Intelligence Division under Rear
Admiral John Godfrey was fully alive to the ways in which intelligence could be used both strategically and tactically. Indeed it was
the desire to use intelligence in time to influence daily events that
caused the Admiralty to set up the Operational Intelligence Centre

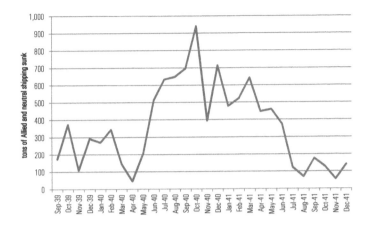

Fig. 2.5. Tons of Allied and neutral merchant shipping sunk per
U-boat per day at sea, 3 September 1939–31 December 1941.

(OIC) which in time became the hub of the Admiralty's control
of the entire naval war. For the Battle of the Atlantic there was a
special focus. The Submarine Tracking Room had the job of trying
to keep tabs on where all the German U-boats were – even while
they were at sea. To do this it needed information, and happily the
German wolf-pack tactics involved a lot of signalling between the
U-boats at sea and Dönitz's headquarters. Unhappily for the British,
the Germans used the 'Enigma' machine to encrypt their messages.
Its use of three different rotors from a choice of up to eight, each
with 26 different settings, which could be placed in any order and
set to start at any of the 26 positions for each rotor, together with
a reflector that sent an electrical pulse each time its typewriter
keyboard was pressed back through the rotors a second time, and
finally a plug board that connected up to ten pairs of letters, meant
that there were billions of possible combinations. Enigma was thus
believed by the Germans to be unbreakable and OIC had a mass of
messages it could not read.

Yet reading (or not) enemy signals traffic was not the only aspect
of signals intelligence that the British were deploying with increasing effectiveness during 1941. Direction finding allowed the OIC
and its subordinate Submarine Tracking Room to work out where

U-boats were, even if they did not know what the U-boats were getting so vocal about. As more direction-finding stations were set up in Iceland and Canada to complement those already established in Britain, so the location information every time a U-boat sent a radio message got better and better, to the point where the Admiralty could try to manoeuvre convoys around the U-boats' patrol lines. Steps were also taken to develop an HF/DF set small enough to be carried on a destroyer so that the escort commander would be able to have an immediate indication if a U-boat was in contact with the convoy and attempting to 'home' the rest of the pack for an attack. By late 1940 the OIC's Submarine Tracking Room was starting to propose changes to convoys' routes in order to miss identified U-boat patrol lines. This evasive routing was a key weapon in the British efforts to frustrate the U-boats.

Nor was this the only signals intelligence tool in use by the OIC by 1941. Traffic analysis could tell much about the unit making the signal without the need to read the message. Short messages might be weather reports or sighting reports, longer ones could mean the U-boat was getting ready to return to base. The man who had to make sense of all this in 1941 was a barrister who had volunteered to help the Navy in any capacity at the outbreak of the war, Rodger Winn. Winn rapidly developed an uncanny ability to understand U-boat operations and predict what Dönitz might do next. But the holy grail of the intelligence war was breaking the codes and ciphers which protected radio messages, to see what the messages actually said.[18]

The German naval Enigma machine had more combinations than its Luftwaffe and Wehrmacht equivalent – a choice of any three from eight rotors, rather than any three from five. This made the naval Enigma settings much harder to calculate, and without each day's settings being known, the messages sent in that 24-hour period could not be read. The Navy needed to capture an Enigma machine with its current settings to give it a toehold in breaking the codes. Commando raids, the capture of German weather ships lurking in the more remote areas of the North Atlantic and, above all, the capture of *U-110* in May 1941 meant that the British code-breaking

centre at Bletchley Park (or 'BP'), using electro-mechanical comput-
ers – 'Bombes' – had been able intermittently to read the German
naval Enigma *Heimisch* (or home waters) code, which was used by
U-boats in the Atlantic, from February to June 1941 but just not
fast enough to be used operationally. Finally, the *Heimisch* code was
effectively mastered from July onwards and was read concurrently
with the Germans – a massive achievement and one that lasted to
the end of the war with at most a 72-hour delay.[19] The Allies called
these Enigma decrypts 'Ultra', for 'Ultra Secret'.

The importance of direction finding and the ability to read
U-boat signals in safeguarding convoys can be seen in the fighting
that occurred around HX 133 in June 1941. This battle saw for the
first time U-boats operating on the far side of the Atlantic – end-to-
end anti-submarine escort for convoys had come not a moment too
soon. When HX 133 sailed from Halifax on 16 June the U-boats had
not had any contact with convoys since 22 May and the Germans
had positioned a patrol line of U-boats running south-east from the
Grand Banks of Newfoundland. HX 133 avoided this line and the
Germans moved their submarines north-east to a line south of Cape
Farewell in Greenland, a move which the OIC did not seem to have
noticed. It was in this new line that *U-203*, some 430 miles south of
Cape Farewell, sighted HX 133 on 23 June.[20]

U-203's sighting report and the response from BdU – the
commander of the German U-boat arm, Karl Dönitz – was intercepted and decrypted by the British, who warned HX 133 that they
had been sighted. As a result the convoy made a substantial altera-
tion of course after dark – just as the U-boats started their attack,
which sank the Norwegian merchant ship *Solôy*. By the early hours
of 24 June several U-boats had joined *U-203* in shadowing the
convoy. During the late afternoon of 24 June, having been silent
for 20 hours, *U-203* informed BdU that HX 133 was heading south-
west – when it should have been heading north-east towards the
UK. BdU did not believe *U-203*, which remained adamant that the
convoy was heading south-west, and BdU then came to the conclusion that there were two convoys close together. BdU was right. A
west-bound British convoy, OB 336, had blundered into the same

area as HX 133 and the crowd of U-boats. That OB 336 was in the same area was due to extreme misfortune. The Western Approaches Command, no doubt on the advice of the OIC, had signalled OB 336 with a new route to keep it well clear of the situation developing around HX 133. But the signaller on the convoy commodore's ship was inexperienced and was unable to decode the message; rather than ask for help he left it on one side for 27 hours, allowing OB 336 to blunder onwards towards the concentration of U-boats. Fortunately only *U-203* attacked OB 336 and only managed to sink one merchant ship before the convoy executed a series of emergency turns and lost contact with its pursuers.[21]

The Admiralty was well aware of the weakness of the escort for HX 133 and the seriousness of the situation by 24 June. Thanks to the OIC, the Admiralty knew that there were no more German U-boats operating to the west of the group around HX 133, so it could strip escorts from west-bound convoys west of HX 133 and send them to reinforce the defences of HX 133. In all, five escorts – four from OB 335 – were directed to reinforce the existing screen of HX 133, and by early evening on 24 June the strengthened screen was in place which carried out spirited attacks in the darkness on U-boats, both real and imagined. The result, however, was that the U-boats could not get into position for a successful attack and on the morning of 26 June HX 133 came within range of Sunderland flying boats which operated over the convoy during the day, forcing U-boats to dive and lose contact with the convoy. Only after the Sunderlands had departed with the onset of darkness were the U-boats able to attack, sinking two merchant ships, but the next day another nine warships arrived to reinforce the escort. Finally, by 28 June it seemed that only *U-651* was in contact with the convoys. She attacked at periscope depth during the day, sinking one merchant ship, but after the attack she was running on the surface when sighted by one of the escorts. After a short chase and gun battle *U-651* was sunk. The battle around HX 133 was over; the Germans had sunk six merchant ships in six days of operations and had lost two U-boats in exchange, but the British use of intelligence had allowed the Royal Navy to shift escorts to the convoy that was in danger in sufficient time to make a difference to the battle.[22]

However, signals intelligence and 'Ultra' generally, or the reading of the German home waters Enigma, was not a panacea for all the problems the Royal Navy faced. Not only was the German Enigma code for foreign waters never broken, but Ultra material had to be very carefully handled to ensure that the Germans received no indication that their code had been cracked. Sometimes this meant that the British had to ignore information because to act on it would give away the 'Ultra secret' – that they were reading German messages. The strategic as well as tactical information was too precious to risk for a quick minor victory. Nor did Ultra prevent several convoys in the autumn and early winter of 1941, such as SC 42, being savaged by well-handled U-boat packs when the action was moving faster than Bletchley Park could decrypt the signals. Yet over all, the advantage seemed to be with the British and Canadian navies, not the U-boats.

Improvements in anti-submarine warfare

At the same time as the British were exploiting their increasing understanding of U-boat signals, the Navy was also making great strides in its tactical approach to the battle. One of the decisions was extremely simple – the increase of the speed that merchant ships had to be capable of if they were to be sent as independently routed shipping that did not have the protection of a convoy. Back in November 1940 the Cabinet had decided that ships capable of 13 knots or more would be sailed independently rather than in convoy. The result of this decision was that the losses suffered by independently routed shipping steadily rose. The Admiralty successfully argued that the speed criteria should return to 15 knots or more, a decision that was implemented on 18 June 1941. The results of this seemingly small change were dramatic. In the three months April–June 1941, 120 independently routed merchant ships were sunk, but in the three months from 1 July to 30 September 1941 only 25 were lost.[23]

Other improvements were more involved and required far more resources than had been available in the summer of 1940. The most significant change was the distance that an anti-submarine escort could accompany an outbound convoy or meet an inbound one. From the fall of France onwards this distance steadily increased from 15°W to 17°W in July 1940 and then to 19°W in October 1940. Following the savaging of HX 126 before its anti-submarine escort had reached it, the Royal Navy and the Royal Canadian Navy introduced a complete transatlantic escort system for the convoys by the end of June 1941 and between the UK and Sierra Leone from mid-July 1941. Not only were the escorts now with a convoy for the duration of the voyage, but they were better trained and equipped as well.

The new convoy escorts that were emerging from British ship-yards from the autumn of 1940 – mostly *Flower* class corvettes – were being put through a 'working up' process to ensure they had absorbed the basics of anti-submarine warfare. Conducted at HMS *Western Isles*, at Tobermory on the Hebridean island of Mull, this was an intensive programme of exercises and drills that would teach these new ships and, above all, their new mostly reservist crews how to fight the U-boats. The training of individual ships was all very well, but it did not extend to training ships to work together as a permanent group. Up until early 1941 the escort for a convoy was drawn from whatever ships were available. This did not allow ships and their crews to learn the strengths and weaknesses of their fellow escorts, or allow the senior officer in charge to develop group responses to a U-boat attack on a convoy. Only in early 1941 were permanent escort groups formed as the number of destroyers and particularly corvettes steadily increased.[24]

Better training also meant that the escorts were able to make better use of their equipment, especially the new tools to search for U-boats that were entering service. The U-boats had been exploiting the fact that while on the surface they were extremely difficult to spot at night and although sonar could and did detect U-boats on the surface, it was not a reliable method owing to the skill level needed by the operator and also because of the impact that temperature and salinity have on the way sound moves through water. The reason why HMS *Vanoc* was able to spot *U-100* in the darkness of a North

Atlantic March night during the battle around HX 112 was down to the deployment of new equipment – radar. The Navy had originally invested in radar to give sufficient warning of an approaching enemy air raid. However, it was very quickly realized that it would also be useful for fighting at night and in low visibility. The first surface-search radar small enough to be fitted in destroyers and other escort craft was the 1.5m wavelength Type 286 and this started appearing from the summer of 1940 onwards. It proved invaluable in helping escorts find their convoys and for detecting straggling merchant ships in bad weather or at night. It was the early version of the Type 286, whereby the ship had to be turned to change the direction of the fixed radar aerial, which *Vanoc* used to such effect on 17 March. However, the Type 286, owing to its 1.5m wavelength, had difficulty detecting an object as small as a U-boat running on the surface with its deck awash, and the best ranges achieved were at about the 1.5 mile mark. A better radar was needed. This came in the shape of the Type 271, a 10cm wavelength set which was more than capable of seeing a U-boat on the surface a few miles away. The prototype 10cm set had been tested in November 1940 and then was rushed into production. It was a godsend for the convoy escorts and started to appear on the North Atlantic routes in the summer of 1941.[25]

Radar also appeared in Coastal Command aircraft. The first version was ASV I, which used a 1.5m wavelength like the Navy's Type 286 radar and was found to be ineffective at finding U-boats, but it did at least help the searching aircraft find the convoy it was supposed to be escorting. The next version, the ASV II, was found to be far more effective, as it had a forward- rather than sideways-facing aerial. However, while it was good enough to allow an aircraft to find a U-boat on the surface in daylight, it was not accurate enough at very close range to allow an attack at night, so Coastal Command remained a daylight-only force. Nor did Coastal Command have a weapon that was effective against submarines. The pre-war anti-submarine bombs were not just ineffective against submarines, but the aircraft did not have bomb sights, so the bombs had to be dropped at very low level if there was to be a slim chance of getting them close enough to do damage. But at low level the bombs had the nasty habit of skipping off the sea and exploding in the air under the aircraft that had just dropped them. The answer to this rather embarrassing problem was to stop using anti-submarine bombs and start dropping modified naval depth-charges, but only after the fall of France was this problem solved.[26]

Even if British land-based maritime patrol aircraft found it difficult to sink submarines, their presence was forcing the U-boats further out into the Atlantic where Coastal Command could not operate. Coastal Command had quickly noticed the effect its patrols and escort work were having on U-boat operations. Where there was no air cover the sinkings were high, where aircraft operated sinkings were low. The commander in chief of Coastal Command thought that the findings of his operational research section were important enough to bring to the attention of the First Sea Lord. However, there was a gap – an air gap – between the area that Coastal Command could cover over the Eastern Atlantic, and that which the Royal Canadian Air Force could cover in the west. Coastal Command was becoming a victim of its own success. The response to this problem was twofold. First, Coastal Command decided to go on the offensive (always a favourite knee-jerk response) in the one area that U-boats could be found that was within the range of the short- and medium-range aircraft coastal Command had available to it – the Bay of Biscay – in an effort to sink U-boats while they were moving to and from their French bases and their patrol areas in the Atlantic. It was not a success. This first 'Bay' offensive started in June 1941 and sank its first U-boat – *U-206* – on 30 November. Without a means of getting close enough to attack at night the Bay offensive was – and remained – a minor nuisance for the U-boats who could dive during the day and surface at night. Fortunately, Squadron Leader Humphrey de Verde Leigh, RAF, had come up with the idea of using a searchlight mounted underneath the aircraft to illuminate the U-boat in the final stages of an attack when it was too close for the radar to be effective. Royal Navy submariners who had been on the receiving end of this new 'Leigh Light' in a trial were full of praise for the idea, but it faced bureaucratic opposition from within the RAF, and although it was ready to go into production in the

Fig. 2.6. HMS *Audacity*, converted from a captured German merchant vessel, was the Royal Navy's first escort carrier and showed how effective ship-borne aircraft could be in deterring U-boats from attacking convoys.

autumn of 1941 it only entered service in numbers in May 1942.[27]

The second solution was to get aircraft that could operate further out into the Atlantic, either by using aircraft carriers or by getting better land-based aircraft. The Admiralty considered small trade defence aircraft carriers the best solution and indeed had produced the first 'escort carrier', HMS *Audacity*, in September 1941. Armed with six Martlet fighters, the *Audacity* was used on the UK–Gibraltar convoy routes where it was felt that air attack was the most serious threat – hence the fighter air group. However, *Audacity*'s fighters proved themselves most adept in making life difficult for the U-boats too, before she was torpedoed and sunk in December 1941 while defending convoy HG 76. Clearly more 'escort' carriers armed with, for example, depth-charge-carrying Swordfish aircraft would be a potent anti-submarine weapon. It was decided that two types of auxiliary or trade protection aircraft carrier would be produced: the small Merchant Aircraft Carrier (MAC) type based on converted merchant ships that still retained cargo-carrying capability, and the much larger escort carrier (CVE), which unlike the MAC ships would be commissioned into the Navy. Unfortunately such were the demands on British shipbuilding yards that work on converting suitable merchant ships could only progress very slowly, and shortages of vital equipment, such as arrestor gear which brought the aircraft to a halt on the short flight decks, further delayed matters. Land-based aircraft would have to be a stop-gap solution.[28]

Fortunately, long-range Catalina flying boats were being supplied by the Americans under Lend-Lease, as the RAF was loath to allow any of the heavy bombers being built in Britain for Bomber Command to be transferred to what it considered to be a misuse of aircraft. B-17 Flying Fortresses were also entering service with Coastal Command, having been rejected by Bomber Command as unsuitable as a night bomber; so too was the B-24 Liberator, which finally gave Coastal Command and the Admiralty the very long-range (VLR) aircraft they were looking for. The Liberator I could patrol for 5.3 hours at 850 nautical miles, able to range far across the air gap. Coastal Command received just seven aircraft in September 1941, and the solitary VLR squadron (120) was plagued with teething troubles.[29]

All of these improvements – important and successful though they were – were not enough to ensure the complete safety of convoys from U-boat packs. The experience of SC 42 was a salutary reminder that things could and would still go the U-boats' way. SC 42 was a large convoy of 64 ships, escorted by a destroyer and three corvettes. On the night of 9–10 September 1941 eight U-boats ran amok in the convoy – up to four were seen moving between the columns of ships; they sank 11 ships that night. The next night another seven were sunk and the escorts only managed to sink two U-boats in return. Only the descent of a thick mist saved the convoy from further losses. Yet the experience of convoys like SC 42 was the exception not the norm. The British were, at worst, holding their ground in the Atlantic.

Then on 7 December 1941 Japan attacked Pearl Harbor, and on 11 December Germany and Italy declared war on the USA. Britain's war was changing out of all recognition and this would have severe ramifications for the war against the U-boat.

CHAPTER 3

The War Against the U-boat
The Battle of the Atlantic 1942–45

Disaster off the US coast

The attack on Pearl Harbor, which brought Japan, Britain and the USA into a war in the Far East, and especially Hitler's declaration of war on the USA on 11 December, helped tip the Battle of the Atlantic in the U-boats' favour. Not only had the war widened to include a significant naval opponent – Japan – which would require resources, ships and men that the Royal Navy could ill spare, but it opened up a new area of operations on the east coast of the USA, away from the well-drilled convoys and their escorts.

Five U-boats – all that the German Navy was prepared to send, despite Dönitz's plea for more to be released – were quickly redeployed to the US east coast and there found a mass of unprotected and unconvoyed shipping. In mid-January they were joined by more U-boats and their experiences became known as their second 'Happy Time'.

The British (and Canadians) were far from happy. They were putting a great deal of effort into convoying merchant ships safely across the Atlantic, but once the ships passed into American waters the US authorities took no meaningful steps to protect them. The Americans did not even order coastal cities and towns to enforce a blackout until mid-April, which allowed merchant ships to be silhouetted by the shore lights and made them easy targets for U-boats loitering off shore. The carnage spread south-west along the US eastern seaboard and into the Caribbean. Nor could Ultra help.

The wolf-packs were not in use on the US eastern seaboard – there was no need for them, and that meant fewer radio signals. Worse still for Bletchley Park and the Admiralty's Operational Intelligence Centre, in February 1942 Dönitz decided to add a fourth rotor to the U-boats' Enigma machines, vastly increasing the possible combinations that had to be broken and requiring Bletchley Park to develop new 'Bombes'. The resulting Ultra blackout in the Atlantic would last until December 1942.[1]

The Americans tried everything except listen to the accumulated anti-U-boat experience of the British and Canadians, and they would not try convoy. So while the loss rate of convoyed ships in the Atlantic fell from 1.5 per cent between July and December 1941 to 0.5 per cent between January and 31 July 1942, the losses of independent ships – non-convoyed – rocketed upwards from 26 per cent to a disastrous 89 per cent, most of which was occurring in American waters. After numerous British protests about the losses occurring in waters under the nominal protection of the US Navy, and mostly because everything else had been tried and failed, the USN finally started adopting the convoy system in June 1942.[2]

In order to help produce escorts for use on the US eastern seaboard, the Americans, British and Canadians pooled ships involved in North Atlantic convoys in early February, which released a number of US destroyers for work along their coast. In mid-February 24 large anti-submarine trawlers were sent across to the US. April saw a further reorganization of the North Atlantic escort force which saw two US escort groups sent back to the American east coast, and later that month the convoy cycle for the HX, SC and ON convoys was opened out by one day, which allowed a reduction in the mid-ocean escort groups from 14 to 12. As a result two more American groups were released for use on US coastal convoys in early May. However, these measures were taking time to have an effect and without convoy – which was only partially introduced to cover the section of coast between Key West and Hampton Roads on 14 May – losses were rocketing, especially in tankers. As a result, in March the British ordered that all their outbound tankers were not to go south of New York and that all UK-bound tankers that were

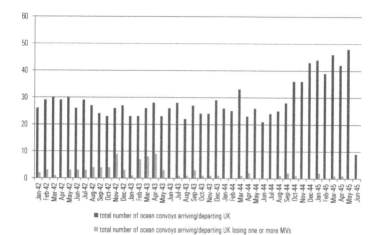

Fig. 3.1. The monthly number of ocean convoys arriving or leaving the UK and the number losing merchant ships, January 1942–June 1945.

loaded with oil and petrol products from the Gulf of Mexico and Curaçao were to be routed across the Central Atlantic to Freetown in Sierra Leone and then to the UK on the SL/HG convoy route rather than proceed up the US east coast to join an HX or SC convoy at Halifax.[3]

While the Germans were busy slaughtering shipping off the east coast of the USA and in the Caribbean – between January and July over 360 merchant ships, about 2,250,000 tons, had been sunk – convoy after convoy was crossing the Atlantic without being attacked. In January 26 convoys passed through what had been the dangerous waters of the North Atlantic and only two had lost one or more merchant ships. In February only three suffered losses; in March only one, in April none. However, with the introduction of convoy progressively along the US eastern seaboard and into the Caribbean, the rich pickings of unprotected merchant shipping dried up. The Germans needed to find a new hunting ground.

The return to the North Atlantic

Dönitz decided that the time was ripe to return to the main battle area, that patch of the North Atlantic that was beyond the effective range of Allied aircraft in Iceland, Northern Ireland, Scotland and eastern Canada where the violence of the weather was soon to be matched by the violence of the enemy. The U-boats were vastly assisted by the fact that in February 1942 the German naval intelligence section's code breakers, B-Dienst, succeeded in breaking the British Naval Cypher No. 3, which was used for all the Allied North Atlantic convoy messages. As a result B-Dienst had a firm grasp on the routes being used by the convoys, especially as the Allies were taking advantage of the U-boats' absence from the North Atlantic to run the convoys along the shortest possible routes from the northwestern approaches to Nova Scotia. Dönitz exploited this knowledge to set in motion a pack operation in May, despite the fact that the bulk of his forces were still most gainfully employed off the east coast of the USA.[4]

A U-boat sighted ON 92, a slow west-bound convoy protected by escort group A3, a mixed US and Canadian group, on 11 May and a small U-boat pack was sent into the attack. A3 had a US destroyer, a US Coast Guard cutter and four RCN corvettes, on paper a reasonable force, if a little small. However, A3 did not have any HF/DF gear, although the convoy's rescue ship did, and it only had one of the new Type 271 radars. Once the U-boat pack of five submarines closed in, the handling of A3 and its protection of the convoy was less than impressive, even allowing for its lack of up-to-date radars and direction-finding equipment. Matters were made worse by the American senior officer taking the two US ships off on an 'offensive sweep' miles ahead of the convoy, leaving just the four corvettes to fend off the attack which the Admiralty had warned was brewing. Before the US ships rejoined the convoy the U-boats had started their attack. *U-124* sank four ships and another was sunk by *U-94* during the night of 11/12 May. The next night *U-94* sank another two merchant ships. In all, seven ships were lost from the convoy of 42 merchant ships – 17 per cent – and no U-boats had been sunk by the defending warships. Dönitz was happy, the British not. Indeed, the British quietly prevailed on the USN to move the commander of A3 into another job. However, the attack on ON 92 in May and the less successful attacks on ON 100 and ON 102 were a clear statement of intent and a reminder that the Germans had not forgotten the Atlantic convoys. It was a message that the Admiralty did not need special intelligence from decrypted U-boat radio signals to read!

With the deployment of a fourth rotor in the U-boats' Enigma machines, rather than the three used for other German models, the Allies had been unable to read the submarine signal traffic in the Atlantic since the start of February 1942. This great blackout lasted until December 1942. However, the absence of Ultra from the OIC's arsenal for combating the U-boats was not critical. Direction finding, traffic analysis and the knowledge of U-boat operations that had already been painstakingly built up meant that the OIC's Submarine Tracking Room and its 'working fiction', which allowed for the vagaries of intelligence and the uncertainty of anti-submarine warfare, ensured that evasive routing was still a major part in the Allied efforts to beat the U-boats. Indeed from July 1942 until the end of May 1943 105 out of 174 North Atlantic convoys – 60 per cent – were rerouted in order to try to avoid U-boat patrol lines and were never located by the Germans. Of the remaining 40 per cent that were sighted, 223 escaped without any losses, 40 sustained only minor losses – sometimes only stragglers. Only 16 North Atlantic convoys lost more than four ships.[5]

But for those convoys that did feel the full weight of Dönitz's renewed attacks in the North Atlantic during the summer and autumn 1942, the experience was terrible. The first to suffer was SC 94, an east-bound convoy of 36 ships stuffed with supplies, escorted by the RN/RCN escort group C1. C1 was nominally well off, with a destroyer and six corvettes, but only the three Royal Navy corvettes had modern radars. The battle around SC 94 started on 5 August when part of the convoy, which had lost touch with the main body in thick fog, was sighted by *U-593* which promptly announced its presence by sinking one merchant ship. By the late evening the convoy had been reunited and was ploughing north-eastwards through intermittent fog, which made air support from Newfoundland – if the aircraft could actually get off the ground in the bad weather there – almost impossible. In the fog the destroyer HMCS *Assiniboine* surprised *U-210* on the surface and a wild close-quarter fight ensured, with the U-boat so close that the destroyer's main guns could not be depressed far enough to hit it and *U-210* could not dive. Both ships sprayed each other with machine-gun fire, the U-boat's 37mm anti-aircraft cannon riddling the *Assiniboine*'s bridge and starting a petrol fire amidships. Finally the *Assiniboine* managed to hit *U-210*'s conning tower with a 4.7-inch shell, killing the U-boat's captain, after which the destroyer managed to ram the submarine twice, fatally damaging it. But the damage to *Assiniboine* was severe: her bows were buckled by the force of the impact and she was riddled with 37mm shell holes and scorched by fire, forcing her to limp back to base. *U-210* may have been sunk, but C1 and SC 94 had lost their only destroyer.

For three nights C1 managed to fend off the gathering wolf-pack. However, on 8 August the U-boats did something new: they launched two simultaneous submerged attacks during daylight – the experience of 1941 was that U-boats attacked at night, en masse, and on the surface. The two attacks sank five vessels and the explosion of one of the sinking ships convinced the crews of three others that they had also been torpedoed and to abandon ship. Two of the crews were persuaded to return to their ships and re-join SC 94, but the crew of the MV *Radchurch* refused and the abandoned derelict was sunk later by *U-176*. Late on 8 August HMS *Broke*, a British destroyer, arrived to reinforce the escort and the next day the Free Polish destroyer *Blyskawica* joined too. But 10 August saw another near simultane-ous submerged daylight attack, this time by *U-438* and *U-660*, which sank another four ships, taking the total losses to 11.

Fig. 3.2. The FH3 ship-borne High Frequency Direction Finding set. Ship-borne HF/DF was an invaluable tool for an escort group commander, telling him if U-boats were shadowing his convoy and massing for an attack.

New tools and new ideas

As summer turned to autumn other convoys suffered in turn. In September ON 127 lost seven merchant ships. Another eight from SC 104 and seven from HX 212 were lost in October, while November saw SC 107 and SL 125 lose 15 and 13 ships respectively. However, this was not a one-sided fight. The Royal Navy had been learning its lessons from the hard battles of 1941, and 1942 saw the introduction of many innovations and technical advances that had been stimulated by the U-boats' first assaults on the convoy routes. Chief among these was better radar. The 1.5m wavelength Type 286 was excellent in helping the escorts find their convoy in the emptiness of the North Atlantic, but it was less good at detecting a small target like a U-boat running on the surface. What was needed was a shorter-wavelength radar that could see small objects at a longer range. These 10cm wavelength 'centimetric' radars were quickly developed and by mid-1942 most British escorts had 10cm Type 271 radars. Unfortunately, the RCN did not, and was still relying on Canadian-built versions of the 1.5m metric radars.

A significant minority of the Royal Navy's escort vessels were also fitted during 1942 and early 1943 with ship-borne HF/DF sets – smaller versions of the land-based listening posts that were doing sterling work keeping the OIC's Submarine Tracking Room supplied with the locations of U-boats. These ship-borne HF/DF sets gave the escort commander a valuable way of assessing the number and rough position of U-boats manoeuvring into position for attack. Escorts (or aircraft if they were present) could then be directed down the HF/DF bearing to force U-boats to submerge and lose contact with the convoy.

The weapons available to the Royal Navy ships fighting the U-boats had improved too. The greatest weakness in an escort's attack was that it had to pass over the position of the U-boat in order to drop its depth-charges. This meant that if the U-boat was very deep it would pass out of the cone covered by the ASDIC (active sonar) some time before the escort could actually fire its depth-charges, giving the U-boat a chance to twist and dodge to get outside the lethal range of the attack. What was needed was an anti-submarine weapon that would throw its bombs ahead of the ship, so the ASDIC could be kept firmly on the target. The first such weapon – 'Hedgehog' – entered service during 1942 and was quickly fitted to navy ships as they went through repairs or refits. Hedgehog was a spigot mortar that fired 24 contact fused bombs in a circle ahead of the hunting ship. A hit by a single bomb was enough to penetrate the U-boat's pressure hull and sink it. There were, however, teething problems, the most serious being that the bombs did not always leave the spigots when fired. The fact that there were not any bangs unless a hit was scored was not popular with the escorts. On the other hand, a succession of non-lethal explosions from depth-charges could create enough cumulative damage to force the U-boat to the surface, which would not happen with Hedgehog. Plans were

Fig. 3.3. The Hedgehog anti-submarine mortar was the first ahead-firing
weapon to reach the Navy's escort force during 1942.

set in motion to introduce a new ahead-firing weapon that would
give the bangs that, even with near misses, did so much to demoral-
ize a submarine.

The British were improving their tactics too. The big lessons from
late 1940 and 1941 was that sinking U-boats was a luxury and the
most important task the escort groups had was the safe and timely
arrival of the convoy. This doctrine had been enshrined during
1941 in the escort's new bible, the Western Approaches Convoy
Instructions (WACIs), which in 1942, with the widening of the war,
had been transformed into the Atlantic Convoy Instructions (ACIs).
Suppressing the desire to seek out the enemy was difficult for the
escort groups, and the Canadian and American groups tended to pay
lip service to the need to safeguard the convoy over sinking U-boats.
The other major lesson from 1941 was that permanent escort groups
were not enough – they needed common doctrine too. WACIs and
ACIs gave the means of sharing the doctrine, but someone had to
develop it in the first place, as each escort group had its own ideas

of how best to deal with a threatened attack or react to a torpedo hitting a merchant ship.

The answer was the Western Approaches Tactical Unit (WATU), the brainchild of Commander Gilbert Roberts. WATU was founded in January 1942 to develop group anti-submarine tactics for the Atlantic. Within a few weeks it was pushing out new tactics for groups to follow – Operation *Raspberry*, a response to a ship being torpedoed at night. Admiral Sir Percy Noble, the commander of Western Approaches Command, was so impressed that he made Roberts an acting captain. Other procedures dealing with different types of U-boat attack followed, as did plans to make searches by aircraft operating under the control of the escort commander. WATU made great use of a 'tactical floor' on which convoy battles could be played out using real-life events. The responses of the escorts to an attack could then be tried and tried again until the best solution was found – without a single real ship being put in danger. Many officers passed through the unit's courses, from junior officers to escort group commanders; often they found that the WRNS plotters, who moved the model ships around during each game and who briefed them on what was going on, knew more about sinking U-boats than they did.[6]

The problem of escorts not having enough fuel to get across the Atlantic was also being addressed. The initial solution during 1941 was to pass the convoys between a series of escort groups covering the whole of its passage. This, however, required large numbers of ships. A longer-term solution that saw dividends from 1942 onwards was the development of refuelling at sea from an oil tanker. This was a new departure for the Royal Navy, as it had previously relied on its network of overseas bases to give it its global strategic reach, but even the bases in Canada and the UK were not enough to solve the problems of escort endurance in the Atlantic. Two methods of refuelling were developed. The first was the alongside method, where the tanker and escort steamed on parallel courses only a few dozen metres apart with fuel hoses between the two suspended from derricks on the tanker. This method, as well as having a reasonable delivery rate, needed less specialized equipment. It also had the

Fig. 3.4. Refuelling at sea was a vital development. Here an
escort is refuelled using the astern method.

added bonus that if the tanker carried spare depth-charges, these
could be transferred to the escort by means of a jackstay between
the two ships. Its main problem was that it needed relatively calm
seas to be used – something that was not common in the high lati-
tudes of the North Atlantic, even in the summer.

The second method of refuelling at sea was for the tanker to
stream a long buoyant hose over its stern as it plodded along. Some
distance behind the tanker was the escort which picked up the buoyant hose over its bows. This method could be used in much rougher
weather and was the most common way of refuelling escorts in the
Atlantic. However, it was a cumbersome process and the hoses,
themselves in short supply, were often parted. There was also the
problem that tankers had a variety of different-sized pipes which the
refuelling gear needed to be able to connect to. It all made for very
slow progress in refuelling at sea. But the biggest problem was the
shortage of tankers, which the massacre of shipping off the east coast
of America and in the Caribbean in the first six months of 1942 had
not helped. Quite simply the Allied bodies responsible for managing

the shipping fleets – like the British Ministry of War Transport – were loath to let tankers be used for refuelling at sea. From the shipping management perspective each tanker used for refuelling at sea meant one less cargo of petrol, oil or lubricants, which were the very lifeblood of the Allied war effort.

Another solution to the endurance problem was the creation of 'long-range escorts'. These were older destroyers, some even World War I vintage *V* and *W* class 1, which had some of their boilers removed to make space available for oil bunkers. Losing some of the boilers meant that these LRE destroyers were not as fast as unmodified ones – around 24 knots compared to 32 knots – but they were still much faster than a U-boat trying to escape on the surface, unlike the *Flower* class corvettes. The conversion also provided more room for the increasing crew sizes that went with new radars, better sonars, HF/DF and Hedgehog. More and better new ships were also coming into service, reducing the reliance on the slow and small *Flower* class corvettes. The increasing numbers of escorts also allowed the British to form 'support groups' in September 1942. These long-awaited groups were tasked with going to the aid of a threatened convoy and its escort, not only to reinforce it but also to give it the resources to hunt U-boats to destruction rather than having to break off the hunt in order to get back to the convoy to ensure its safe and timely arrival at its destination. The convoy was now becoming not just a defensive arrangement but also one where the Allies could mount local offensives against the U-boats.[7]

No sooner had the first support groups been formed than they had to be broken up to provide the escorts for the Allies' first major combined offensive – Operation *Torch*, the invasion of French North Africa. While the invasion convoys suffered almost no losses to U-boats, the drain of resources from the North Atlantic helped make November 1942 a dreadful month for shipping losses: 807,754 tons in all areas, 508,707 in the North Atlantic. In particular, SC 107 and SL 125 suffered their shattering losses because of the need for anti-submarine escorts for the *Torch* convoys. Only the awful weather in December 1942 and January and February 1943 kept the U-boats at bay.

Yet while the escorts had been fighting in the Atlantic during 1942 the Admiralty had faced another battle. The wolf-packs might have returned to the North Atlantic, but during the latter half of 1942 the British had internal issues to be resolved – the RAF and Royal Navy were at war with each other in the corridors of Whitehall.

Maritime airpower 1942–43 and the 'Battle of the Air'

The 'Battle of the Air' was an argument over resources. On one side there was the Royal Navy and the RAF's Coastal Command. On the other were the Air Ministry, the Air Staff and Bomber Command. The issue was the supply of aircraft by the Air Ministry for both the Royal Navy and Coastal Command – the reason these aircraft were needed was to attack U-boats. This was not the first time that the two different approaches to the use of airpower – maritime and strategic – had come to bureaucratic blows during the war. During 1941 there had been significant pressure to try to get Bomber Command to pay as much attention to the massive U-boat pens being constructed in the French Biscay ports as they did to trying (and failing) to damage German munitions factories in the Ruhr.

This time the debate was over the supply of air cover to convoys. The Navy had long recognized the usefulness of aircraft in anti-submarine warfare and once the Battle of the Atlantic was under way the Navy had wanted to supply air cover using small escort carriers. It had been decided that two types of auxiliary or trade protection aircraft carrier would be produced: the small Merchant Aircraft Carrier (MAC) type based on converted merchant ships that still retained cargo-carrying capability, and the much larger escort carrier (CVE), which unlike the MAC ships would be commissioned into the RN. The first auxiliary carrier, HMS *Audacity*, had considerable success during late 1941 against the German FW 200 Condor reconnaissance aircraft which located convoys for the U-boats. Furthermore, despite the fact that *Audacity*'s air group was not configured for anti-submarine warfare, her F4F Martlets had attacked surfaced U-boats, forcing them to submerge. This indicated to the Admiralty and Coastal Command by the end of 1941 the potential of this type of ship, especially if equipped with Swordfish aircraft armed with depth-charges.[8]

The desire to bring MAC auxiliary carriers into production was frustrated by the severe lack of shipbuilding and repair capacity which caused great reluctance on the part of the Ministry of War Transport to release suitable ships. At the 24th meeting of the Battle of the Atlantic Committee on 11 November 1941 it was expected that the first six MACs would be available in March 1942, but that the next six would not be delivered until 1943. Unfortunately the programme was delayed further by problems in the supply of arrestor gear. As a result of these delays the first MAC did not enter convoy service until 29 May 1943. At the same time, some convoy commodores expressed reservations over the effectiveness of the MACs in service owing to the size of the vessels: 'the North Atlantic weather conditions in winter often made flying impossible from the pitching decks of these smallish ships'. Displacing approximately 15,000 tons with an air group of up to 16 aircraft, CVEs were a different proposition. However, the woeful state of British shipbuilding, with its small and poorly designed yards, obsolete technology and restrictive working practices, played a major part, forcing reliance on American shipyards. Unfortunately the British CVEs were delayed further by the Royal Navy improving the American-built vessels so that they could carry out full fighter operations rather than just anti-submarine work. The Admiralty also had serious reservations about some of the design aspects of the American-built CVEs and after the loss of two such vessels remedial work further delayed their entry into service. The cause for Admiralty concerns about these vessels was down to the circumstances of the loss of HMS *Avenger* and HMS *Dasher*.[9]

Both HMS *Avenger* and HMS *Dasher* were in the first group of CVEs built for the Royal Navy in the USA – the other being HMS *Biter*. On 15 November 1942 HMS *Avenger* was hit by a single torpedo fired by *U-155* and practically disintegrated, with only 12 out of over 550 crew surviving. An inquiry concluded that the torpedo set off depth-charges and bombs that were stored next to the ship's hull. As a result the Admiralty ordered that all CVEs were to be modified to ensure that depth-charge and bomb magazines were at least 10 to 15 feet from the ship's side. This meant more delays in getting CVEs into service. HMS *Dasher* sank in eight minutes following an internal explosion on 27 March 1943 while operating aircraft in the Firth of Clyde. It seems that petrol vapour from refuelling aircraft exploded and devastated the ship. Only 148 out of the 526 crew were saved. The board of inquiry ordered to establish the cause of the explosion concluded that the American petrol-handling system, which was very different from that used on British-built aircraft carriers, was the root of the problem (the USN said that it was because the British, used to a different system, were not operating the equipment correctly). The Admiralty ordered that the petrol-handling facilities on CVEs were to be replaced with British equipment, and all electrical systems removed from compartments used as part of the petrol-handling system, or that the electrics were uprated to the same standard as those used in explosive magazines. The result was more delays in getting CVEs into service.

Fig. 3.5. A convoy of troop ships forming part of Operation *Torch* are escorted by a CVE, possibly HMS *Biter*.

The attitude of the Royal Navy – and indeed the problem of fighting a global war against three very different navies – also prevented
the CVEs having much impact on the Battle of the Atlantic from
autumn 1942 until early summer 1943. As a CVE could carry nearly
half the aircraft of an *Illustrious* class fleet aircraft carrier, it was far
too tempting for the Admiralty to use CVEs on major fleet operations to ease the strategic overstretch caused by the Navy's lack of
fleet carriers. To this end CVEs were employed on the *Torch* and
Husky operations as well as the Arctic convoy route to Russia. Not
until April 1943 did HMS *Biter* appear on the North Atlantic convoy
routes, the first British-manned CVE to do so.[10]

Given the delays that beset the MAC and CVE programmes from
the very outset of 1942 the Navy wanted more support from Coastal
Command. Coastal Command, however, was the most neglected
of the RAF's commands and had suffered from a number of failed
rearmament plans for its long-range flying boats. Using long-range
bombers converted into anti-submarine aircraft was a solution to
this problem, but this brought Coastal Command into conflict with
the Air Ministry, Air Staff and Bomber Command who wanted to
bomb Germany, not ensure the safety of raw materials that would
keep their aircraft flying.

Coastal Command was also a victim of its own success and
of the entry of the USA into the war. So effective were Coastal
Command's efforts in inhibiting U-boat activities in 1941 (even if
they were not sinking many) that the U-boats moved further out
into the Atlantic where the flying boats and converted bombers
lacked the range to operate. Coastal Command now had to find a
way of using its admittedly limited resources in a way that could
bring them into contact with U-boats. The routes the U-boats took
from their Biscay bases out into the North Atlantic was an obvious
area that was within striking distance of the medium- and long-
range aircraft that formed the bulk of Coastal Command's aircraft,
especially if they operated from bases in south-west England. While
in 1941 the Bay offensive had had very little success, thanks to a
lack of suitable weapons and the means to press an attack at night,
1942 saw the combination of ASVII, a 1.5m airborne surface-search

radar, and the Leigh Light, a high-powered searchlight that could be used to illuminate at night a submarine on the surface in the final stages of an attack when a radar target became hidden by false echoes. It was used with great effect by Coastal Command, especially in their Bay offensive, and now that Coastal Command were using depth-charges set to explode close to the surface, there was a chance of doing serious damage to the U-boats before they reached the convoys. Unfortunately, an ASVII-equipped aircraft crashed in Vichy French Tunisia in April 1942 and the Germans got hold of the radar. They set about building a receiver that could detect the ASVII radar and warn the U-boat it was in danger long before the aircraft could attack and allow it time to submerge.

Coastal Command needed a new radar system that this 'Metox' receiver could not detect. Happily, there was in development an airborne version – ASVIII – of the centimetric radar that was proving so useful to the Royal Navy's escorts. Unfortunately the RAF's Bomber Command also wanted it to use as a radar bomb sight (H2S) to help them overcome the problem that many of the bombs they were dropping on Germany, as the Singleton and Butt reports showed, were not hitting their targets. Both ASVIII and H2S had some common components and it was even possible to use H2S sets as centimetric search radar. The result was that there were bitter arguments over the supply of the radar sets. Bomber Command, unsurprisingly, resisted the transfer of any H2S sets to Coastal Command on the mistaken assumption that the H2S technology could not be used in the maritime role. Unfortunately the long-term policy for ASVIII and H2S could not be settled rapidly as the chiefs of staff could not reach an agreement. Again the issue had to be referred back to the Anti U-boat Committee who on 23 December decided in favour of Bomber Command receiving priority on the advice of Portal, Cherwell and Watson-Wyatt, who all believed that H2S would make a significant improvement to Bomber Command's accuracy. But no matter how effective Coastal Command got in the Bay of Biscay area, it could not close the gap in air cover in the North Atlantic where from summer 1942 onwards the bulk of the merchant ship losses was occurring.[11]

What was needed were very long-ranged aircraft (VLR). Only these VLR aircraft had the range and endurance to operate in the 'air gap' that existed in the mid-Atlantic beyond the range of normal aircraft operating from Canada, Iceland and the UK. In September 1941 Coastal Command received seven VLR Liberator aircraft under Lend-Lease and divided the solitary squadron (120 Squadron RAF) equipped with them between Northern Ireland and Iceland. However, all subsequent deliveries of US long-range and VLR Liberators went to RAF bomber squadrons in the Middle East or to the civil airline, BOAC. The only aircraft Coastal Command was getting were Lend-Lease aircraft from America and only then because the American bomber types had proved to be useless for Britain's night bombing offensive. Then when the USA entered the war in December 1941 the Americans needed to expand their own air forces and the Lend-Lease supply of bombers and of the long-range Catalina flying boat faltered. The supply of home-grown aircraft was also causing problems with Sunderland flying boat production suffering particularly: out of a target of 15 Sunderlands per month from four different firms, only one firm was in production at a rate of four aircraft per month and two of the three remaining firms had not made any deliveries at all.[12]

From late 1941 and throughout 1942, Coastal Command also had to face the problem that the numbers of VLR aircraft (seven in total) were unsustainable as the Liberator I was out of production. The Admiralty and Coastal Command made repeated requests for more VLR aircraft to help in the Battle of the Atlantic, but they were constantly rebuffed by the Air Staff and the bomber barons in the RAF. The arguments became increasingly bitter as 1942 drew on. The new commander in chief of Bomber Command, Air Marshal Sir Arthur Harris, even wrote to Churchill to tell him that Coastal Command was achieving 'nothing essential to our survival or to the defeat of the enemy' and that it was 'merely an obstacle to victory'.[13]

It was even more unfortunate that the Liberator IIs that had been delivered would require substantial conversion to obtain the same performance as the Liberator I and had anyway been completely allocated to Bomber Command. By November 1942 the situation regarding the supply of VLR aircraft had deteriorated as the Liberator II was itself out of production and all of these aircraft, save a few for transport duties, has been allocated to overseas commands. Not only were all the 1942 deliveries of Lend-Lease Liberators sent to the Middle East but, as the Chief of the Air Staff, Air Chief Marshall Sir Charles Portal, explained to Churchill in March 1942, 'the Americans were already restive about the Fortress squadron in Coastal Command which was being used on tasks other than high-level bombing for which these aircraft had in the first instance been supplied to the RAF'.[14]

Therefore, any hope of improving the supply of VLR aircraft would rely on the supply of Liberator IIIs converted to VLR Liberator Vs. Appeals to the Americans bore fruit, allowing Churchill to minute Pound on Trafalgar Day 1942 that General Eisenhower was ready to make all American Liberators and Fortresses available for anti-submarine warfare. None of this solved the issue of the provision of VLR aircraft or Coastal Command's numerical weakness during the proposed conversion period to Liberator Vs. Indeed 59 Squadron (which had converted to the Liberator III from the Hudson in August 1942) lost their Liberators in December of that year, until the Liberator V was issued to them in May 1943. At the third meeting of the Anti U-boat Warfare Committee the matter was raised again and this time Portal promised Halifax heavy bombers to replace the Liberators undergoing conversion to the VLR type. Yet despite Portal's assurances, during the intervening five months, 59 Squadron operated the Fortress with a corresponding drop in radius of action.[15]

In order to try to disarm the bitter dispute over allocation of aircraft, the Anti U-boat Committee was formed in November 1942. The long debate over the supply of aircraft was brought to an end by a thorough evaluation of the situation by the committee. It rapidly came to the conclusion that the Admiralty's request for only 40 more VLR aircraft, at a time when Bomber Command was losing nearly that number a night, was entirely reasonable, especially as the RAF's latest plan to expand Bomber Command had been declared impossible to achieve. However, the aircraft would have to be supplied by the Americans, not come from Bomber Command, and supply problems meant that this was not as quick as the Navy and Coastal Command had hoped. Happily the Casablanca Conference in January 1943 to decide joint Allied grand strategy made the supply of VLR aircraft for the North Atlantic a high prior-ity. The first new aircraft started arriving in February 1943 and the few that did enter service by May 1943 proved to be just enough.[16]

The defeat of the U-boats

At the same time as the internecine warfare between the Navy and the RAF was dying down with the formation of the Anti U-boat Committee in November 1942, there came a change at the very top of the Royal Navy's efforts to beat the U-boats. Sir Percy Noble, who had headed Western Approaches Command through the dark days of 1941 and 1942, was replaced by Admiral Sir Max Horton, a submariner who had been Flag Officer Submarines, so that Noble could move to head up the British delegation in Washington – a vital task in ensuring inter-Allied cooperation. Noble was the architect of the efforts to defeat the U-boats, but Horton would reap the benefits and the victory. Similarly, in February 1943 Air Marshall Sir John Slessor replaced Philip Joubert de la Ferté at Coastal Command; Joubert had to face up to the Air Staff and the bomber lobby in the battle for resources, but Slessor would be the officer that got to wield the weapon that Joubert had created. But first, the Royal Navy, assisted by Coastal Command, had to deal with the increasing pressure the U-boats were placing on the convoys.

TM 1 was a special convoy of nine tankers from the Caribbean to Gibraltar. It was sighted by *U-514* on 3 January 1943. The Germans moved a wolf-pack to intercept and on 8 January TM 1 steamed straight into the waiting U-boats; seven tankers were sunk. Such losses were clearly on the minds of the most senior Allied commanders and politicians when they met later that month in Casablanca, where finally it was decided to commit enough Allied resources, rather than just British, to win the battle. Unfortunately implementation of decisions and the procurement of extra resources took time before any appreciable moves could be taken to strengthen the Allied position in the Atlantic.

At the start of February it was SC 118 which took the brunt of the U-boat attack. Twenty-one submarines massed to attack the convoy from 4 February onwards in an exhausting five-day-long battle. Thirteen ships were sunk; in return the escorts managed to sink three U-boats as well as badly damaging another two. What alarmed the British was that the escort was especially strong, having had sufficient reinforcements to lift its strength to 12, double the normal number and including no fewer than five destroyers. Yet the U-boats still managed to devastate the convoy. Worse, as far as the Navy was concerned, this disaster had been overseen by one of its own escort groups, B2. Not only was the case for support groups to reinforce the close escort of a threatened convoy made abundantly clear – if indeed it needed making at all by this stage in the campaign – but also that these reinforcements could not just be cobbled together at the last minute. The rationale for permanent escort groups so painfully learned in 1941 – that teamwork and trust cannot be created out of thin air – logically had to be extended to any new support groups when they were created. Nor were the U-boats done for February. At the end of the month they fell on ON 166 in an ambush that was made possible by the Germans reading the Allied convoy codes. Unfortunately Bletchley Park was unable to decode the U-boat Enigma signals fast enough to allow the OIC to realize what the Germans intended. The result was another 14 ships sunk over five days of bitter fighting. The Allied losses for the month were therefore most depressing: 63 ships sunk by U-boats – 27 from two convoys alone.

On 1 March the Allies convened the Atlantic Convoy Conference which was to allow some of the problems facing the Royal Navy, RCN and USN, together with those confronting such parts of the Allied air forces involved in the anti-submarine battle, to be ironed out. The Americans caused consternation by demanding the with-drawal of the few ships they had committed to North Atlantic convoy escort duties to allow them to concentrate on the Central Atlantic and their convoys from the USA to their forces in North Africa. A compromise was reached, however, which saw the USN agreeing to supply a support group and a CVE for the North Atlantic. The boundaries of the operational areas were redrawn too, with the RCN getting its own operational area. But the most important work was over the supply and deployment of the small number of VLR aircraft entering service which provided, for the first time, VLR aircraft to operate from Canada. When these aircraft were deployed it would, together with those in the UK and Iceland, mean the closing of the air gap where so many ships had been sunk. But there was no breathing space for the Allies. Early in March the U-boats struck again.

In March 1943 there was a series of massive battles around the convoys SC 121, SC 122, HX 228 and HX 229 which saw significant merchant ship losses, despite the efforts of the Royal Navy and Coastal Command and the Royal Canadian Air Force. In all, 77 merchant ships were sunk while in convoy during March 1943. Between 6 and 11 March SC 121 lost 13 ships either in convoy or straggling out of 57 in the convoy. The efforts to defend the convoy from the U-boats was hampered by the violent storm that was raging, but while this scattered the convoy and caused many ships to straggle, it also scattered the waiting U-boat patrol line and allowed the convoy to limp past unseen on 5 March before being sighted by *U-405* from a second group the next day. Despite the weather, seven U-boats were in contact with SC 121 by 7 March and they were attacking the convoy as well as picking off stragglers. Only when the storm got above Force 10 on 10 March did the U-boats have difficulty in torpedoing the convoy's many stragglers and their attack was called off the next day.

HX 228 of 60 merchant ships and escorted by B3's four destroyers and five corvettes crewed by the Royal Navy as well as the Free Polish and Free French navies, following a more southerly route, got off more lightly. In support there was also the USN support group with its escort carrier USS *Bogue*. During the U-boats' first attack on 10/11 March the destroyer HMS *Harvester* sighted *U-444* on the surface. The U-boat tried to escape and crash-dived, but depth-charges blew it back to the surface where it was rammed. The act of *Harvester* riding over the top of *U-444* did severe damage to the British destroyer's propellers and she could only crawl along on one engine. The French corvette *Aconit* came to *Harvester*'s assistance and rammed and sank *U-444* which was still afloat. *Aconit* was ordered by *Harvester* to rejoin HX 228 while she limped along as best she could, but the next day *Harvester*'s remaining engine broke down and as she lay motionless was torpedoed by *U-432*; nearly all *Harvester*'s crew and the survivors she had already picked up were drowned. The *Aconit*, back with HX 228, saw the column of smoke far astern that marked *Harvester*'s destruction and turned back, quickly gained ASDIC contact, and depth-charged *U-432* to the surface, where after a short gun battle the U-boat was rammed and sunk. Between 10 and 13 March four merchant ships out of HX 228's 60 vessels and HMS *Harvester* were sunk in exchange for two U-boats. Again the weather made defence difficult and the storms made attempts to operate aircraft from the USS *Bogue* ineffective.

The 38 merchant ships of HX 229 suffered next both from storms and then the U-boats. Unfortunately the escort was weak and there was no rescue ship. As the U-boats attacked, the escorts found themselves tied up in efforts to rescue the survivors as the merchant ships detailed to help survivors steamed past without stopping. The U-boats had little difficulty in making their attacks, 12 ships being sunk from the night of 16/17 to 18 March. Indeed with up to 38 U-boats ordered to operate against the convoy, it is remarkable that the losses were not heavier. SC 122 with 51 merchant ships was badly scattered by storms too, and from 17 to 19 March the U-boats sank nine ships that were straggling or still in the convoy. Only one U-boat was sunk in exchange for the losses in HX 229 and SC 122.[17]

The convoy battles around HX 228, HX 229, SC 121 and SC 122 in March 1943 have frequently been described as the crisis of the whole Battle of the Atlantic. When the fighting around these four convoys only is considered it is easy to come to the conclusion that the Allies, and the Royal Navy in particular, were losing the battle. To lose 38 merchant ships – 18½ per cent – from a total of 206 in the four convoys and sink only three U-boats in exchange was not good. However, it did not threaten to cut Britain's supply lines. The losses in March were bad, but not the worst. As the Admiralty's own assessment of the fighting in March pointed out, it did not mean the value of convoy was diminished, as the total percentage of ships lost was roughly constant. Where there was a crisis – and one that had been bubbling away in the background for a while – was the global shipping shortage that the Allies faced. But this shortage was not caused by ships being sunk, although this clearly did not help. In fact the Allies had been building more ships each month than the Germans were sinking since July 1942 (with the exception of November 1942). The shortage of shipping was caused, quite simply, by the Allies mismanaging what shipping they had and neglecting to allow for the amount of shipping needed when they produced their plans to attack Germany and Japan. The American military were particularly bad at shipping management, especially in the Pacific where merchant ships were often used as warehouses rather than being unloaded, preventing them from being assigned to new tasks. Crisis or not, one thing was clear at the end of March 1943: with the increasing numbers of U-boats at sea in the North Atlantic and the Germans reading the Allied signals to and from the convoys, evasion was no longer an option. The convoys would have to be fought through to their destinations in Britain and the new world.[18]

April saw several large pack attacks on convoys, but Bletchley Park's successful cracking of the four-rotor U-boat Enigma machines – 'Shark' – was bearing fruit. There were several convoys, such as HX 230, HX 231, ON 176 and ONS 4, which, thanks to the OIC, Bletchley Park, the newly reformed support groups, aircraft, both land-based – especially the increasing numbers of VLR aircraft – as well as HMS *Biter*, the Royal Navy's first CVE to be used on the North Atlantic convoy routes, and USS *Bogue*, a USN CVE, were able to fight off determined attacks for very few losses, if any. Ultra decrypts also showed that the U-boat crews were getting increasingly wary of air attack. The result was that the U-boats only managed to sink 56 merchant ships (327,943 tons).[19]

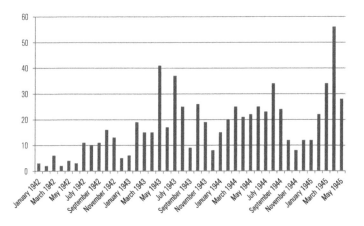

Fig. 3.6. U-boats sunk (all causes), 1 January 1942–9 May 1945.

The numbers of German U-boats were such at the start of May
that the OIC assessed that all routes across the Atlantic were now
blocked. There were two wolf-packs of 15 and 17 U-boats loitering along the western edge of the air gap, another pack of 13 south
of Cape Farewell, Greenland, and a final pack of 13 across the
Gibraltar route to the west of the Bay of Biscay. Into this mass of
U-boats steamed ONS 5. For once the weather worked in the Allies'
favour and the massive storm that engulfed ONS 5 ensured that the
U-boats lost contact before an attack could be mounted. However,
on 4 May the U-boats regained contact after three days of searching. Fortunately the first of two support groups had already arrived
to reinforce the convoy escort and the warships started the arduous
running battle with the U-boats, which lasted for three days. During
the battle the U-boats managed to sink 12 merchant ships from the
convoy, but lost seven of their own to aircraft and warships.[20]

The next convoys in the German sights were HX 237 and SC
129. The OIC tried unsuccessfully to steer both convoys round the
massive concentrations of U-boats, but the Germans' ability to read
the convoy codes allowed them to match the OIC move for move.
HX 237's escorts, which included the CVE HMS *Biter*, managed to
sink three U-boats for the loss of only three merchant ships. HX
237 also saw the first use by the Allies of an air-dropped homing

torpedo, the 'Mark 24 mine' – it destroyed *U-266*. SC 129 also put up an impressive fight, sinking two U-boats in exchange for two merchant ships sunk. The U-boats could not sustain this level of losses and worse was to follow. Air and surface escorts protecting SC 130 managed to sink three U-boats for no loss during a battle that lasted from 18 to 20 May. It was the same with the attack on HX 239 between 21 and 23 May where no merchant ships were sunk, but one U-boat was. On 24 May Dönitz ordered the U-boats away from the North Atlantic into areas that might be less well defended. In all, 41 U-boats were sunk in May 1943, over twice the number of the previous worst month of losses. They had been defeated.[21]

One force that had been present in the Battle of the Atlantic since 1941 and had made the battle its own was missing from the campaign during the spring 1943 – the Royal Canadian Navy. One of the first things that Max Horton, the new commander of Western Approaches Command, had done was examine the relative losses suffered by convoys escorted by the Royal Navy, US Navy and Royal Canadian Navy. The findings showed that the convoys escorted by the Royal Canadian Navy suffered higher losses than the others. In part this was due to the fact that the Canadians tended to escort the SC and the slower ON convoys, which, because of their slow speed, were easier targets for the U-boats. However, the level of losses could not be explained by this alone. Clearly the massive expansion of the RCN was part of the problem – experience levels were diluted which meant less effective crews, but again this was only part of the story. Quite simply the Canadian escort groups had worse equipment and worse training. They were based and equipped on the other side of the Atlantic to where the anti-U-boat research and development was taking place, which meant they were not as good at anti-submarine warfare. This was a bitter pill for the RCN to swallow given the effort and sacrifices its men and ships had made in bringing convoy after convoy cross the Atlantic, but it was something that could no longer be ignored. The savaging of ON 154 in December while being escorted by the Canadian group C1 was the last straw: 14 ships had been sunk. The Canadian escort groups were withdrawn from the battle and sent to the UK. Here they were extensively reequipped with the most up-to-date anti-submarine sensors and weapons the British had available. The Canadians were also given a major re-training package at the individual ship level – to make sure the crews could use their new weapons and sensors properly – and at the escort group level – to make sure that the senior officers could effectively use their ships against a sustained U-boat pack attack. The Canadians were not alone in this; training was something of a fetish for Horton and the early months of his command at Western Approaches saw an increased emphasis on training at the individual and group levels. Difficult though this was for the Canadians, their escort groups were transformed by the process and emerged to share in the defeat of the U-boats.

The Germans may have suffered a defeat, but they were carrying on with the fight. In September 1943 the wolf-packs returned to the North Atlantic convoy routes, this time armed with homing torpedoes. But the Royal Navy and the RCN were ready and waiting: six merchant ships were sunk from ONS 18 and ON 202, as well as three escorts, in exchange for three U-boats in a four-day battle. However, the German success was short-lived. The countermeasure to the German acoustic homing torpedo was already in development, thanks to an earlier intelligence scare that such weapons were about to enter service. The Western Approaches Tactical Unit rapidly developed a method of approaching a U-boat that would ensure that the attacking escort would remain out of the area where it could be detected by the homing torpedo. Both the Royal Navy and RCN also developed towed decoys that made so much noise that they would attract any homing torpedoes rather than the sound of the ship's propellers – the RCN version was simpler, smaller and easier to use. More ominously for the Germans, the low U-boat losses in September quickly rose. By mid-November Dönitz again had to admit defeat and withdraw from the convoy routes to go in search of less dangerous areas. The days of wolf-pack attacks were ending.[22]

During the winter of 1943/44 many convoys made the Atlantic crossing without any attempts by the U-boats to stop them. From January 1944 at least one CVE or MAC ship could be sailed with every convoy. The air support during the day over the convoys and day and night across the U-boat transit routes from their bases forced the U-boats to remain submerged during the day and only operate on the surface at night to charge their batteries. As a result the time to get across the Bay of Biscay and out into the Atlantic was lengthening; the U-boat operating areas were steadily moving to the east and into the coastal waters of Britain.

The Allies deployed better weapons too. The Squid anti-submarine mortar was first used in January 1944; it exploited the information from more advanced sonars like the Type 147 which had entered service in the autumn of 1943. Better radars meant that air and surface units could spot the snorkel masts used by U-boats in 1944/45 to recharge batteries while they were submerged. Sonarbuoys were introduced in December 1943 which allowed aircraft to listen for the sound of a submerged U-boat, increasing the usefulness of the Allies' homing torpedoes. Magnetic Anomaly Detectors, which indicated the presence of a submerged U-boat, were used successfully by aircraft in February 1944. Life was getting very difficult for the U-boats and as their losses mounted the Allied merchant ship losses fell.[23]

That the Royal Navy was now an excellent anti-submarine force was beyond any doubt. Now with more than sufficient resources to defend the convoys, the escorts could also be used to hunt down U-boats wherever they could be found – round convoys, given away by the decoding of their Enigma signals, refuelling in the Atlantic, or in the outer fringes of the Bay of Biscay. Commanders like Peter Gretton or 'Johnnie' Walker – whose 2nd Escort Group destroyed six U-boats between 31 January and 19 February 1944 – were past masters at sinking U-boats. Walker, however, would not survive the war: he died of a stroke, having refused any rest during three years of conflict.[24]

With war material pouring into Britain unhindered by the U-boats from May 1943 onwards, the invasion of Europe was only a matter of time. But the invasion when it came would need all the skills of the Royal Navy's now crack anti-submarine force to protect the vulnerable invasion shipping.

The inshore battle 1944–45

Nor could the Germans achieve any appreciable successes against the mass of shipping that was launched across the English Channel in June 1944. Protecting the Allied invasion fleets was a layered anti-U-boat defence of ships and aircraft. Coastal Command flew intensive patrols in the Bay of Biscay and the mouth of the English Channel. Below the aircraft and along the flanks of the assault convoy routes were ten escort groups – 54 ships – poised to hunt any U-boat that was detected. If a U-boat made it past these layers of hunting aircraft and ships it still had to get past the close escort of the individual assault convoy.

As soon as the Germans realized the invasion was under way the U-boats started sailing from their Biscay bases and the fighting began. In the five days from 6 June there were 40 sightings of U-boats, with 24 being attacked – 18 of those at night. Six U-boats were sunk by air patrols, another three by aircraft and ships, two more by hunter-killer groups and finally one by a convoy's close escort. Yet despite loss after loss, the U-boats still kept trying to attack, although now only with vessels that had been fitted with snorkels to allow them to use their diesel engines to recharge their batteries while they were submerged. Fortunately, improvements in the radars fitted to Allied ships and aircraft made it possible for them to detect the top of a snorkel as it stuck above the surface of the waves and the noise of the diesel U-boat engines running while the snorkel was up also made them easy to hear on ASDICs that were used in the passive, or listening, mode. But the fight in the inshore waters was not easy.

Anti-submarine warfare in the shallow waters of the south-western approaches, English Channel and Irish Sea was very different from the deep waters of the open ocean. Now the flotillas of anti-submarine vessels had to deal with water eddies, wrecks and underwater rock formations, all of which could produce an ASDIC echo that might sound similar to a U-boat. Also in the shallow waters the U-boat could sit on the bottom to try to escape the attentions of the Navy. Often the response of the hunting warships was

massive overkill with depth-charges, Squid and Hedgehog attacks
against a damaged or flooded U-boat on the seabed in order to rip
open the U-boat's pressure hull and provide indisputable evidence of
the U-boat's destruction – human remains. In all, the Allies sank 36
U-boats operating in the Bay of Biscay and the English Channel in
June, July and August 1944. Moreover, with the breakout of Allied
land forces from Normandy, the German hold on the Biscay bases
was in danger and the U-boats were evacuated to Norway, losing
more of their number en route.[25]

The greatest technical challenge was yet to come, however. The
Germans finally started receiving new designs of U-boats – the Type
XXI and Type XXIII – which were very fast underwater, indeed
faster than some of the Allied escort vessels, threatening to under-
mine the hard-won Allied anti-submarine superiority. But they
arrived too late. The first of the Type XXI ocean-going U-boats only
became operational on 30 April 1945, while the Type XXIII, which
was operational from January, only carried two torpedoes, limiting
its ability to be a serious threat in coastal waters. The delay in the
German construction plans was due in no small part to the Allied
strategic air forces' attacks on the German transport system during
the winter of 1944/45 (against the wishes of Bomber Command).
These attacks slowed the rate of production of the submarines by
delaying the movement of the pre-fabricated submarine components.

With the German unconditional surrender on 7 May 1945, the
Admiralty signalled that all U-boats were to surface at noon on 8
May and make for designated British ports; over 150 did so, but 221
scuttled themselves at sea or in harbour rather than surrender. As
the U-boats made their way on the surface in accordance with the
Admiralty's order, they flew the Royal Navy's white ensign above
their own flag. The Battle of the Atlantic was over.[26]

CHAPTER 4

Home Waters and the Home Fleet 1940–45

The combination of the fall of France and the German victory in Denmark and Norway was a catastrophe for the British and for the Royal Navy. Between 9 April, when the German invasion of Denmark and Norway commenced, and 25 June, when the armistice between France and Germany came into effect, Britain's war plans were completely overturned. For the Royal Navy this was an unmitigated disaster; the enemy now controlled the European coastline from Hendaye on the Franco-Spanish border to Kirkenes in the Arctic Circle. Britain's main naval and military ally had been knocked out of the war. With the European coast under German control, and with so much territory in occupied Europe now available to Germany to exploit and loot, the British ability to impose an economic blockade on Germany was severely diminished.

But Britain was not, contrary to the popular imagination of World War II, alone – and nor was the Royal Navy. Backing Britain were the Dominions – Canada, New Zealand and Australia, all of whom had navies that were a vital part of the British war effort – and the wider empire, providing the United Kingdom with a vast economic and military potential. There were also those parts of various countries' armed forces and civilian populations who had escaped the onrushing Germans and successfully fled to Britain to form the 'free' forces of France, Poland, Holland, Norway and Belgium, which again enhanced the Royal Navy's strength, albeit in a small way.

Britain might not have been 'alone', but she was facing a fight for survival, and that survival would depend on the Royal Navy and the war at sea. The first task of the Navy following the fall of France was a very distasteful one – that of ensuring that French warships did not fall into German hands. In the Mediterranean Admirals Cunningham and Somerville had to deal with the majority of French ships that had escaped from France or were deployed before the armistice (see Chapter 4), while French ships that were in British ports were seized. Once the Vichy French naval forces in the UK had been neutralized, attention returned to the Germans. With the Germans encamped on the French Channel coast, invasion was the chief British fear, and the Royal Navy was required to carry out its most important traditional role – defending Britain from invasion.[1]

The Royal Navy saves Britain, summer 1940

In order to combat the threat of invasion, large numbers of destroyers were taken off convoy duties and, supported by cruisers, placed where they could strike at German invasion forces crawling across the English Channel. Patrols of auxiliary craft in the Channel were stepped up to give warning of any approaching German armada. Cruisers and destroyers shelled the German-held Channel ports in order to destroy the invasion barges. The RAF's Bomber Command devoted its rather paltry forces to ineffectively attacking the invasion ports from the air. Meanwhile, RAF Fighter Command duelled with the German Luftwaffe and everyone waited for the invasion that never came.

The myth of the Battle of Britain is that Fighter Command defeated the Luftwaffe and thus prevented a seaborne invasion. Yet it seems that the German Luftwaffe had achieved air superiority over the coastal regions of south-east England by early September 1940, something that was considered an essential precursor to a successful invasion. Many of the vital sector stations engaged in covering the likely invasion area within Fighter Command's 11 Group had been severely damaged. Large formations of German aircraft were able to penetrate inland and widen their attacks. By September the

Luftwaffe had gained at worst 'air parity' – the ability to control the air over friendly forces – but given their wide-ranging attacks and the increasingly ineffective response by 11 Group, it is more realistic to credit the Germans with having achieved a degree of local air superiority over south-east England – the ability to carry out operations without prohibitive interference from the RAF. Only when the Germans attacked London – beyond the effective range of their own fighters – could the RAF mount serious opposition.[2]

Yet having apparently achieved local air superiority, the German invasion did not come. Why? It is difficult to say with any certainty; after all it is unclear whether the Germans were really serious about an invasion – Operation *Sealion* – or whether they hoped to terrify Britain into capitulation with the threat of an all-out attack on British cities from the air. But the idea that the Battle of Britain was only about giving credence to a threat to attack cities is unsatisfying. Why then did the Germans go to the trouble of gaining local air superiority over the potential invasion areas and then throw it away to fight in an area in which the RAF was still able to operate effectively – over London? The often disregarded role of the Royal Navy is a possible answer.

If there was any one factor that caused the Germans to abandon their invasion plans – if indeed they were ever that serious about it – it was the fear of what British destroyers and cruisers, let alone battleships, would do to a German invasion force in the waters off south-east England. The relationship between the Royal Navy and the non-invasion of Britain is quite straightforward – the Germans had to invade by sea and were therefore at the mercy of the Royal Navy. The Germans knew this; indeed they had had first-hand experience of how dangerous a foe the Royal Navy was during their very recent invasion of Norway, where the British had inflicted huge damage on the Kriegsmarine, and used Fleet Air Arm Skua dive-bombers to sink the light cruiser *Konigsberg*, while the Norwegians had destroyed the cruiser *Blucher*. At the same time, the *Gneisenau, Scharnhorst, Lutzow, Nurnberg* and *Leipzig* had been damaged and were still under repair. Even at Dunkirk, where the Royal Navy's freedom of movement was severely hampered by having to evacuate the BEF, the Luftwaffe sank only five of the 56 British destroyers that were deployed. The result was that by late August the Germans had just one heavy cruiser, five light cruisers and ten destroyers to face, in the invasion area alone, eight cruisers, 36 destroyers with another 40 in reserve, plus the entire weight of the Home Fleet. So, unlike the Kriegsmarine, the Royal Navy was still able to fight a serious battle.[3]

More importantly, air superiority in this period lasted only as long as good weather and daylight. Clouds, night or bad weather meant that ships could operate with little chance of being successfully attacked. The German Luftwaffe in 1940 was not as accomplished at attacking warships as it was to become in 1941 in the Mediterranean, and the weather in the Channel was not as kindly as that over Crete. The inability of the German Luftwaffe to protect the invasion force at night made it vulnerable to the Royal Navy's destroyers and cruisers. The Royal Navy knew this. Admiral Sir Charles Forbes, the commander of the Home Fleet, deplored the frittering away of his force in penny packets around the coast on anti-invasion duties when he considered that an invasion, if it occurred (which he doubted), could be defeated at night within 24 hours of it being launched without bringing his battleships south from Scapa Flow. He made his views very clear to the First Sea Lord and to Churchill. However, standing up to Churchill was never a safe career move and Forbes was replaced in December 1940 by Admiral Tovey. Even the government seemed to realize that an invasion was unlikely, dispatching large numbers of tanks, soldiers and fighter aircraft to the Middle East in August 1940.[4]

Propaganda, political expediency and myth-making do not, however, change the essential facts of 1940. During an invasion scare in the Napoleonic Wars Lord Barham, the First Lord of the Admiralty, reputedly told anxious politicians that he had not said that the French could not come, only that they could not come *by sea*; this was also true in 1940. Germany might have gained sufficient local air superiority to prevent the RAF interfering in Operation *Sealion* if it went ahead, but not the Royal Navy. German airpower in 1940 was effective in daylight and good weather only.

It was just not possible for a German invasion fleet improvised from slow barges to get from embarkation ports – especially those in the shelter of the Scheldt estuary – to England and back in the hours of daylight. If the Germans had mounted Operation *Sealion*, it is almost certain that British cruisers and destroyers would have inflicted devastating losses on the invasion force by night – and the German navy was acutely aware of its own weakness and British strengths.

The Battle of Britain might have come and gone, but the Battle of the Atlantic was in full flow and now the Home Fleet, rather than the escorts of the Western Approaches Command, would be called on to play a full part in the battle.

Combating the German surface fleet

Despite the punishment the German surface fleet had received during the Norwegian campaign, once repairs had been made to the damaged heavy cruisers, pocket battleships and battlecruisers, the Germans would have a force that could pose a serious threat to the Royal Navy and Britain. More worrying for the British was the fact that new German warships would soon enter service, notably the battleships *Bismarck* and *Tirpitz*. The first German move came towards the end of 1940 when they deployed the pocket battleship *Admiral Scheer* and the heavy cruiser *Admiral Hipper* into the Atlantic.

Following a long refit in East Prussia, the *Admiral Scheer* had sailed from Brunsbüttel via a passage through the Kiel Canal just after 11:00 on 27 October and broke out into the Atlantic via the Denmark Strait between Iceland and Greenland on the 31st. The orders for her commanding officer, Captain Theodor Krancke, were straightforward: to upset the dispositions of British escort forces by first attacking a convoy from Canada to the UK, then move to the South Atlantic and the Indian Ocean to cause as much confusion, dislocation and damage to merchant shipping as possible.[5]

The first indication the British had that the *Scheer* was on the loose in the Atlantic was a radio message from the homeward-bound convoy HX 84 on 5 November 1940. The convoy of 38 merchant ships (one vessel had straggled from the convoy on 2 November) had sailed from Halifax on the morning of 28 October; its only escort was the armed merchant cruiser HMS *Jervis Bay*. The *Scheer* was sighted at 16:50 with less than two hours of daylight left in which she could destroy the convoy. The *Jervis Bay* went at once to full speed and closed the *Scheer*, who had also announced her presence by a salvo of heavy shells that had exploded harmlessly amongst the convoy. While *Jervis Bay* charged towards the pocket battleship, the convoy turned away and the order was given to scatter. The *Scheer*'s third salvo hit *Jervis Bay*, putting the steering gear, the forward control position and the radio office out of action as well as causing several fires; she kept closing, however, firing from a single gun at maximum elevation, but all her shells fell short of the *Scheer*, which continued to score hits. At 17:05 *Jervis Bay* was effectively out of control and still the *Scheer* pounded her with both her main and secondary armament. By 17:20 *Jervis Bay* was burning furiously as well as starting to sink by the stern; at 17:45 the order was given to abandon ship and still the *Scheer* kept firing for another 15 minutes. Finally, at 20:00, *Jervis Bay* sank. When news of the ship's gallant, if futile, resistance became known, her captain, Captain E.S.F. Fegen, was awarded a posthumous Victoria Cross. The *Jervis Bay*'s sacrifice was not in vain; in the gathering darkness the *Scheer* was only able to sink five ships from the convoy.[6]

The response of the British was immediate. Two convoys from Canada to the UK were recalled to Halifax, and a Bermuda convoy to Halifax was also turned round; in all, six convoys were disrupted. All independent sailings through the *Scheer*'s likely operating area were also suspended until 7 November. Only with HX 89, which sailed on 17 November, did the normal convoy cycle resume. Furthermore, the ocean escorts were augmented, older battleships were used in place of the armed merchant cruisers, and the convoys affected by the disruption were sailed in two groups of three.[7] It was assumed that the *Scheer* would run for a French Biscay port such as Brest to attempt to pass back to Germany. As a result the Home Fleet was disposed to watch the Greenland–Iceland–UK gaps and cover the possibility of a dash to France. But the *Scheer* had disappeared into the emptiness of the South Atlantic and would remain there, sinking solitary merchant vessels until she passed back through the Denmark Strait and reached Germany undetected in March 1941.[8]

Right at the end of November, the German heavy cruiser *Admiral Hipper* sailed from Hamburg with orders to attack the Atlantic and Gibraltar convoy routes. Like the *Scheer* she entered the Atlantic via the Denmark Strait, although the *Hipper* flew British colours during her breakout. Once in the Atlantic the *Hipper* faced two weeks of gales and nagging machinery problems, with the result that her captain decided to move further south. On the evening of 24 December a convoy was detected on *Hipper*'s radar and during the night she launched a torpedo attack that missed and went completely unnoticed by the convoy and its escorts. When the *Hipper* attacked again in the half-light before dawn, she made the rather unpleasant discovery that the convoy was being escorted by British cruisers, not the expected anti-submarine escort of sloops and corvettes which posed little threat to a ship like the *Hipper*. In a brief battle between 06:40 and around 07:15 the cruisers *Berwick* and *Bonaventure* engaged the *Hipper* as she retreated and eventually escaped in a rain squall.

The convoy was the troop convoy WS 5A, which accounts for its heavy escort of three cruisers and two aircraft carriers, HMS *Argus* and HMS *Furious*. Despite the element of surprise, the *Hipper* only managed to lightly damage one troop ship, the *Empire Trooper*. The *Berwick* received some damage but also scored a hit on the *Hipper* amidships. Deteriorating weather prevented the aircraft carriers from launching an air strike on the fleeing *Hipper* during the day. As with the earlier appearance of the *Scheer* as a surface raider, the British reinforced convoys at sea with heavier escorts from the Home Fleet – notably for convoys HX 97, SC 16 and SL 59, while HX 98 returned to Sydney, Nova Scotia, and was combined with HX 100 and sailed on New Year's Day 1941. The strength of the British reaction, which was reported to the *Hipper* thanks to the German version of Britain's 'Y' or direction-finding service, persuaded the *Hipper*, despite having sunk only one independently routed merchant vessel on the day of her brush with WS 5A, to head for the safety of German air cover from France and make for port at Brest, where she arrived on the evening of 27 December after a high-speed passage to avoid the net the Royal Navy was trying to catch her in.[9]

On 23 January it was the turn of *Gneisenau* and *Scharnhorst* to slip out of Kiel and head up the Norwegian coastline in order to break out into the North Atlantic. Alerted by intelligence – it seems that the German ships were sighted moving through the Great Belt between Denmark and Sweden – the Home Fleet put to sea in order to be ready to intercept the German ships as they passed between Greenland and Scotland. After an aborted attempt to break out on 28 January – the German ships were very briefly sighted by the British cruiser *Naiad* before losing contact – the two battlecruisers success-fully entered the Atlantic on 3/4 February. They sighted convoy HX 106 on 8 February, but this east-bound convoy was escorted by the battleship HMS *Ramillies* and the German ships broke off rather than risk the damage that would occur if they fought. The presence of a British battleship was not an accident. It was now policy to sail as many convoys as possible with an old battleship as protection before the anti-submarine escort joined as the convoy approached Britain – the Royal Navy's armed merchant cruisers, as the experience of *Jervis Bay* showed, were just not strong enough to fend off an attack by a German heavy ship. However, on 22 February the German battle-cruisers found a group of unescorted merchant ships some 500 miles east of Newfoundland. The merchant ships were all from a recently dispersed outbound convoy and as such had no protection; five ships were sunk, but several managed to make raider reports which alerted the Admiralty to the presence of the German ships. Moving south-east the *Gneisenau* and *Scharnhorst* sighted and were sighted by HMS *Malaya*, which was escorting the Sierra Leone-bound convoy SL 67, but again took no action. The Home Fleet was by now deployed to try and trap the Germans, but the *Scharnhorst* and *Gneisenau* had no inten-tion to try to get back to Germany. Instead they headed for Brest, arriving there on 22 March, where they were regularly attacked by Coastal Command and Bomber Command aircraft.[10]

Attention now turned to two new German ships, the battleship *Bismarck* and the heavy cruiser *Prinz Eugen*, which were thought to be getting ready for their own sortie into the Atlantic. Unfortunately the Admiralty's Naval Intelligence Division was very much in the dark about the German plans, as indeed they had been about the previous German surface ship sorties. The British were not yet able to decipher the German naval Enigma machine codes. However, Bletchley Park could read the German air force Enigma codes, thanks to sloppy procedures and poor communications security in the Luftwaffe. This was not perfect, but it was a start. The other problem the Navy faced was that once the Germans were at sea, without knowledge of their intentions, the British would have to rely on the Germans breaking radio silence to give a chance of locating the raiders by radio direction finding – an unlikely occurrence. The British were therefore almost totally reliant on a net of searching aircraft and ships to back up the Admiralty's and the Commander in Chief Home Fleet's best guesses as to where the Germans would go once they were at sea.

The German plan was an evolution of a concept that the commander of the Kriegsmarine, Admiral Erich Raeder, had been formulating since the early raids on British and Allied shipping in 1940 and early 1941. Given the dislocation that these earlier raids had achieved, out of all proportion to the resources employed, and the strain they had placed on an already stretched Royal Navy that did not have enough cruisers, fast battleships or aircraft carriers to deal with a major surface threat, Raeder felt that a raid by the *Bismarck* and another major unit would do irreparable damage to the British convoy system in the Atlantic. Fortunately for the British, Raeder was not prepared to wait for *Bismarck*'s sister ship, the *Tirpitz*, to finish her working-up period, and the most obvious support for a sortie – the *Scharnhorst* and the *Gneisenau* at Brest – were unavailable: the *Scharnhorst* was under repair following engine problems, while the *Gneisenau* had been hit by a torpedo while in Brest harbour from a suicidal attack by Coastal Command aircraft as well as suffering minor damage from bombs while in dry dock, courtesy of the RAF.

The *Bismarck* sailed from Gotenhafen in the Baltic on 18 May 1941; by the 19th she had met her consort for the foray into the Atlantic, the *Prinz Eugen*. As the two ships passed through the Great

Belt that separated Denmark from Sweden as well as the Baltic from the North Sea, they were shadowed by the neutral Swedish cruiser *Gotland*, which informed the Swedish naval authorities about the German force. Then a Swedish naval officer passed the news to a friend in the Norwegian embassy in Stockholm, who immediately informed the British. By 21:00 on 20 May the Admiralty were aware that a German attempt to break out into the Atlantic was now a possibility and it tied in with decrypted Luftwaffe signals that indicated that it had been paying unusual attention to the position of the edge of the pack ice between Jan Mayen Island and Greenland.

The British countermeasures swung into operation. The warships on patrol in the Greenland–Iceland–UK gaps were warned to be extra vigilant. Coastal Command was ordered to search the Norwegian coast and it was a photo-reconnaissance Spitfire that found the German ships at anchor in Bergen on 21 May. This confirmed the likelihood of a breakout and the Home Fleet was put on short notice for steam while the Admiralty reinforced the Home Fleet by allocating to it the battle cruiser HMS *Repulse* and the new aircraft carrier HMS *Victorious* which had been tasked to escort a large troop convoy. At the same time, the Commander in Chief Home Fleet, Admiral Sir John Tovey, ordered Vice Admiral Lancelot Holland to sail with the battlecruiser HMS *Hood*, the brand-new battleship HMS *Prince of Wales* and five destroyers to cover the cruisers HMS *Norfolk* and HMS *Suffolk* who were watching the Denmark Strait. Bad weather stopped an air attack on the *Bismarck* or *Prinz Eugen* at Bergen and prevented Coastal Command's reconnaissance aircraft getting any more sightings of either ship. The British waited nervously for news, news that was eventually provided on 22 May by a Fleet Air Arm aircraft flying from Hatston in the Orkneys on the initiative of the base commander. The Fleet Air Arm aircraft managed to fly under the clouds along the Norwegian coast and into Bergen harbour; it confirmed that the German ships had sailed. Just before 23:00 on 22 May Admiral Tovey took the battleship HMS *King George V*, the aircraft carrier *Victorious*, four cruisers and six destroyers out of Scapa Flow and into the Atlantic. With the dispositions made, all that could be done was to wait and see what the Germans would do.

Fig. 4.1. The German battleship *Bismarck* is seen here in action
during the battle with HMS *Hood* and HMS *Prince of Wales*.

At 20:32 on 23 May the waiting ended: the German ships were
sighted by the cruisers *Norfolk* and *Suffolk* in the Denmark Strait.
The weather that night in the strait was foul, but the two British
cruisers continued to shadow the German ships, aided by information from *Suffolk*'s radar. The sighting reports made by *Norfolk* and
Suffolk were received by Admiral Holland in HMS *Hood*, who shaped
a course to intercept the *Bismarck* and *Prinz Eugen* on 24 May.

The *Bismarck* and *Prinz Eugen* were sighted by the *Hood* and
Prince of Wales at 05:35 and they closed to attack. Just after 05:50
the range was down to about 25,000 yards and the *Hood* opened
fire, followed a minute later by the *Prince of Wales*. The German
ships replied with great accuracy and concentrated their fire on the
Hood, rapidly starting a fire amidships. At 06:00 the *Bismarck* fired
her fifth salvo of the battle and at least one or more 15-inch shells
hit the *Hood*, causing a massive explosion in her after magazines.
The *Hood*'s forward section was seen to rear bows up and sink out
of sight in a matter of minutes, while the after section of the ship
had disappeared from sight in the cloud of the explosion. When the
smoke cleared there was nothing to be seen of the interwar pride of
the Navy but floating debris torn from the bowels of the ship as she

sank. There were only three survivors from her crew of more than 1,400 officers and men.

Despite the loss of the *Hood*, the *Prince of Wales* continued the fight and was hit repeatedly by 15-inch and 8-inch shells, including one that passed through the bridge without exploding but still killing or wounding almost everyone there. At 06:13 the *Prince of Wales* turned to open the range and as she did so the ship's giant after quadruple 14-inch gun turret jammed, reducing the battleship's firepower by 40 per cent. This wasn't due to damage, but rather to the newness of the ship: the *Prince of Wales* had not had the chance to work up properly; she had even sailed to fight the *Bismarck* with dockyard workers still onboard, frantically trying to persuade A and X turrets, each with four 14-inch guns, to behave. The battle had lasted only 20 minutes, but in that time the *Prince of Wales* had inflicted sufficient damage to the *Bismarck*'s fuel tanks that the German commander, Admiral Günther Lütjens, decided that the *Bismarck* and *Prinz Eugen* should separate and the *Bismarck* head for St Nazaire on the French Biscay coast for repairs.

The German force thus divided, the *Prinz Eugen* successfully slipped away from the British shadowers to carry out attacks on merchant ships and convoys. However, she achieved nothing and arrived at Brest on 1 June. The *Bismarck*, on the other hand, was still very firmly in the British sights. Indeed that night at around midnight Swordfish torpedo bombers from HMS *Victorious* managed to locate and attack the *Bismarck*, but it seems that no hits were made. The British then lost touch with her.

For over a day the British groped blindly in all directions trying to find the *Bismarck*, but without success. She had in fact turned south-east towards Brest rather than west to go deeper into the Atlantic or north-east to head back between Greenland and the UK in order to return to Germany. Finally, during the mid-morning of 26 May, an RAF Catalina flying boat sighted the *Bismarck* nearly 700 miles west of Brest. It seemed that, barring a miracle, only Force H, coming up from Gibraltar and between the *Bismarck* and France, could stop the battleship reaching safety – the rest of the British fleet was too far behind.

Fortunately Force H had an aircraft carrier, HMS *Ark Royal*, and thus an air strike to slow down the *Bismarck* was launched. Unfortunately the Swordfish aircraft attacked not the *Bismarck* but the British cruiser *Sheffield*, which was in the briefed target area unbeknown to the aircrews. The weather was so bad that the Swordfish had to use radar to search the area and, having located what they thought was the correct target, attacked. Happily all 11 torpedoes that were launched at the *Sheffield* missed. Once the mistake was realized the Swordfish returned to the *Ark Royal*. There was, however, despite the mistake, enough time to launch one more strike against the *Bismarck*. Fifteen Swordfish took off and flew back to the *Sheffield* which then signalled the range of bearing of the *Bismarck*. This time the strike went off as planned and two, possibly three, hits were seen, despite heavy anti-aircraft fire from the *Bismarck*. One of the hits was on the port side amidships, but it did not do any serious damage. The other hit, on the starboard side right aft, was a different matter – it jammed the rudders and flooded the steering gear compartment. Frantic efforts managed to centre the starboard rudder, but the port one remained obstinately stuck at 12° to port and it proved impossible to steer the battleship using her engines alone. Indeed it proved impossible to do anything but steam directly into the rising gale – straight back towards the British Home Fleet.

The British were mightily relieved at the news that the *Bismarck* had turned round and was steaming slowly towards them. The battleships *King George V* and *Rodney*, plus a gaggle of appreciative cruisers and destroyers, would now be ready to engage the *Bismarck* after dawn on 27 May. Before that main engagement, however, the destroyers were let off the leash to attack the *Bismarck* during the night with torpedoes. Despite their efforts, they did not gain any hits and the German battleship retaliated with radar-controlled gunfire which straddled but did not damage the attacking destroyers – she was still an enemy to be wary of.

By morning a gale was raging and at 08:20 HMS *Norfolk* signalled that the enemy was 16 miles away; a few minutes later the *Bismarck* came into sight. At 08:47 *Rodney* opened fire, followed a minute later by *King George V*; at 08:54 *Rodney* scored two hits with her third 16-inch salvo, one on *Bismarck*'s forecastle, the other amidships. Eight minutes later another 16-inch shell hit the *Bismarck*, destroying her forward two gun turrets. Soon only one of the two aft turrets remained in action and at 09:31 she fired her last salvo. By 10:15 the *Bismarck* had been battered into a flaming wreck, ablaze almost from end to end and listing to port, but it seemed that gunfire alone would not sink her. HMS *Dorsetshire* was sent in to finish things off with torpedoes. Following two hits to starboard and one to port, *Bismarck* capsized and sank.

While the *Bismarck* had been dealt with, there still remained a number of major German warships ready to go into action, three of which – the battlecruisers *Gneisenau*, *Scharnhorst* and the heavy cruiser *Prinz Eugen* – were perilously close to the North Atlantic convoy routes in Brest. To deal with this threat the Admiralty could only deploy a ring of submarines and Coastal Command patrol aircraft to watch the port while enjoining Bomber Command to attack the German ships so as to damage them enough to make a sortie impossible. Bomber Command was less than enthusiastic and torpedo bomber attacks were limited by the small numbers of aircraft available to Coastal Command. Yet damage was inflicted often enough to make life difficult for the Germans. All the British could do was watch and wait and try to decide if a raid into the Atlantic was likely or an operation to get the ships back to Germany was the enemy's objective.

In fact by February 1942 the British had come to the conclusion that the Germans would themselves remove this dangerous threat to Britain's sea communications by shifting their ships from Brest to Germany and thence to Norway. Unfortunately for the Royal Navy, the Germans chose to send their ships via the English Channel. The British plan to stop such a move, which relied heavily on the RAF, proved to be a dismal failure. The British had accurately predicted how the Germans would conduct the operation; the problem was that the British thought that the passage past Dover would set the timescale for the operation. The Admiralty predicted that the Germans would pass Dover close to high tide in order to minimize the threat from mines and make the most of around 14 hours of darkness to protect them as they went up the Channel. However, the Germans thought it more important to hide their departure and rely on surprise, speed and air cover to get them past Dover in daylight, irrespective of the time of high tide. By disguising their time of departure the Germans hoped to ensure that a move south by the Home Fleet from Scapa Flow in time to intercept them off Holland would be impossible.[11]

Sir Bertram Ramsey, Vice Admiral Dover, had only six Fleet Air Arm Swordfish torpedo bombers, six destroyers, the minelayer HMS *Welshman* and up to six motor torpedo boats with which to stop the Germans. His plan was to launch a coordinated torpedo attack with the motor torpedo boats and the Swordfish aircraft in the Straits of Dover. This striking force would not be enough to sink the three German ships, but it could cripple one or more of them within range of the shore batteries around Dover. The six destroyers, on the other hand, would attack in the southern North Sea, 30 miles to the north-east of the Westhinder sandbank. Here they would have room to manoeuvre away from the enemy's shore batteries on the French side of the straits and also be clear of the British minefields in the area. Additionally, it was expected that the RAF's Bomber Command and Coastal Command would launch heavy air attacks on the German ships.

At 19:30 on 11 February 1942 the *Scharnhorst*, *Gneisenau* and *Prinz Eugen* left Brest. Two of the patrolling RAF aircraft suffered radar failures and did not detect the German departure. Nor did the RAF alert the Admiralty to the fact that there were holes in the net cast for the Germans, nor replace the aircraft that had been recalled owing to broken equipment. The first indication the Navy had that the Germans were forcing the Channel was at 10:25 when a radar station at Hastings reported a convoy south-west of the Dover straits. At 11:25 the Admiralty confirmed that these were the three German heavy ships. The limited forces at Dover and Harwich went into the attack as planned – five motor torpedo boats (MTBs), six Swordfish aircraft and six destroyers.

First to make their attack were the five MTBs supported by

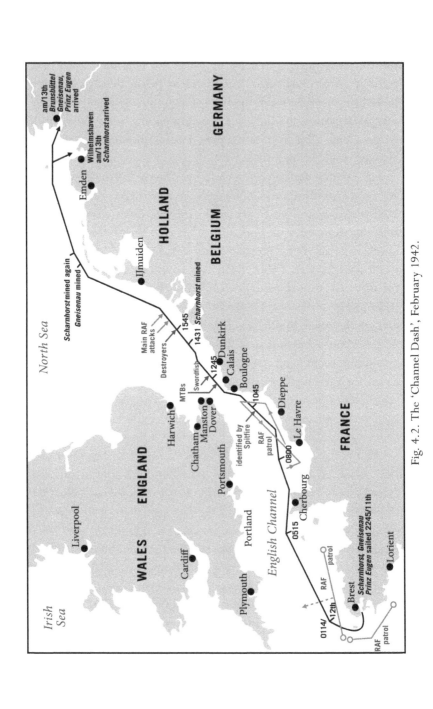

Fig. 4.2. The 'Channel Dash', February 1942.

motor gunboats. Under heavy fire from the outer screen of German E-boats and destroyers, which were also faster than the British MTBs, there was no real option except to fire the torpedoes at long range. This gave the Germans plenty of time to alter course to avoid them and consequently the MTBs scored no hits. Just as the MTBs were attempting to withdraw, the six Swordfish and a fraction of the promised escort of three squadrons of RAF Spitfires commenced their attack – the two additional squadrons of Spitfires tasked with attacking the German anti-aircraft gunners did not arrive at all. Attacking in two sub-flights of three aircraft, the Swordfish were mercilessly attacked by German fighters; by the time the first sub-flight passed over the screen of E-boats and destroyers, all three had been damaged and the leading aircraft flown by Lieutenant Commander Eugene Esmonde had had one of its lower wings almost completely shot away. Esmonde, whose aircraft got to within 3,000 yards of the German battlecruisers before being hit again and crash-ing into the sea, was awarded a posthumous Victoria Cross for his bravery. The remaining two aircraft continued to close and both dropped their torpedoes before crashing. Again no hits were scored. The second flight of three Swordfish torpedo bombers were last seen flying straight towards the German ships. Once they passed beyond the ring of E-boats and destroyers, they were not seen again.

Throughout the afternoon Bomber Command aircraft – a total of some 242 in three waves – tried to find the German ships, but only 39 actually managed to do so and attack. All failed to score a hit. Some also managed to bomb the Royal Navy's destroyers which were closing on the German convoy from the north-west, although happily in this case the RAF's aim did not improve. In part the failure by Bomber Command to damage the German ships was due to the poor weather; cloud cover made it difficult to find the ships – a clear reminder of the limitations of airpower in this period. However, the impact of RAF doctrine cannot be ignored. The RAF doctrine – some might say doctrinaire approach – was that airpower was indi-visible and flexible. This meant that a centrally controlled bomber force could be used against a wide range of targets without the need for it to be broken up into small packets and farmed out to those who wanted air support. However, hitting warships from high altitude was extremely difficult and Bomber Command, as evidenced by the Butt and Singleton reports of 1941 and 1942, had problems hitting cities, let alone fast-manoeuvring ships. Meanwhile, snow was hampering the move of 28 RAF torpedo bombers to the area from the north of Britain; they were able to attack only after the Germans were well past Dover and again scored no hits.[12]

While this massive and, from a British perspective, frustratingly ineffective air battle was taking place over the southern North Sea, the destroyers based at Harwich launched their own torpedo attack on the German ships. Fortunately the destroyers earmarked for this task under Admiral Ramsey's plan were already at sea, but one of the six had to turn back almost immediately with engine problems. The remaining five – all worn-out World War I veterans that normally escorted convoys up and down Britain's east coast – picked up the German ships on their radars and the worsening weather hid their approach until they were about four miles from the enemy. Attacking in two divisions, the ships came under an extremely heavy and accurate fire from both the battlecruisers and the escorting German destroyers. HMS *Worcester* received very heavy damage and after frantic efforts to put out fires and repair damage to her engines, managed to make her way back to Harwich, aided by the other destroyers. Despite the determination and bravery shown by the five ships in pressing home their attacks while under heavy fire and in worsening weather, no torpedoes hit their targets. Only as the German ships neared home did they suffer damage – from mines; the *Gneisenau* was slightly damaged, the *Scharnhorst* more seriously. The failure of the RAF, and the Navy in particular, was a terrible blow to British prestige. *The Times* summed up the situation, saying that:

> Vice-Admiral [Otto] Ciliax has succeeded where the Duke of Medina Sidonia failed: with trifling loses he has sailed a hostile fleet from an Atlantic harbour, up the English Channel, and through the straits of Dover to safe anchorage in a North Sea port. Nothing more mortifying to the pride of sea-power has happened in home waters since the seventeenth century.

Plate 1. *The Battle of Matapan* by David Cobb.

Plate 2. *Empire Day 1941* by Paul Wright. HMS *Hood* is depicted on fire moments before she exploded.

Plate 3. A recruiting poster for the Women's Royal Naval Service (WRNS).

Plate 4. British landing craft carries American troops, c. May–June 1944.

Despite this damning and accurate assessment, at least the 'Channel Dash' was a strategic defeat for the Germans – they had made the Royal Navy's tasks much easier by removing such a direct threat to the Atlantic convoys.[13]

Waiting in the wings, however, was the Bismarck's sister ship, the Tirpitz. It was imperative that the Germans were deterred from using the Tirpitz against the Atlantic convoys. Fortunately there was only one dry dock big enough to hold her for repairs and maintenance – the Normandie dock in St Nazaire. It was decided that a joint attack by commandoes and the Royal Navy could destroy the dock and prevent its use by the Tirpitz – the Navy had been used as a springboard for commando raids along the coast of occupied Europe since 1940. Such was the importance of the raid that the Navy was prepared to sacrifice a destroyer to ensure the destruction of the Normandie dock gates. But the attack would not be easy. St Nazaire lay five miles from the sea up the Loire river. The harbour, as a U-boat base and the only one capable of repairing a Tirpitz-sized battleship in France, was heavily defended with gun batteries of various calibres along the estuary leading to St Nazaire; even the anti-aircraft guns protecting the area could be used against an approaching force.

The attack went in during the early hours of 28 March 1942. The destroyer HMS Campbeltown had been altered to look like a German torpedo boat to help the force penetrate the Loire estuary; she had also been packed with three tons of explosives to destroy the dock gates. Three-quarters of a mile from the dock gates the Germans realized what was happening and opened fire on the Campbeltown and the motor launches carrying the commandoes, but to no avail. At 01:34, four minutes later than planned, the Campbeltown crashed into the dock gates and her embarked commandoes swarmed ashore. The motor launches, too, were landing their commandoes under a very heavy fire. Such was the strength of the German resistance that it proved impossible for the unarmoured motor launches to come back in to pick up the landing force and instead they attempted to escape over land, but were all captured. As the naval force withdrew, the losses continued to mount, but just before noon that morning *Campbeltown* blew up, demolishing the dock gates and making it unusable. The raid had been a success but at a heavy cost: out of 16 motor launches 12 were lost, out of 622 naval personnel and commandoes who took part in the raid only 228 returned to England; five more escaped overland to Spain, 169 were killed and 215 captured. The losses might have been heavy but the objective had been attained: the only dock the *Tirpitz* could use was put out of action and she never operated in the Atlantic. Instead she lurked in Norwegian fjords – a dark brooding presence for those embarking on the Arctic convoy route.[14]

The Arctic convoys

On 22 June 1941 Germany invaded Russia. Churchill immediately committed Britain to providing military aid to the USSR, despite his well-known anti-communism. Finally on 18 July the Russians accepted – somewhat grudgingly – the British offer of aid. That aid could only be delivered either via an overland route through Persia or by sea round the top of Norway and to the north Russian ports of Murmansk and Archangel – the Arctic run was thus initiated.

The political decision to run convoys to north Russia added greatly to the Royal Navy's problems and those of the Home Fleet in particular. The convoy route was hemmed in by polar ice to the north and by Norway to the south and east. Furthermore, Norway provided ample anchorages and bases in its deep fjords for German warships and U-boats, as well as numerous airfields for the Luftwaffe. Arctic convoys could therefore expect to experience a range of attack far greater than the norm in the Atlantic, turning each convoy into a major naval operation. Worse still, during the summer months, near constant daylight would deprive the convoy of any chance of hiding in darkness, while in winter the polar ice would force the convoys much closer to German bases in Norway. All the time there was the dreadful weather, the freezing water that would kill anyone within minutes of entering it and the constant battle against the build-up of ice on ships, which would threaten to sink them if ignored.

The first Arctic convoy – Operation *Dervish* – sailed in August from Iceland; it consisted of six merchant ships loaded with raw materials that the Russians desperately needed. The *Dervish* convoy had a close anti-submarine escort, in many respects similar in role to that of an Atlantic convoy, but here the similarity ended, as over the horizon the Home Fleet's aircraft carrier HMS *Victorious* and two cruisers waited to pounce on any German surface ships that tried to intervene. The convoy was a success and all the merchant ships arrived safely in north Russia. The next convoy was run at the end of September – PQ 1 with 11 merchant ships – and at the same time a return convoy (QP 1) sailed from Murmansk. In all 12 PQ/QP convoys sailed before the end of 1941 and only one merchant ship out of 108 was lost to German action. This would not remain so during 1942.[15]

From March 1942 the Germans began to react violently against the PQ/QP convoys; in particular the surface threat to the convoys was escalated. In February 1942 the German's 'Channel Dash' had brought the *Scharnhorst*, *Gneisenau* and *Prinz Eugen* back from Brest to strengthen naval forces in Norway, but the *Gneisenau* was soon gutted by an air raid on Kiel while the *Prinz Eugen* was torpedoed and very heavily damaged by the submarine HMS *Trident* off Trondheimsfjord in late February 1942. However, the most important change was the German decision in early 1942 to base their new *Bismarck* class battleship *Tirpitz* in Norway where it could either try to break out into the Atlantic convoy routes or operate against the Arctic convoys. This made every Arctic convoy a major fleet operation for the Royal Navy. German reinforcements meant that the quiet passages of the early convoys were soon forgotten.

PQ 13 in March was lashed by a severe gale, causing the convoy to disperse as the ships fought the elements rather than the Germans. When the gale abated to merely very bad weather, with storms reducing visibility, the escorts set about rounding up the merchant ships and fending off German air attacks and three German destroyers which had sailed to intercept the convoy. Fortunately for the British the German capital ships such as the heavy cruiser *Hipper* that were based in northern Norway were immobilized by a lack of fuel. In poor visibility but with the warning of radar, HMS *Trinidad*, a *Colony* class cruiser and part of PQ 13's covering force, surprised the three large German destroyers. One, *Z26*, suffered heavy damage from *Trinidad*'s salvos of 6-inch shells. However, owing to a gyroscope failure, one of the cruiser's torpedoes reversed back on itself and hit the *Trinidad*. While the crew tried to save their ship, the destroyer HMS *Eclipse* pursued the escaping *Z26*, but as she was delivering fatal damage to the German ship the other two German destroyers appeared out of the snow squalls and drove her off. But it was too late for *Z26*; she soon capsized and sank. Other British destroyers, which were busy either searching for stray merchant ships or shepherding the gaggle of vessels that answered to the name PQ 13, hastened to help the stricken cruiser. Soon *Trinidad* was limping towards the Kola Inlet at 7 knots, arriving there on 30 March. But PQ 13 was still at sea and despite the efforts of the escorts to round up strays and protect the convoy, German U-boats and aircraft managed to sink five of the 19 merchant ships.[16]

Nor was PQ 13 the only convoy to suffer during the spring and early summer of 1942. In April PQ 14 suffered severe damage from icebergs; only eight out of the 24 merchant ships were able to head towards the Kola Inlet and German aircraft managed to sink one of them. The next pair of convoys, PQ 15 going to Russia and QP 11 bringing empty ships back to Britain, lost the cruiser HMS *Edinburgh*. In May PQ 16 was heavily attacked and lost 20 per cent of its merchant ships; the cruiser *Trinidad*, patched up in Russia, was damaged again on its way home to the UK and had to be scuttled. Then in July came the convoy that has become synonymous with disaster – PQ 17.

PQ 17 had sailed from Iceland on 27 June, the day after the returning convoy, QP 13, had left Archangel. Ice damage and a grounding as PQ 17 sorted itself out forced two merchant ships to drop out from the convoy, leaving 34 plodding towards Russia. The Germans found the convoy during the afternoon of 1 July, but sank nothing until 4 July when three merchant ships were sunk and one was damaged. However, the day before, the Admiralty discovered that the *Tirpitz* was not at her moorings and there was no certain information as to her whereabouts. The First Sea Lord and others at the Admiralty felt there was a strong possibility that the *Tirpitz* and possibly other German units were at sea. Naval Intelligence disagreed, alluding to the absence of any Ultra decrypts indicating that the Germans had sailed, but this was not enough for the First Sea Lord. The convoy was ordered to scatter. Shorn of their protective escorts, as the merchantmen made their separate ways towards Russia they were exposed to the full weight of German U-boat and air attack. Eleven merchantmen survived to reach Archangel. It was the worst convoy disaster of the war; *Tirpitz* had returned to harbour without ever menacing the convoy. Only one more PQ convoy was run before Operation *Torch* absorbed the warships that were needed on the Murmansk and Archangel runs, forcing the suspension of the Arctic convoys.[17]

When the Arctic convoys resumed in December 1942 they received new code letters: 'JW' for Russian-bound convoys and 'RA' for homeward ones. Admiral Tovey also ensured that they were given a much stronger destroyer escort so that they could stand a chance of fighting off a German surface force rather than have the convoy scatter. The new arrangements were tested on 31 December 1942 when the German pocket battleship *Lutzow*, the heavy cruiser *Hipper* and six destroyers attempted to attack convoy JW 51B. The convoy had an escort of five *O* class fleet destroyers, an older destroyer, plus other escorts with a covering force of two cruisers further off. As was usual on the Arctic convoy routes, JW 51B experienced an atrocious storm which caused some straggling as well as heaping misery on the crews of the merchant ships and their escorts; as the gale died away the convoys ploughed on through the obligatory snow storms. The battle, once the German ships were sighted, took place in the twilight of the Artic winter.

Despite the gloom and blinding snow squalls it was a brilliant example of convoy defence. For an hour, while the cruisers HMS *Sheffield* and HMS *Jamaica*, both armed with 6-inch guns, charged down from the north, the four destroyers held off what should have been an overwhelming force. The German commander had divided his force to allow both sides of the convoy to be attacked, *Hipper* from the north and *Lutzow* from the south, each with three destroy-

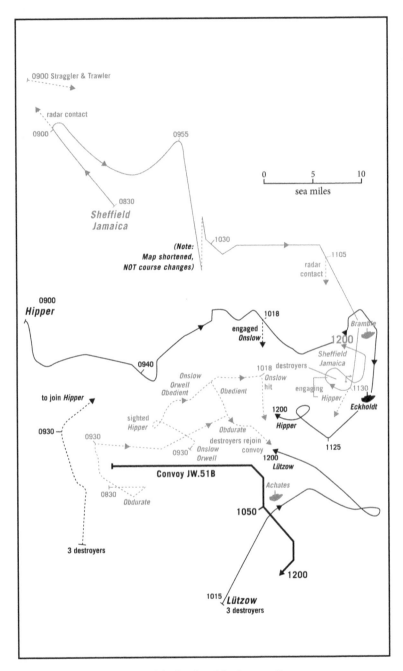

Fig. 4.3. The battle of the Barents Sea.

ers in support. It was the German destroyers of the northern group that first brushed against the convoy, and on being charged by HMS *Obdurate* at 09:30 fell back on the *Hipper*. By 10:00 the four *O* class destroyers had placed themselves between the *Hipper* and the convoy, opening a rapid fire on the German cruiser, before HMS *Obdurate* and HMS *Obedient* were sent back to cover the convoy. *Hipper* then timorously turned away to the north – straight towards the closing British light cruisers. About ten or 15 minutes later *Hipper* turned back south and her lacklustre gunnery rapidly improved, severely damaging HMS *Onslow* and wounding the escort commander, Captain Robert Sherbrooke, before she again swung away to the north, leaving the *Onslow* crippled.

Meanwhile, the *Lutzow* had managed to pass by the convoy until it too lay on the same side of JW 51B as the *Hipper*, invalidating the German plan of attack. At 11:00 *Lutzow* was sighted by the escorts and they again moved to place themselves between the German ships, now both on the eastern side of the convoy. As the *Lutzow* moved south-east it allowed *Hipper* to concentrate her fire on HMS *Achates* which was industriously laying smoke to conceal the merchant ships. After several large-calibre shell hits, the *Achates* slowly started to sink, burning furiously, but the anti-submarine trawler *Northern Gem* went alongside her as she capsized and rescued the survivors in a brilliant display of seamanship. Finally the *Lutzow* moved towards the convoy at just the moment that the cruisers under Rear Admiral Robert Burnett sighted the *Hipper* and opened fire at a range of seven miles, scoring damaging hits. Surprised and realizing that the pincer attack had failed, the Germans broke off the battle and escaped westwards with Burnett's cruisers in pursuit. Then two of the German destroyers mistook Burnett's cruisers for their own side and tried to join the British ships. At point blank range HMS *Sheffield* swept past the *Friedrich Eckholdt* and practically blew her out of the water, while HMS *Jamaica* drove off the other German destroyer, the *Richard Beitzen*. At 14:00 the British cruisers that had continued to pursue the Germans through the use of radar finally lost contact. The convoy continued unmolested to the Kola Inlet, arriving on 3 January; the badly injured

Captain Sherbrooke was awarded a Victoria Cross.[18]

In March 1943 the Admiralty decided that it could no longer run Arctic convoys. The decision to suspend them, however, is not straightforward and is not an indication of a crisis in the Battle of the Atlantic or that the destroyers committed to the convoys were needed to fight the U-boats. The First Sea Lord, Dudley Pound, advised the Cabinet's defence committee on 16 March that the route should be suspended, which was the day that HX 229 was sighted and the day before SC 122 was discovered and subsequently attacked by U-boats. The explanation for the suspension of the Arctic route is more to do with the shortage of capital ships in the Royal Navy rather than an escort shortage. By mid-March the Arctic nights were shortening quickly, increasing the exposure of a convoy and its escort to air and surface attack in conjunction with the existing submarine threat from U-boats based in Norway. Air attack could be dealt with by the use of the Royal Navy's few escort carriers that were trickling into service, carriers which also provided anti-submarine air cover during the passage to and from Murmansk, but it was the surface threat that was the real problem, especially when combined with air and submarine attacks.[19]

The German surface threat based in Norway was by March 1943 considerable, comprising the battleship *Tirpitz*, the battlecruiser *Scharnhorst*, the pocket battleship *Lutzow* and the cruiser *Nurnberg*. To deal with a potential attack by these German ships required an extremely strong British close and distant covering force from the Home Fleet to protect the convoy. But once the battleships and fleet carriers of the Home Fleet were inside the Barents Sea they would be at the mercy of the U-boats and the German Luftwaffe. Admiral Tovey, the commander of the Home Fleet, considered such a risk unacceptable. It might only need a single lucky German U-boat or torpedo-bomber attack to leave the Home Fleet weakened enough to allow German warships to stage a breakout into the Atlantic. This was a scenario that the Admiralty found more disturbing than what was happening in the Atlantic convoy battles.[20]

Clearly the Royal Navy needed to find some way of dealing with the German ships, especially the *Tirpitz*, even if the Germans

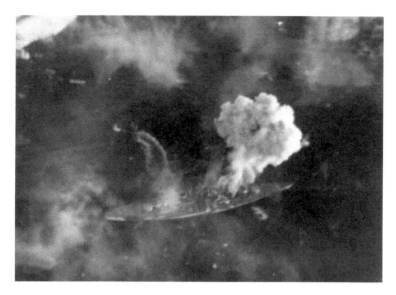

Fig. 4.4. The German battleship *Tirpitz* under attack by
Fleet Air Arm Barracuda torpedo/dive-bombers.

refused to come out and fight. The Navy had tried in October 1942 to cripple the *Tirpitz* with 'chariots' – British versions of the Italian two-man 'human torpedoes' – but the attack failed. In September 1943 they tried again, this time with midget submarines – X craft. The attack succeeded in crippling the *Tirpitz* although the *Scharnhorst* was undamaged. When the *Tirpitz* was finally ready for sea trials, the Navy struck again, this time from the air. The Fleet Air Arm launched a well-executed attack – Operation *Tungsten* – in early April 1944. Forty Fairey Barracudas, escorted by 79 fighters launched from HMS *Victorious*, HMS *Furious* and four escort carriers, succeeded in hitting or near missing the *Tirpitz* 16 times, leaving her crippled again. Improved German air defences frustrated subsequent FAA efforts to get another successful attack in, so the immobile *Tirpitz* was left for the RAF's Bomber Command, which finally sunk her on 12 November 1944.[21]

By the time the *Tirpitz* was sunk, the *Scharnhorst* had also met its end. In December 1943 the Germans attempted to intercept

convoys JW 55B and RA 55A. On 26 December, in the darkness
of the Arctic winter and the teeth of snowstorms and a raging gale,
the *Scharnhorst* was detected and hunted by radar-equipped British
cruisers and the battleship *Duke of York* – radar was even used to
control the British ships' gunnery in the darkness. Ultra decrypts
had given the British warning and allowed them to spring their trap.
A running fight developed as the *Scharnhorst* tried to escape. Slowed
by hits from the British cruisers as well as repeated hits by 14-inch
shells from HMS *Duke of York*, the *Scharnhorst* was finished off with
torpedoes fired by fleet destroyers summoned from their task of
escorting RA 55A.[22]

In all, 40 convoys sailed from Iceland and the UK to Russia –
809 merchant ships in total; 65 (8 per cent) were sunk by enemy
action or marine causes during the east-bound passage. A total of
3,964,231 tons out of 16,366,747 tons of British, Canadian and US
aid to Russia went by the Arctic route; this included ammunition,
raw materials, tanks, artillery, stream trains, electronics, machinery, small arms and vehicles, all of which played an important part
in stemming the German onslaught on Russia, and enabling the Red
Army to take the war to Germany. Across thousands of miles of
steppe, forest, marsh and town across Eastern Europe and Russia,
wherever the Red Army was fighting, Allied – British – seapower
was being felt in some small way. It enabled the liberation of Europe,
from the east but also from the west.[23]

The liberation of Europe

From the moment the evacuation of British forces from Dunkirk had
been completed in June 1940, the liberation of Europe was under
consideration – which meant a seaborne invasion. However, the
experience of Gallipoli in World War I and the debacle of Norway
in 1940 had shown that amphibious assaults against modern weapons were not to be undertaken lightly. A great deal of planning and
preparation would be needed, procedures would need to be worked
out, command and control problems identified and resolved, and
equipment – both landing craft and for the landing force – would

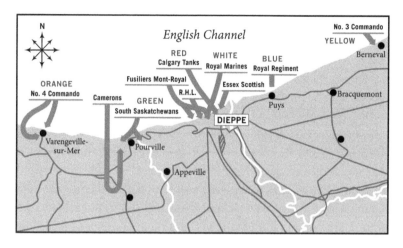

Fig. 4.5. The raid on Dieppe.

have to be designed, built and tested. While the Allies had had
some successes with a variety of commando raids in Europe and the
Mediterranean, as well as the attack on Madagascar in May 1942,
these were not big enough to put ashore sufficient forces or develop
sufficient firepower to batter a way through the German coastal
defences in France.

The first operation designed to see how difficult such a landing
might be was the raid on Dieppe on 19 August 1942. The raid was
a frontal assault on a defended harbour; elements of two Canadian
infantry brigades and a Canadian tank regiment, plus supporting
commando units, including a Royal Marines commando unit, were
to overwhelm the German garrison, destroy everything of military
value in the area and remain in possession of the town from low
tide to the next high tide. An important consideration was whether
it was possible to attack and capture a port intact so that follow-up
forces could be easily landed and fed into the battle – a vital consideration if the subsequent landings to liberate Europe were to be a
success.[24]

The raid was a disaster. As the landing force approached by sea,
part of it bumped into a German coastal convoy, which altered the
defences as well as reduced the force landing on Yellow Beach to

levels where they could not achieve their objectives. On Blue Beach the infantry were pinned down as they landed. Without tanks or heavy naval gunfire support they could make no progress; the naval landing craft that attempted to evacuate the landing force suffered heavy losses. On Green Beach the South Saskatchewan Regiment made an unopposed landing but ran into German defensive positions as soon as it tried to move inland. In the centre, the main assault on Red and White Beaches saw heavy casualties as the infantry tried to make headway against entrenched defences. Even the presence of tanks did not help, as many were unable to get off the beach owing to the height of the sea wall, and those that did were unable to get into the town to support the infantry as their paths were blocked by anti-tank obstacles. By 09:00, four hours after the landings began, it was clear that the main assault was a failure and evacuation was needed sooner than planned. But the German fire on the beaches and their approaches made the evacuation extremely difficult and only a few hundred troops could be taken off while the landing craft

Fig. 4.6. The landing craft off the beach during the raid on Dieppe.

suffered heavy losses. By 12:40 it was all over and the landing force had started to surrender. Out of a landing force of 6,088, 3,625 were killed, wounded or captured – just under 60 per cent. An invasion of Europe on these lines was clearly impossible.[25]

However, important lessons had been learned. The raid demonstrated the difficulty of seizing a port by direct assault, the need for very heavy naval gunfire support (only eight destroyers were present off Dieppe), the need for permanent naval assault forces, headquarters ships, better close air support, and specialized armoured vehicles to clear the beaches and immediate area of tank traps. The invasion of Europe would be a very different affair than the raid on Dieppe.

Planning for the seaborne invasion of Europe initially coalesced around Anglo-American plans for Operations *Roundup* and *Sledgehammer* – ideas to invade in late 1942 in order to take the pressure off the Russians. It was realized that the plans were impracticable, not least because of the experience of the Dieppe operation, and the planners' attention moved to the Mediterranean and Operation *Torch*. Serious planning restarted in spring 1943 and an outline plan was presented to the Combined Chiefs of Staff (the Anglo-American coordination committee) and the British and US political leadership at the Quebec Conference in August 1943. In October the complexities of the operation were becoming clear and it was decided that a separate naval commander would be needed; Admiral Sir Bertram Ramsey was chosen for the job. Finally, in January 1944, the invasion plan was increased from three assault divisions to five in response to criticisms by the new land force commander, General Sir Bernard Montgomery. The naval plan – Operation *Neptune* – would have to do several things. First, it would need to land sufficient troops to overwhelm the defences. Second, it would need to provide gunfire support from warships to compensate for a lack of army artillery in the opening phases. Third, it would need to defend the embarked landing force and follow-up waves from German interference on, below or above the waves. Finally, it would have to ensure that sufficient reinforcements and supplies could be transported from the UK and USA and landed to build up the land force to a level where it

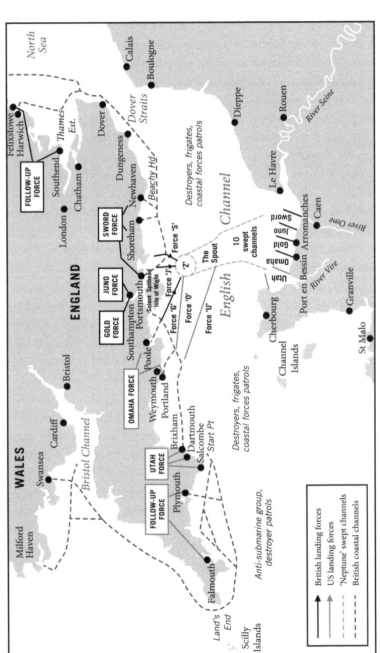

Fig. 4.7. Operation *Neptune*.

could beat the German units that would be rushed to the area to contain the invasion.[26]

The invasion fleet was divided in two: the western task force consisting of Force U, bound for Utah Beach, and Force O, heading for Omaha Beach; and the eastern task force with Forces G, J and S, which were heading for Gold, Juno and Sword Beaches respectively. Each of the five naval forces bound for the assault beaches was responsible not just for the protection of the landing force but also for providing fire support for the assault. It was a massive undertaking. In all, there were 138 warships allocated for bombardment duties, including seven battleships, 23 cruisers and over 100 destroyers. In addition, another 226 ships acted as escorts for the ships carrying the assault and follow-up forces; 287 minesweepers were used to clear the sea routes of German mines, while 4,125 landing ships and landing craft plus 864 merchant ships with their precious cargoes of men and equipment were shepherded to the landing zone. Further up and down the Channel, large naval forces stood ready to intercept any attempt by German U-boats and torpedo boats to attack the invasion convoys. It was quite simply the greatest naval operation ever mounted – and the majority of the ships and men were provided by the Royal Navy.[27]

Perhaps the most difficult task in the planning stage was not the organization of the assault but rather the organization of the reinforcements needed after the initial phase of the invasion had come to a conclusion towards the end of June. The raid on Dieppe had demonstrated that seizing a port would be prohibitive in terms of losses, so the Royal Navy, Combined Operations Command and others developed during 1943 a portable harbour – the Mulberry. There was one for the British sector and one for the US, which would give the Allies port facilities at the beach itself rather than rely on capturing Cherbourg intact at an early stage of the operation. Additionally, the 'Pluto' scheme developed a means of quickly laying fuel pipes across the seabed to carry petrol from England to Normandy. Together they were a highly innovative approach to the logistical problems of liberating Europe.

On 6 June 1944, after a delay of 24 hours due to poor weather,

Fig. 4.8. A merchant ship has been beached to allow rapid unloading during the early days of the Normandy invasion.

the assault began. The moment that the first landing crafts were due to touch down on each beach varied: 06:30 at Utah and Omaha Beaches, 07:25 at Gold Beach, 07:35 at Juno Beach and, lastly, 07:45 at Sword Beach, thanks to the need for the tide to cover offshore reefs. From a naval point of view the landings were a complete success. By the end of the day, all the assault divisions were ashore, the follow-up forces were starting to be fed into the beachhead and over 75,000 men and their vehicles had been landed. Naval gunfire had been highly effective in suppressing the German defences and then breaking up hostile probes and counterattacks, responding well to the calls for assistance from the infantry. Yet the casualties for the seaborne landing force were very low – around 3,000. The majority of these occurred on Omaha Beach due to a lack of specialized assault armour as deployed on the British beaches and poor weather, which sank many of the amphibious tanks after they are launched.[28]

With the landing force safely ashore and the beachhead expanding – if not as quickly as had been hoped – the naval effort moved
towards building up British, Canadian and American armies, as
well as continuing to provide gunfire support until the front line
moved beyond the range of the warships' guns. The construction
of the Mulberry harbours at Gold and Omaha Beaches started
on D-Day +1 and they were in full swing by 9 June. Congestion
caused by ships waiting to unload while the Mulberries were being
built, especially bad in the American sector at Omaha Beach, was
solved by the simple expedient of beaching the ships and unloading
them directly on to the sand as the tide went out. In the first six
days of the operation, 326,547 men, 54,186 vehicles and 104,428
tons of supplies were unloaded. Once the Mulberries came into
operation the daily average of men, supplies and vehicles unloaded
in Normandy between 15 and 18 June was 34,712 men, 24,974
tons of stores and 5,894 vehicles. Then, in the early hours of
19 June, a gale blew up and raged for three days. The American
Mulberry harbour at Omaha Beach was destroyed and never
rebuilt; the British one at Gold Beach was heavily damaged but
repaired – possibly because the British were keener on the concept
than the Americans. Despite this, in the week after the gale the
daily average of vehicles landed was actually higher than before the
storm. On 26 June the first of the ship-to-shore fuel pipelines to
unload tankers came into use. The end of June also saw the capture
of Cherbourg. Unfortunately the Germans had comprehensively
wrecked the port and a new task fell to the British and US navies
– clearing captured harbours of obstacles and restoring the quays,
cranes and docks to working order.

At sea the Royal Navy's 10th Destroyer Flotilla had intercepted
and destroyed a raid by four German destroyers based in Cherbourg
in the early hours of 9 June. Further out in the naval cordon around
the invasion area the U-boats were suffering too at the hands of the
Navy's anti-submarine forces – 12 were sunk in the Bay of Biscay
or the English Channel during June. Such was the density of British
anti-submarine forces that from the middle of June only U-boats
fitted with snorkels could be used and even then they had a slim

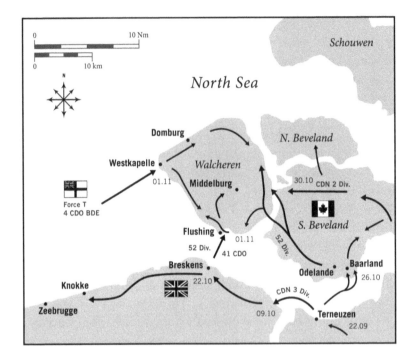

Fig. 4.9. The operations to clear the Scheldt
estuary and the assault on Walcheren.

chance of survival. On 24 June the decision was made to wind up
the Operation *Neptune* aspects of *Overlord*, and by the end of the
month *Neptune* was over.[29]

But the Royal Navy's part in the liberation of Europe was not
over – the Allied armies still needed supplies, which could only
arrive by sea. The need to keep the forces supplied and on the move
became especially acute after the breakout from Normandy on 25
July. By the end of August the Allied armies were crossing the
Seine, Paris was liberated on 25 August, on 3 September Brussels
fell as the Allies charged forward and by the middle of the month
they were ranged along the Dutch frontier and then south-east of
Luxemburg and into Alsace. There were not enough supplies to keep
all the armies moving, a problem that was exacerbated by General
Eisenhower's broad-front policy which meant that all Allied units

Fig. 4.10. The seaborne assault on Walcheren; landing craft and amphibious
tracked armoured personnel carriers approach the beach.

were supposed to be attacking all the time.

The key was Antwerp. Admiral Ramsey, on the day Brussels
fell, had emphasized its importance and that it was useless unless
the Scheldt estuary that led to the port was cleared of German gun
batteries. The next day Antwerp was captured intact by the British
11th Armoured Division, but both banks of the Scheldt remained in
German hands. While their guns commanded the approaches to the
port, British minesweepers could not operate and the port would
remain closed to Allied shipping. Generals such as Eisenhower and
Montgomery were focused on getting into Germany and across the
Rhine – clearing the approaches to Antwerp was effectively forgotten and supplies still had to be dragged from the Normandy beachhead. It seems that Admiral Ramsey was not regularly included in the
senior generals' strategic conferences and so the problems of opening
Antwerp were not given due consideration. Only on 16 October did
clearing the Scheldt estuary become a priority for the Allies.[30]

As British and Canadian units struggled across flooded and waterlogged countryside to clear the German defences, the Royal Navy was on hand with its landing craft to ferry units between islands and to bypass Nazi positions. By 31 October all that was left of the German defences was the island of Walcheren – but it was an exceptionally difficult target. An amphibious assault was the answer. A two-pronged attack took place on 1 November, at the same time as the Canadians tackled the causeway that led to the island from the east. The eastern assault was led by 4 Commando (Royal Marines), with 52 Division as the follow-up; all were ferried across the Scheldt by landing craft to capture Flushing. The western assault faced a more heavily defended sector of the island and was supported by the battleship HMS *Warspite* – her last engagement in a career going back to Jutland – as well as monitors and a full supporting chorus of landing craft. The Navy put three battalions of Royal Marine commandoes from 4 Special Service Brigade ashore, together with supporting armour. After very heavy fighting and many casualties, the last German position on Walcheren surrendered on 6 November, opening the way for shipping to access Antwerp. Within three weeks, the German minefields had been cleared and on 28 November the first supplies were landed at Antwerp, vastly reducing the Allies' logistics problems.[31]

With the supply situation restored, and the December German counterattack in the Ardennes defeated, the battle for Germany could begin. By March the Allied armies were at the Rhine. In the north, where the river was at its widest and the current strongest, the problems in mounting an assault crossing were severe. Again the Royal Navy was present, using landing craft to support the main British attack with amphibious LVT7 personnel carriers. Finally on 8 May, as the Royal Navy continued its unremitting war against the U-boat and enemy mines, Germany surrendered. The war in Europe was over.[32]

CHAPTER 5

The War in the Mediterranean

The opening moves

At just before 18:00 on 3 July 1940, the battlecruiser *Hood*, and the battleships *Valiant* and *Resolution*, two supporting cruisers, the aircraft carrier *Ark Royal*, and 11 destroyers, comprising the newly reformed Force H, attacked a mixed force of two battleships, two battlecruisers, a seaplane carrier and six destroyers while they were in harbour. The engagement was brutal and short: the British capital ships had opened fire at a range of 15,000 yards and used aircraft to spot their fall of shot; the British gunnery was very accurate. Aircraft from the *Ark Royal* also laid magnetic mines in the harbour mouth to help pin the ships inside. The third British salvo found the magazine of one of the battleships and caused a massive explosion, destroying the vessel. After just a few minutes, it was seen that the opposition had ceased firing back at Force H and the British ships ceased fire too. None of Force H's ships had been hit, although the return fire from the ships being pounded in the harbour had fallen close to the British vessels and in some cases achieved the precursor to a direct hit – a straddle, where shells fell closely on either side of the target, showing that the gunnery was accurate and hits would result.

As the smoke from the gunfire and the numerous explosions of heavy shells on the ships in the harbour drifted away, the British could see that one of the battleships had blown up, the other was damaged and apparently run aground, as was one of the battlecruisers, and the seaplane carrier was burning, together with one of the destroyers. However, at 18:20, it was reported that the remaining battlecruiser was trying to leave the harbour. In response the *Ark Royal* launched a strike of six Swordfish armed with 250lb semi-armour-piecing bombs to try to stop her. The Swordfish claimed at least one hit, but the battlecruiser continued to try to escape, so a second strike of six Swordfish, this time armed with torpedoes, was launched. Attacking in the dusk the Swordfish reported two possible hits, but they failed to slow the battlecruiser. As Force H was running low on fuel, its commander, Vice Admiral Sir James Somerville, decided to call off the chase.

The destruction or damage of so many vessels for so few British casualties should have been cause for celebration; after all, putting out of action two battleships and a battlecruiser was not an every-day occurrence, even for a force as aggressive and professional as the Royal Navy. However, the ships the Royal Navy had destroyed and damaged were not German, or even Italian, but French – the British had apparently turned on their ally.

With the outbreak of the main German attack in the west on 10 May 1940, attention naturally focused on France and the Low Countries, especially as the Allied intervention in Norway fizzled out from late May onwards. Despite the collapse at Sedan, the fall of northern France and Holland and the evacuation of the BEF, Italy remained on the sidelines and an uneasy peace remained in force in the Mediterranean. On 5 June the German armies turned south and launched a widespread attack on the reconstituted French lines running behind the line of the rivers Somme and the Aisne. After heavy fighting, the Germans broke through near the Channel coast and drove deep into Normandy. On 10 June Paris was declared an open city and Italy entered the war on the German side. The war had reached the Mediterranean.

The fall of France had a significant impact on the Royal Navy. Until the French were forced to the armistice table by events on land, the naval responsibility for the Mediterranean had been divided between Britain and France. The British Mediterranean Fleet, based at Alexandria, was responsible for the eastern basin; the French Mediterranean Fleet, based at Toulon and Mers-el-Kébir, the western basin. With the collapse of France, a naval force was needed to prevent the Italian fleet having effective control of the western Mediterranean or worse, breaking out into the Atlantic. The result was the creation of the Royal Navy's Force H, based at Gibraltar and as such able to operate either in the Mediterranean or the Atlantic as the situation required. Comprised of units transferred from both the Home and Mediterranean Fleets, Force H would in a relatively short period of time come to have two battleships, a battlecruiser, an aircraft carrier, three cruisers armed with 6-inch guns and 16 destroyers, compensating for the loss of French naval forces. In many respects basing a significant naval force at Gibraltar was an old idea; the fleet redistribution of 1905 planned by Admiral Sir John Fisher included basing a fleet at Gibraltar that would be able to support either the Mediterranean Fleet or the Channel Fleet.

The problem the British faced was that if the French turned over their fleet to either the Italians – or more likely the Germans, given which country had the greater responsibility for knocking France out of the war – the Royal Navy would be at a serious disadvantage and the Germans would be able to replace the ships sunk and damaged during the Norwegian campaign at a stroke. Steps had to be taken to end any chance of the French Fleet ending up in German hands. The result was Operation *Catapult* – the attack on Mers-el-Kébir, with Churchill impatiently demanding results as quickly as possible. Such a ruthless turning on a former ally demonstrated one thing that no other event could in the chaos following the fall of France and the pressure from certain British politicians to reach a negotiated settlement with Nazi Germany – that Britain was still prepared to fight and do what it felt was necessary to further its cause. However, at the other end of the Mediterranean in Alexandria, Admiral Cunningham managed to persuade the French admiral commanding a battleship and several cruisers there to disarm his ships rather than fight.

**Table 5.1. Composition of British, French and Italian
Mediterranean Fleets, June 1940.**[1]

	Battle-ships	Battle-cruis-ers	Air-craft carriers	Cruisers (8 inch)	Cruisers (6 inch)	Dest-royers	Sub-marines	Escort vessels
Britain	5	0	1	0	9	31	12	5
France	3	2	1	7	7	44	46	22
Italy	5	0	0	7	12	111	107	10

Getting the measure of the Italians

Having dealt with the problem of the French fleet – in Cunningham's case by negotiated disarmament, or in Somerville's by sinking it – the Royal Navy could turn its attention to its new enemy, the Italian fleet and air force. The threat of air raids had ensured that Malta had been evacuated as a fleet base before the outbreak of hostilities and instead was only a forward operating base for light forces and submarines. On the other hand, Malta was potentially an important asset if it could be defended from air attack, as it sat astride British lines of communication between Gibraltar and the Suez Canal, and also commanded Italian communications between the mainland and its Libyan empire.

The tone of the war in the Mediterranean was quickly set by the need by both sides to pass supplies through the Mediterranean, generally along an east–west axis via Malta for the British and across the sea north–south avoiding Malta for the Italians. The result of this was that the fighting centred on or around convoys from an early juncture. The first of many such actions was in early July 1940 when the British sought to pass two convoys from Malta to Alexandria, and hopefully bring some parts of the Italian Fleet to action – Operation *MA5*. Coincidentally the Italians were also trying to pass a convoy from Italy to Libya, so their fleet was also at sea.

The British plan was quite simple: the Mediterranean Fleet was to sail from Alexandria and penetrate the central Mediterranean to within 25 miles of the Italian coast, while Force H would sail from Gibraltar and operate off Sardinia to launch an air strike on Cagliari. Both sides had received indications that their opponents were at sea, as both were able to read each other's codes to a greater or lesser extent. On the basis of the information received, each side decided to try to surprise the other. Admiral Cunningham planned a very aggressive move northwards with his fleet to get between the Italians, commanded by Admiral Campioni. The Italians planned a coordinated attack by submarines, surface forces and land-based aircraft. But Cunningham's aggressive move to get between the enemy fleet and its base left the submarine part of the Italian ambush far behind. Unfortunately the Italian air force did manage to find the British fleet and subjected it to heavy high-level air attacks during the day on 8, 9, 11 and 12 July. Only HMS *Gloucester* was hit, by a single bomb on 8 July, but it failed to prevent her continuing as part of the British force.

The violence of the air attacks was something that was also to become a feature of the war at sea in the Mediterranean, dominated as it was by the ability of the belligerents to project airpower far over the sea – depending on who controlled what territory. Indeed it was the very likelihood of heavy air attack from land-based aircraft that had driven the construction of the Royal Navy's new armoured fleet aircraft carriers with their thick armoured flight decks. The first of these new aircraft carriers, HMS *Illustrious*, had only been commissioned in May 1940 and was, at the outbreak of war in the Mediterranean, still 'working up'. This meant that the only aircraft carriers in the Mediterranean were the modern *Ark Royal* with Force H – though she was not as heavily armoured to withstand air attack as the new armoured fleet aircraft carriers – and the elderly and rather small HMS *Eagle* which was with Cunningham's fleet and carried only two Sea Gladiator biplane fighters and 17 Swordfish torpedo bombers. The result was that the Navy had to rely heavily on RAF support for reconnaissance, as well as for fighter defence and strike aircraft. But such support was not always available.[2]

The two fleets sighted each other just before 15:00; both sides' cruisers were exchanging fire at extreme range by 15:14, with the British battleship *Warspite*, the fastest of the three battleships

Cunningham had with him, charging ahead and intervening in the cruiser fight. Then at 15:48 the two Italian battleships joined the fray, but at 16:00 *Warspite* succeeded in hitting the Italian battleship *Giulio Cesare* at the unprecedented range of 26,200 yards – over 13 miles. A hit at such a distance unnerved the Italian naval force which withdrew at high speed under the cover of a smokescreen. As Cunningham noted after the battle, while the action might not have resulted in heavy damage to the Italians, it established a degree of moral superiority over them. By 16:49 the battle off Calabria was over – with the exception of air attacks by the Italian air force, which in a display of even-handedness bombed both British and Italian fleets but did not succeed in hitting anything.[3]

The start of July also saw a significant setback for the Royal Navy's war against Italy. The intelligence the British had been receiving from their decryption of the Italian navy's codes started to dry up. This may have contributed to a lull in the Mediterranean between July and October 1940. During this period the Mediterranean Fleet made 16 sweeps into the eastern and central Mediterranean but only sighted Italian warships on three occasions. Worse yet, the Royal Navy and RAF only managed to intercept about 2 per cent of the 690,000 tons of shipping the Italians used to keep their Libyan forces supplied between June and December.

More important were the British operations to reinforce Malta and the Mediterranean Fleet itself. At the start of August, 12 modern Hurricane fighter aircraft flew to Malta from the venerable (indeed obsolete) aircraft carrier HMS *Argus*. At the end of that month the Mediterranean Fleet received badly needed reinforcements that were passed through the Mediterranean via Force H in Operation *Hats*. The reinforcements consisted of the Royal Navy's new (and at this stage only operational) armoured fleet carrier, HMS *Illustrious*, the battleship HMS *Valiant*, the heavy cruiser HMS *York* and the anti-aircraft cruisers HMS *Coventry* and *Calcutta*, as part of Operation *Hats*, while HMS *Ajax* arrived via the Suez Canal in place of HMS *Neptune*. Nor was *Hats* the end of the reinforcements: another heavy cruiser, HMS *Kent*, soon joined Cunningham's fleet.

The arrival of the battleship *Valiant* was a significant improvement

Fig. 5.1. HMS *Illustrious*, the Royal Navy's first armoured fleet carrier, was designed to operate in waters like the Mediterranean where the threat of land-based air attack was high and the probability of support from the RAF low.

on the unmodernized HMS *Malaya*, as *Valiant* had received a major reconstruction in the late 1930s and had been fitted with radar sets for air warning and gun ranging, as had HMS *Ajax*, while the anti-aircraft cruiser *Coventry* carried air-search radars. HMS *Illustrious* too was fitted with the new radar sets, and its arrival as an additional aircraft carrier was a particular boon to the Mediterranean Fleet, for not only did it have radar but also came with an air group of 19 badly needed modern Fulmar fighters and 18 Swordfish torpedo bombers. More important still, the *Illustrious* was fully conversant with the concept of 'fighter direction' using information from radar sets, a technique pioneered by *Ark Royal* in the Norwegian campaign, thanks to the two ships' brief period together in Gibraltar as the start of Operation *Hats*.[4]

Taranto and after

Having two aircraft carriers with the Mediterranean Fleet and another one based at Gibraltar with Force H not only increased the Navy's reconnaissance and air defence capabilities in the Mediterranean theatre, but also its strike capability. For centuries the Navy had been wrestling with the problem of what to do if an enemy refused to do the decent thing and come out and be crushed by British seapower and instead sulked in harbour where he would be difficult to get at. Now the Mediterranean Fleet had enough aircraft carrier and torpedo planes to contemplate an air attack on the Italian fleet which had so frustratingly managed to avoid being brought to battle.

From the outset Rear Admiral Arthur Lyster, who had arrived with HMS *Illustrious* to command the Mediterranean Fleet's aircraft carrier squadron, wanted to attack the Italian fleet's main base at Taranto at night using Swordfish torpedo bombers launched from HMS *Illustrious* and *Eagle*. Cunningham, unsurprisingly, was enthusiastic about this aggressive idea for getting at an enemy that had been eluding him. Indeed, it wasn't a new idea at all – parts of the Navy had been mulling over such an idea since the Abyssinian crisis in 1935, when there was the distinct possibility of war in the Mediterranean between Britain and Italy.

It was Cunningham's intention to celebrate Trafalgar Day on 21 October by sinking as much of the Italian fleet as possible in the manner proposed by Admiral Lyster. Unfortunately a fire in *Illustrious*'s hangar meant the operation had to be delayed until mid-

November when moonlight would next be available for the attack.

On 28 October, however, Italy invaded Greece; the result was that the next day the Royal Navy started transporting army and RAF personnel and equipment to Crete, where a major base was planned in the Suda area, as well as to mainland Greece. The result was that the attack on Taranto – Operation *Judgement* – was dovetailed in with a series of fleet operations to cover convoys to and from Greece and the Aegean. Indeed between 4 and 14 November no fewer than ten operations were mounted by the Royal Navy in the Mediterranean.

That the Mediterranean Fleet and Force H could mount ten interconnected operations shows the degree of command of the ocean that the Royal Navy had achieved against a nominally superior naval force and a vastly numerically superior land-based air force. The British suffered only the most minor of losses and destroyed an Italian convoy of four merchant ships totalling 16,938 tons. Then, of course, there came the thunderous success of the Fleet Air Arm attack on the Italian fleet at its base in Taranto harbour.

It had been intended that both HMS *Eagle* and HMS *Illustrious* would be used for the attack, but the *Eagle* had severe problems with her aircraft fuelling system, so only the *Illustrious* was available to make the attack – although aircraft and experienced aircrews were transferred to the *Illustrious* to augment the strike force. The *Illustrious* and her escort force of four cruisers and four destroyers parted company with Cunningham's main force at 18:00 on 11 November, having received the latest aerial reconnaissance photographs of Taranto taken by Malta-based planes which showed that there had been no changes to the Italian fleet. The attack was an outstanding success. Three battleships were hit: the *Conte di Cavour* was so badly damaged by a single torpedo hit that she never went to sea again, the *Littorio* suffered three torpedo strikes and was out of action for four months, while the *Caio Diulio* was sidelined for six months. Additionally, the cruiser *Trento* and some destroyers were hit by bombs. It was the single most devastating air attack on a force that any navy had yet experienced.

Nor was Taranto the end of the Royal Navy's offensive against

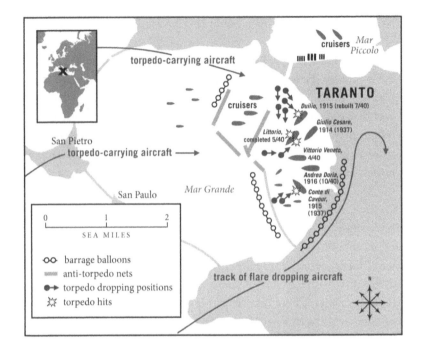

Fig. 5.2. The Fleet Air Arm attack on the Italian fleet in Taranto harbour.

the Italian navy. At the end of the month, on 27 November, Force
H clashed with an Italian force consisting of two battleships, seven
heavy cruisers and 16 destroyers which had put to sea as soon as
the Italians had become aware that the British were mounting a
major operation. The British aim was to pass a small number of
fast merchant ships through the Mediterranean from Gibraltar to
Egypt with urgent equipment. Somerville, commanding Force H
(*Ark Royal*, *Renown*, *Sheffield*, *Despatch* and nine destroyers), was fully
aware that his prime task was, according to the Navy's tactical bible,
Fighting Instructions, the safe and timely arrival of the convoy he was
protecting. The result was that when the Italians were engaged
by Somerville's force just after noon on 27 November off Cape
Spartivento as well as by ships detached from Cunningham's fleet to
support the operation, the battle turned into a chase, with only the

battlecruiser *Renown* having anything like the speed needed to keep her guns in range of the rapidly retiring Italian force. Having driven off a superior surface force Somerville gave up the chase as the running battle neared the Sardinian coast on the basis that the safety of the convoy was of prime importance. Unfortunately London (Churchill) disagreed, and Somerville was in the ignominious position of having a board of inquiry convened to examine his actions before he had even returned to port after the operation. The board sat, listened to all the evidence and then endorsed Somerville's actions.

Enter the Germans

The naval situation in the Mediterranean was most satisfactory at the end of 1940, with the Royal Navy having trounced the Italians. On land the Italian army attacking Greece was being held quite nicely by the Greek army, while the Italian forces in Libya had only managed to advance about 65 miles into Egypt before refusing to move any further. In December General Richard O'Connor, commander of the Western Desert Force, launched Operation *Compass* to drive back the Italian forces. What started as a raid on the Italian positions rapidly turned into a decisive victory, for by 11 December the Italians were collapsing and retreating headlong back down the coast road to Libya, being shelled by HMS *Terror* and supporting gunboats on the way. In January O'Connor's force resumed the offensive; on 22 January the British captured Tobruk and the rapid British advances caused the Italians to evacuate Cyrenaica. By early February the British had cut the coast road at Beda Fomm, trapping the Italian 10th Army; in all 130,000 Italian troops were captured as well as hundreds of tanks and artillery guns. However, at sea the balance of power was on the verge of shifting – the German Luftwaffe had arrived in strength.

In early January there were intelligence indications that German air force units were moving into Sicily. As Force H and the Mediterranean Fleet carried out another of their periodic interlinked operations to get merchant ships to and from Malta and from

Gibraltar to Egypt – Operation *Excess* – the Luftwaffe's Fliegerkorps X, a specialist anti-shipping force of over 150 bombers and dive-bombers plus supporting fighters, announced its arrival. In the early afternoon on 10 January Cunningham's Mediterranean Fleet was attacked by about 36 aircraft 55 miles west of Malta. Unfortunately these were not Italian aircraft, but were German Ju-87 and Ju-88 dive-bombers. Between 18 and 24 of the dive-bombers concentrated on HMS *Illustrious*. In the space of a few minutes, six 1000lb armour-piercing bombs and three more very near misses reduced *Illustrious* to a shambles. Three bombs caused only superficial damage, but the other three, one of which penetrated the armoured flightdeck, landed on or near the after aircraft lift causing a major fire in the after hangar which spread to surrounding compartments, while the near misses caused a total steering failure; for nearly three hours *Illustrious* was out of control. That evening she limped into Malta's Grand Harbour for repairs – where she was bombed by German and Italian aircraft – until sufficient repairs had been made for her to get first to Alexandria, where more repair work was done, and then to the USA, where she arrived in May. She remained under repair in New York until December 1941.[5]

The next day Fliegerkorps X found the cruisers *Gloucester*, *Southampton* and *Diamond* as they moved to reinforce the escort of convoy ME 6. The British cruisers had no warning of the attack by a dozen dive-bombers that came out of the sun, until the whistle of the bombs falling was heard aboard the ships below. The *Gloucester* was hit by a single bomb which struck the 6-inch gun director tower and penetrated five decks, but luckily the bomb did not explode. HMS *Southampton* was not so fortunate. She was hit by two, possibly three, 550lb bombs which exploded in her forward boiler room and the gunroom flat and caused almost fatal damage and massive fires. Her crew battled to control the fires; though at no time was she out of control or the fight, the fires slowly spread and it proved impossible to flood some of the magazines that were threatened by the flames. After nearly five and a half hours of desperate attempts to extinguish the fires it was decided to take off the *Southampton*'s crew and sink her with torpedoes.[6]

Fig. 5.3. Force H. HMS *Ark Royal* can be seen launching
Fulmar fighters with HMS *Renown* in attendance.

Despite the savage mauling of HMS *Illustrious* and the loss of HMS
Southampton, even German aircraft could not dominate two areas at
the same time. Therefore a raid by Force H on Genoa was planned
for February. Weather caused the first attempt to be aborted but
almost as soon as he returned to Gibraltar, Somerville was looking
for a new date to get Force H in a position to attack. The date of the
bombardment was fixed for 9 February and on 6 February Force H
slipped out of Gibraltar. Before dawn on the appointed day all was
ready; the 15-inch guns of HMS *Malaya* and HMS *Renown*, together
with the 6-inch guns of the cruiser HMS *Sheffield*, were trained on
Genoa and awaiting the order to fire, while aircraft from HMS *Ark
Royal* were poised to lay mines in Spezi harbour and bomb the oil
refinery at Leghorn. The force opened fire at 07:14, 20 minutes
before dawn, achieving complete surprise. Aircraft from the *Ark
Royal* supported the attack by spotting the fall of shot; unfortunately
they did not see the battleship *Caio Duilio*, which had been damaged
by the Fleet Air Arm at Taranto, and was in dry dock in Genoa for

repairs. The attack lasted just 31 minutes and at 07:45 Somerville's ships ceased fire and disappeared over the horizon. Despite major efforts the Italians failed to catch Force H, which reached Gibraltar on 11 February without meeting the searching Italian fleet or suffering any air attacks. Indeed Force H carried out training exercises on its return passage.[7]

Somerville's raid on Genoa caused great damage, with salvos of heavy shells hitting factories, storehouses and dock facilities with one of *Malaya*'s salvos of 15-inch shells missing the damaged battleship *Caio Duilio* by a small margin. It was also a major propaganda coup for a naval force to penetrate so far north and escape detection. But raids like this one would not decide the course of the war in the Mediterranean.

As Cunningham had realized, the German air attacks against his fleet on 10 and 11 January 1941 had completely altered the balance of power in the central and western Mediterranean. Whereas the Italian air attacks, although heavy, had not prevented the Mediterranean Fleet from operating as it saw fit – even close to the Italian mainland – the arrival of German dive-bombers able to deliver heavy and, above all, very accurate attacks meant this was no longer possible until the British had increased the levels of land-based fighter cover for the Navy. Nor could Cunningham's Mediterranean Fleet rely on its own resources for air defence against such an enhanced air threat – its only modern aircraft carrier had been gutted in a single attack and a replacement, HMS *Formidable*, would take months to reach the theatre.

Worse still, intelligence was suggesting that soon German forces would join the Italian attack on Greece and, thanks to the diversion of British army units from Libya to form an expeditionary force to aid Greece during spring 1941, O'Connor's successful offensive across half of Libya had been halted well before it had occupied all the possible ports that the Axis could use to revitalize the shattered and dispirited Italian forces in North Africa. The British position was looking tenuous on land and sea in the Mediterranean; perhaps the only question in the spring and summer of 1941 was how bad the new onslaught would be.

The answer was: bad.

In the Balkans the situation was deteriorating with increasing signs that German intervention was imminent. Britain's War Cabinet explored various options for assistance to Greece, culminating in the decision to offer an expeditionary force to the Greek government on 24 February – a decision that was reaffirmed on 7 March. On 1 March Bulgaria declared for the Axis and the next day German troops started to cross into that country from Romania; the Bulgarian army mobilized and massed along the Greek frontier. Yugoslavia signed the Tripartite Pact on 25 March but then a pro-British coup deposed the pro-Axis government. On 6 April Germany invaded both Yugoslavia and Greece.[8]

The British decision to commit an expeditionary force vastly increased the already heavy burden being shouldered by the Mediterranean Fleet, as convoys to carry the army and RAF to Greece had to be organized and the ships found to protect them against air, surface and submarine attack. The first of these convoys sailed on 4 March and for most of March and April the Mediterranean Fleet was almost completely absorbed with the tasks of supporting the land forces in Greece and the remaining British army formations in the western desert. The logistical problems the Navy faced were made worse by the mining of the Suez Canal by Axis aircraft in this period. As a result of this, the arrival of the Mediterranean Fleet's new aircraft carrier, HMS *Formidable*, was delayed, as was the sailing of the patched-up HMS *Illustrious* to the USA for repairs. However, the near constant stream of Allied shipping heading across the sea from Africa to Greece was a tempting target and the Italian fleet sought to disrupt this vital, if unglamorous, theatre of war.[9]

A German intelligence report that Cunningham's fleet only had one operational battleship was the spur for the Italians to mount a major operation to catch and destroy one of the British convoys heading to Greece. Indeed the fact that the Italians contemplated the sortie because they believed that only HMS *Valiant* was ready for action shows the wariness of the Italian navy and the moral ascendancy the British had achieved. Yet this was the same service that in a daring raid with explosive-filled motor boats had penetrated the imperfect defences of Cunningham's forward operating base at Suda Bay, Crete, and damaged his only heavy cruiser, HMS *York*, so badly that she had to be beached. Unfortunately for the Italian fleet the German report was wrong and the British knew the Italians were coming.[10]

For the first time since the start of the war in the Mediterranean, British intelligence and specifically that derived from the decryption of enemy signals, was timely and accurate. Intelligence showed that a major operation against British convoys between Greece and Egypt was in motion for 26 March. The decrypts of Italian naval messages and the Admiralty's appreciation of likely enemy movements were passed to Admiral Cunningham, who prepared to take his fleet to sea once night fell on 27 March, and ordered convoys out of the danger area while he carried out his own personal deception plan to help mask his fleet's movements.[11]

Cunningham believed that the supposedly neutral Japanese consul in Alexandria was passing information on the Mediterranean Fleet's movements to the Italians and Germans. Cunningham, who like the Japanese consul was a keen golfer, made sure that he was seen at the club house with his clubs and an overnight bag to give the erroneous impression that the fleet had settled down for the night. After darkness fell Cunningham returned to his flagship, HMS *Warspite*, and the fleet set sail.[12]

In the early morning of 28 March four light cruisers commanded by Vice Admiral Henry Pridham-Wippell, which had been covering the convoys to and from Greece, were 25 miles south of the island of Gavdos making towards the main British force (three battleships, the aircraft carrier *Formidable* and destroyers) coming up from the south-east. An air search had been flown off by *Formidable* at just before six that morning and at 07:20 one of the searching carrier aircraft sighted eight enemy ships – four cruisers and four destroyers heading south-east about 25 miles south of Gavdos. When this report was received by both Cunningham and Pridham-Wippell they both felt that the aircraft had misidentified the British cruisers that were indeed close to that location and heading south-east. Another of *Formidable*'s aircraft made a new enemy sighting report of four cruisers and six destroyers only 25 miles from the first sighting report, and it was again thought that it was Pridham-Wippell's cruisers that had been spotted.

In fact both sighting reports were broadly correct; there were indeed two enemy forces only a couple of dozen miles apart and very close to Pridham-Wippell's blissfully ignorant ships. Pridham-Wippell was still mulling things over when at 07:45 he was rather rudely disabused of the notion that the reports referred to his own ships; smoke was sighted astern and a minute later a number of enemy warships were visible. The British cruisers increased speed, at first to 23 knots and then to 28 knots, when it was feared that the enemy ships could be heavy cruisers that were faster and with longer-ranged guns than the British force. Pridham-Wippell decided that his only course of action was to try to lead the enemy force on to the guns of Cunningham's battleships some distance to the south-east.

The situation was much worse than Pridham-Wippell realized. To his north-east, in a position to get between him and Cunningham, was another force of Italian cruisers and only just over the horizon to the north-west were the Italian battleship *Vittorio Veneto* and her escorts. Just before 09:00 the Italian cruisers broke off the action and started to retire westwards and Pridham-Wippell followed them. Having followed them for nearly two hours, the British cruisers received a very unpleasant shock when the *Vittorio Veneto* was sighted to the north and started showering the British ships with salvos of 15-inch shells. Pridham-Wippell only had one choice: withdraw to the south as quickly as possible; even HMS *Gloucester*, whose speed was apparently limited to 24 knots, found the sight of an enemy battleship extremely motivating and she too was soon speeding south away from the Italians at 30 knots.[13]

Cunningham reacted to the news by detaching the fastest of his three veteran *Queen Elizabeth* class battleships, HMS *Valiant*, to support Pridham-Wippell, while the *Warspite* and *Barham* came up as fast as they could. Fortunately Cunningham had a carrier, HMS *Formidable*, with him as well as FAA Swordfish at Maleme airfield in Crete and RAF medium bombers from Greece. HMS *Formidable*'s

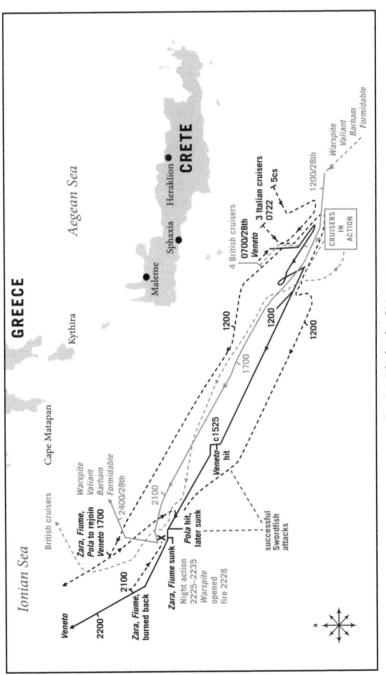

Fig. 5.4. The battle of Matapan.

Albacore torpedo bombers were the first on the scene at 11:27, having been launched at 09:56. This strike of six torpedo bombers attacked the *Vittorio Veneto*, but without success. The appearance of British aircraft, however, persuaded the Italians to give up their pursuit of Pridham-Wippell's force and retire north-west, making it harder to bring the Italian force to action with Cunningham's battleships. Then at 12:05 three FAA Swordfish from Maleme airfield arrived and attacked the Italian cruiser force, again unsuccessfully; a couple of hours later RAF Blenheims attacked the Italians from high level, but also achieved zero hits. It was, however, the first time the RAF in the Mediterranean had operated with the Navy in an attack on an enemy fleet at sea.

There was then a pause in the action as the British tried to catch up with the retiring Italian force and readied themselves for action, but it was soon clear that unless the Italian fleet was slowed by an air attack, they would escape. A second strike of torpedo bombers from HMS *Formidable* was sent in, attacking the *Vittorio Veneto* between 15:10 and 15:25 and achieved one hit which slowed her down. It looked like Cunningham's battleships might just catch up and force a night action with the Italians; thus the cruisers and destroyers were let off the leash to find, attack and disorganize the enemy fleet, followed by the three British battleships.

A third air strike from HMS *Formidable* was launched, again consisting of only a handful of torpedo bombers, which in turn was joined by two Swordfish from Maleme as the aircraft neared the Italian force. At 19:25 the attack went in as the sun was setting. In the deepening darkness most of the aircrews thought they had successfully attacked the *Vittorio Veneto*, but only the heavy cruiser *Pola* was hit, bringing her to a complete stop.

In the darkness the cruisers and destroyers searched for the enemy force, but it was the battleships that found it. Following up a radar report from the cruisers of a stopped ship, the battleships closed on the position until at 22:03 HMS *Valiant*'s radar detected the target at a range of eight or nine miles on the port bow. Then at 22:23 the silhouettes of two large ships (the cruisers *Fiume* and *Zara*) and a destroyer were sighted on the starboard bow about four miles away. These ships had been sent back to aid the stricken *Pola* but now seemed likely to become casualties themselves as they were totally oblivious to the presence of the British.

The British fleet turned to bring the *Fiume* and *Zara* to action (the aircraft carrier *Formidable* being told rudely to 'get out of the bloody way') and at 22:28 a searchlight stabbed through the darkness and illuminated the Italian ships. *Warspite*'s main armament guns crashed out at the extremely short range of 2,900 yards followed seconds later by both the *Valiant* and the *Barham*. In less than five minutes it was over: both the Italian cruisers had been totally surprised by the British and utterly destroyed by the close-range 15-inch shell salvos that crashed into them without warning.

By the morning, as the British fleet reassembled following the night actions, three Italian cruisers had been sunk – the *Zara* and *Fiume* by the battleships and the *Pola* by the destroyers – together with two destroyers that had also been hunted down by Cunningham's aggressive destroyer flotillas. The prize, the *Vittorio Veneto*, had, however, eluded the searching British ships and escaped. The battle off Cape Matapan was a welcome victory for the British but not a decisive one.

The warm glow of victory did not last long. Indeed even before the battle of Matapan, the situation was deteriorating. In the western desert Rommel, the new German commander of the Axis forces in Libya, had probed the British positions at El Agheila and, having found them weakly held, launched an offensive that by 14 April had bundled the British back to the Egyptian border while the garrison at Tobruk was under siege and reliant on the Royal Navy for supplies – a siege that would last for 242 days.

In the Balkans too the situation rapidly grew desperate. In Greece the Germans quickly pushed back the British, Imperial and Greek forces that were attempting to hold them. On 21 April the decision was made to evacuate British and Allied forces from Greece starting on 24 April. In order to carry out the evacuation, Vice Admiral Pridham-Wippell had seven cruisers, 19 destroyers, two sloops, two corvettes, two of the *Glen* class infantry-landing ships and eight transport ships. The evacuation lasted five days and succeeded in rescuing over 50,000 Allied troops and civilians for the loss of two destroyers and three transports sunk by German air attacks.

Just three weeks after the British evacuated Greece, the German airborne attack on Crete commenced. The Navy's role in the defence of the island was straightforward: stop German units reinforcing their airborne landings by sea and keep the British and Imperial forces fighting on Crete supplied. The execution of these duties, however, was extremely difficult as heavy German air raids had forced the abandonment of Suda as a forward operating base, compelling the Navy to operate from Alexandria. Worse, there was effectively no fighter protection for naval forces in the vicinity of Crete and, to achieve both its aims, the Royal Navy would have to operate under the very noses of German airbases in newly occupied Greece.

The aim of preventing German seaborne invasion forces reaching Crete was achieved with some success on 21 and 22 May, as neither of the two German seaborne invasion forces carrying 2,300 and 4,000 troops respectively reached the island. One of the convoys was intercepted during the night of 21/22 May by Force D, consisting of three cruisers and four destroyers; the other force was intercepted by Force C (two cruisers and three destroyers) and turned back under the cover of smoke. Efforts to get British supplies and reinforcements to the island were made much more difficult by the German command of the air. As a result supplies could only be landed by night, and in practice it was found that only warships of high speed and manoeuvrability had a chance of getting through.

The air attacks on the British ships were incessant. On 21 May the destroyer *Juno* was bombed about 20 miles south-east of Crete; she sank in about two minutes. On 22 May the destroyer *Greyhound* was hit by two bombs and sank by the stern in 15 minutes. The loss of *Greyhound* was followed a few hours later by a much heavier blow: the cruisers *Fiji* and *Gloucester* were sunk. The next day the destroyers *Kelly* and *Kashmir* were attacked by German Ju-87 dive-bombers and overwhelmed, sinking ten miles south of Gavdos island. Thanks to the almost continuous air attacks, the fleet was running seriously short of anti-aircraft ammunition and had to retire to Alexandria on 23 May to rearm.

On land the initial German airborne invasion was in trouble; the attempt to take Maleme airfield had failed with the destruction of almost the entire German force that landed on target, and elsewhere the Germans were under severe pressure from Allied forces and Cretan civilians who immediately rose up to fight the invader. Unfortunately the situation on Crete deteriorated during 21 May, despite the success of the Navy in preventing German reinforcements from reaching the island by sea. A tactical error by the New Zealand troops defending Maleme airfield allowed the Germans to occupy a key feature, Hill 107, which gave them effective control of the airfield. The Germans flew in reinforcements directly to Maleme, braving heavy losses as the transport aircraft landed in what was effectively no man's land. With an airfield in their hands the Germans were able to reinforce at will by air, despite the blockade the Royal Navy had placed around the island. An effort to destroy Scarpanto airfield, which was believed to be the source of much of the German airpower, was made by the Fleet Air Arm flying from HMS *Formidable* on 26 May, achieving complete surprise but only destroying a few aircraft. HMS *Formidable*, however, was attacked by about 20 dive-bombers that afternoon and was heavily damaged by two bombs. As the German forces consolidated and advanced, an evacuation of the British and Imperial forces on the island was only a matter of time.

The decision to evacuate was taken on 27 May following the final collapse of British and Imperial forces in the Suda-Maleme area after six days of extremely heavy fighting and almost constant German air attack. The evacuation from Heraklion and Sphakia cost the Navy dear. In all, over 16,000 troops were transported to Egypt, but the naval losses were extremely heavy. The Mediterranean Fleet's only aircraft carrier was badly damaged and the repairs took six months; three battleships had been damaged – *Warspite* was out of action for seven months, *Barham* for two, while *Valiant* was never out of action. Three cruisers were sunk, *Fiji*, *Gloucester* and *Calcutta*, while another six were damaged and likely to be under repair for up to 25 weeks. Lastly, six destroyers were sunk and seven more damaged. Worse still, most of these large-scale repairs were beyond the capability of the facilities in Egypt, ensuring that ships had to be sent vast distances for permanent repairs, thereby lengthening the time they would be unavailable. Both *Warspite* and *Formidable* had work done in the USA, as did *Orion* and *Dido*; *Barham* was repaired in South Africa and *Perth* in Australia.

The losses suffered by the Mediterranean Fleet during the battle for Crete represented a significant reduction in Cunningham's fighting strength. The impact was almost immediate and long lasting through the summer of 1941. The losses of cruisers and destroyers, both sunk and damaged, coupled with a lack of air support ensured that the Mediterranean Fleet was effectively immobilized for long periods for want of a screen to be able to both locate an enemy force and shield the fleet. The damage to its only aircraft carrier, *Formidable*, meant that the battlefleet was constrained to operating at night or under the rather limited range of land-based fighters, particularly as no long-range fighters were available to British forces in the eastern Mediterranean. The air cover situation was made worse by the German occupation of Crete, Greece and the eviction of the British army from Libya, allowing the Axis to establish airbases on either side of the eastern Mediterranean. At the same time, the collapse of the military situation in Libya and the need to supply Tobruk as well as Malta placed an increasing demand on the Navy's light forces, especially destroyers – the very ships needed to screen the battleships.[14]

Nor could reinforcements be obtained from the UK. Quite simply there were no carriers to replace the damaged *Illustrious* or *Formidable*. Furthermore, the widening of the war to involve Russia, following the German attack on the USSR in June 1941, meant that the Royal Navy had to protect a new convoy route, the Arctic convoys, from August 1941 onwards. Moreover, there was the ever present eastern menace of Japan to be deterred, if possible. With the added demands of the Arctic convoy route and the need to provide a force to deter the Japanese, modern battleships, aircraft carriers, cruisers and destroyers were going to be in even more short supply than they had been.[15]

Fig. 5.5. A convoy arrives at Malta.

The enforced inactivity of the battlefleet and the inability
to get at the enemy was enough to drive Cunningham mad. By
September Churchill was complaining about the relative passiv-
ity of the Mediterranean Fleet, but with the demands on the
Mediterranean Fleet's light forces made by the Malta and Tobruk
runs, as well as operations in the Red Sea and off Syria, there was
little that Cunningham could do. The weight of the war at sea in the
Mediterranean in the summer and autumn of 1941 was very firmly
on Force H at the other end of the sea.[16]

After its operations in the Atlantic against the *Bismarck* in May,
Force H spent the next few months ferrying supplies and aircraft
to the besieged and beleaguered island of Malta. Following on from
the 'Tiger' convoy at the start of May, which in conjunction with
the Mediterranean Fleet saw five merchant ships loaded with tanks
for the 8th Army in the western desert pass successfully through the
Mediterranean – only for the tanks to be thrown away in an over
hasty attack in June, Operation *Battleaxe* – Force H made five trips
to fly fighters in to Malta between April and June, while during July

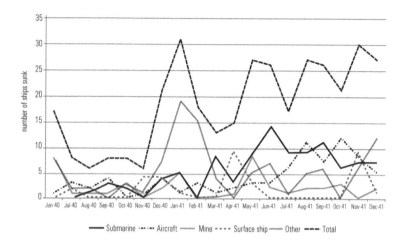

Fig. 5.6. Axis merchant vessels sunk in the Mediterranean, 1940–41.

and August the emphasis was on resupplying Malta.

The purpose of these operations was, of course, to keep Malta in the war. It was not just a matter of providing adequate defences for its own sake, but more importantly to keep the island as a viable base from which to strike at the Axis supply lines to Libya. In striking at these routes the Navy was at the forefront of Malta's battle, thanks to the Fleet Air Arm, submarines and surface ships, especially when it seemed that the weight of air attack was not as bad as had been feared. However, from the opening of hostilities until the arrival of Force K (two cruisers and two destroyers) on Trafalgar Day 1941, no surface forces were based at Malta; the main effort from Malta would be made by aircraft and submarines. Indeed the focus of Malta's submarines was the sinking of Axis merchant ships, not warships.[17]

The Admiralty's decision on 17 July 1940 to impose a 'sink-on-sight zone' for all Italian shipping found within 30 miles of the Italian coast or the coast of Italian processions in North Africa immensely aided the effectiveness of British submarines, especially those based in Malta. When Germany became involved in the Mediterranean war, the British sink-on-sight zone was extended as of 22 February

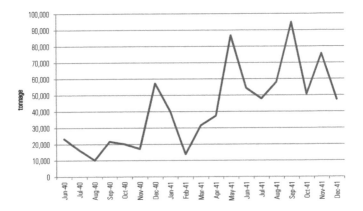

Fig. 5.7. Axis merchant ships sunk (by tonnage), June 1940–December 1941.

1941. The impact of such zones was straightforward: submarines, warships operating from Gibraltar or Alexandria and even aircraft could attack enemy vessels without warning rather than conform to the 'Prize Rules' of stop, search and taking as a Prize.

While the achievements of the British anti-shipping effort are impressive, sinking 352 ships of over 800,000 tons between June 1940 and December 1941, it must be contrasted with the unfortunate fact that large numbers of Axis ships were getting through. In the first six months of the war in the Mediterranean over 690,000 tons of Italian shipping, successfully used the Mediterranean and despite British efforts, only suffered a loss rate of less than 2 per cent. In fact the real crimp on German and Italian land forces in Libya was not down to the Royal Navy but more mundane factors – the North African ports like Tripoli and Benghazi (Tobruk remained in British hands during 1941) simply did not have the capacity to deal with the large volumes of stores, food and liquids that a modern army needed, a situation that grew worse the further an army moved away from its bases, with the result that there were more supplies waiting in Axis-controlled North African ports then could be moved to the front line.[18]

Nor were the British successes, such as they were, bought cheaply. The Royal Navy's submarines suffered particularly heavily,

Fig. 5.8. *U* class submarines alongside in Valetta harbour, Malta.

as the clear waters of the Mediterranean made them especially
vulnerable to being spotted from the air, even when they were at
considerable depths. In the six months from June 1940 the Royal
Navy lost nine submarines in the Mediterranean and in 1941
another eight failed to return from patrol. There were, however,
some notable successes by British submarines and surface ships:
Lt Cdr Malcolm Wanklyn of HMS *Upholder* in one attack torpedoed two 19,500-ton liners which contributed to his personal tally
of over 90,000 tons of Axis shipping sunk, winning him a Victoria
Cross in the process. On 9 November 1941 Force K, which had been
established in Malta in late October, sank or set afire every one of
a seven-ship convoy. These and other actions from September 1941
onwards contributed to less than 40 per cent of Axis supplies reaching Libya in November 1941. But just as the successes of the Navy's
submarines and light forces were being savoured, disaster struck at
both ends of the Mediterranean.[19]

On 13 November, Force H was returning to Gibraltar after
yet another sortie ferrying in fighters to Malta. The weather was
excellent and the sea calm as the warships zigzagged as a precaution

against Italian and now German U-boats that were operating in both western and eastern basins of the Mediterranean. At 15:41, just after the force had turned onto the latest leg of the zigzag and *Ark Royal* steadied on a new course to launch aircraft for a patrol, a single torpedo fired by *U-81* hit the starboard side of the carrier. A massive hole was blown in her side and the *Ark Royal* immediately listed to starboard; 20 minutes after the explosion the list was 18°. The flooding affected the starboard boiler room, but despite the damage it was hoped the ship might be saved. Tugs were dispatched from Gibraltar and efforts were made to get up steam again. At 20:55 the disabled carrier was being towed at 2 knots towards Gibraltar and the list had been reduced. However, the boiler uptakes ran under the hangar deck and became flooded due to the list. Fires broke out in the port boiler room due to the heat from the fumes, and the compartment had to be abandoned. The list increased back past 18° and by 04:00 on 14 November it was 27° when the decision was made to abandon the efforts to save the ship. At 06:13 the list reached 45° and the *Ark Royal*, the ship the Germans and Italians had repeatedly claimed to have sunk, capsized and disappeared under the waves.

Towards the end of November it was Cunningham's turn to suffer a major loss. On 24 November the battlefleet was at sea support-ing the efforts of Force K and Force B to find and destroy a convoy of desperately needed reinforcements and supplies for Rommel's Afrika Korps. HMS *Barham* was hit by three torpedoes fired from the German submarine *U-331*; the mortally wounded battleship rolled over and her magazines exploded, ripping the ship apart. Of *Barham*'s crew of slightly fewer than 1,200 officers and men, 856 were killed.

Nor were British woes in the Mediterranean over. On 14 December the cruiser *Galatea* was hit by two torpedoes and sank. Then Force K, which had done sterling work harassing and sink-ing Axis shipping between Italy and North Africa, blundered into a newly laid Italian minefield that was in surprisingly deep water and some distance from the coast during the night of 19/20 December. HMS *Neptune* hit two mines, and attempted to go astern out of the

Fig. 5.9. HMS *Barham* capsizing after being hit by three
torpedoes; moments later she exploded.

minefield, but then hit a third mine that left her stopped in the
water. Meanwhile, HMS *Aurora* and HMS *Penelope* had also struck
mines and suffered too much damage to be able to help *Neptune*. Two
of the four destroyers screening the cruisers attempted to get close
enough to pass *Neptune* a tow, but one of them, HMS *Kandahar*, hit a
mine and had her stern blown off and later sank; *Neptune* warned the
remaining ships to keep clear. With daylight approaching and close
to an enemy-held coast, the rest of Force K had to leave *Neptune* and
Kandahar. The *Neptune* then drifted helplessly into a fourth mine and
capsized. Only one survivor from the crew of 765 was alive on a raft
five days later when it was discovered by an Italian torpedo boat. In
one stroke Force K was reduced to one cruiser – HMS *Penelope*.

The same night as Force K was suffering such grievous losses, the
Italians struck at Cunningham's fleet while it was in the supposed
safety of Alexandria. The Italians launched an audacious attack using
frogmen riding 'human torpedoes' which carried them through the
harbour and allowed them to place limpet mines on the bottom
of HMS *Queen Elizabeth* and HMS *Valiant*. Just before 06:00 on 20
December the mines exploded and the two British battleships sank

to the bottom of the harbour. However, the harbour was so shallow that the upper decks of the ships were still clear of the water and, indeed, shipboard life continued as normal until sufficient repairs were made to raise the ships off the harbour's bottom.

The battle for Malta

The year 1942 therefore opened with the Mediterranean Fleet in woeful condition, without an aircraft carrier or a single operational battleship. Nor were any reinforcements likely to improve Cunningham's lot. Thanks to the fast deteriorating situation in the Far East, the Admiralty had informed Cunningham that all reinforcements would be heading for the Eastern Fleet, not his command. At the other end of the Mediterranean, Force H was without a modern fleet aircraft carrier following the loss of HMS *Ark Royal* the previous November. Instead the obsolete and small HMS *Argus* was Force H's only carrier from mid-December 1941 until it was joined by the slightly larger but still obsolescent HMS *Eagle*. The Royal Navy was faced with the unpalatable conclusion that it was not big enough to fight Germany, Italy and Japan in three different operational theatres, that the direst shortages in ships were modern fast battleships and aircraft carriers, and that given the state of British industry, the need to repair and refit damaged shipping and the demands for resources by the other services it was unlikely that any shortfall in major warships could be quickly rectified.

Meanwhile, Malta's position was deteriorating under the siege that the Germans and Italians had thrown round the island and the incessant air raids. By February fuel was running short, threatening the ability of the Navy's submarines and the FAA and RAF aircraft that were based there to strike at Axis supplies heading to North Africa. Cunningham therefore attempted to run three fast merchant ships to Malta and take back the empty shipping already there. Unfortunately the attempt was smashed by Axis airpower – while the four empty ships reached Alexandria safely, the Malta-bound ships were heavily bombed, two had to be sunk as they were so badly damaged, while the third managed to reach Tobruk. Indeed

Fig. 5.10. HMS *Euryalus* during the heavy air attacks that
were unleashed on the ships of Operation *MG1*.

so heavy were the attacks that the escort had to cope with that the
three *Dido* class light cruisers, commanded by Rear Admiral Philip
Vian, which provided the only protection against an enemy surface
attack, fired off approximately 3,700 rounds of ammunition from
their dual-purpose 5.25-inch guns. This represented another head-
ache for Cunningham, as only 1.3 replacement sets of 5.25-inch
ammunition remained for the cruisers of the Mediterranean Fleet.

In March another attempt was made to get supplies through –
Operation *MG1*. It was very carefully planned by Cunningham's
staff in an effort to mitigate the British weakness at sea. Submarines
were posted to watch the Italian fleet harbours, the RAF suppressed
enemy airfields in Libya and Sicily and the Long-Range Desert
Group mounted diversionary raids on Libyan airfields. Yet despite
the planning and great effort that went into easing the passage of the
convoy it was, unfortunately, a failure. The convoy consisted of only
four merchant ships, yet the escort under Vian was as strong as the
Mediterranean Fleet could make it – three light cruisers, 11 fleet
destroyers and a close escort of an anti-aircraft cruiser and six *Hunt*

class destroyers. However, there were no battleships and aircraft carriers to intercept the Italian fleet if it tried to attack the convoy. Vian, in command of the cruisers, which were the heaviest escort ships available, carried out a textbook defence of the convoy, holding off superior Italian surface ships, including a modern battleship, twice during 22 March, once in the early afternoon and then during the dog watches. Using smoke screens to hide the retreating convoy, the light cruisers and fleet destroyers turned back the first Italian force following a brief long-range gunnery duel – indeed so thick were the British smokescreens that many of the British ships did not even sight the enemy before the Italians broke off the action. While this was happening the convoy was itself under heavy air attack. However, the Italian cruisers, now joined by the battleship *Littorio*, regrouped and again attempted to engage the convoy. In a running battle that lasted over two hours, Vian's cruisers and destroyers again held off the Italians, who would not pass through the smokescreen while the convoy fled to the south-west. Unfortunately the delays this imposed on the convoy meant that the merchant ships were unable to reach Malta before dawn broke on 23 March. Axis aircraft mercilessly attacked the ships as they straggled towards the island and while the surviving ships were being unloaded. Only 5,000 tons out of 26,000 tons of supplies reached Malta.[20]

This was, however, Cunningham's last battle as Commander in Chief Mediterranean. On 1 April 1942 he was relieved by Admiral Sir Henry Harwood, the victor of the battle of the River Plate. Cunningham left for Washington to head up the British delegation there – probably the only British naval officer with the professional standing and temperament to stand up to the irascible head of the US Navy, Admiral Ernie King, who was a far from willing partner in the coalition that Britain and America were now in as they sought to defeat the Axis, first in Europe and then in the Far East. The commander of Force H, Admiral Sir James Somerville, had also moved on in February. Somerville was to command the reconstituted Eastern Fleet; he was replaced in Force H by Admiral Syfret.

The British naval position in May 1942 was so weak and such were the demands on the fleet as a whole that it was decided that no convoy could be run from Gibraltar to relieve Malta. However, the aerial pounding the island was receiving made reinforcing the air defences absolutely imperative if Malta was to survive. As no British aircraft carrier was available in April, the USS *Wasp* was borrowed from the USA and used to launch 47 Spitfires to fly on to the island, only for them to be destroyed in the days following their arrival. The operation was repeated in early May, but this time the USS *Wasp* was joined by the elderly British carrier HMS *Eagle*. The two ships launched 64 Spitfires, 61 of which reached Malta on 9 May. The next day these new aircraft were successfully in action defending Malta and starting to turn back the Axis tide in the central Mediterranean. HMS *Eagle* made three more runs to fly in Spitfires, once more in May and twice in June, adding another 55 fighters to the island's arsenal.

Fighters were, however, only part of Malta's needs. Some materials could and were sent in by submarine or by one of the Navy's fast minelayers such as HMS *Welshman*, but only in small amounts. What was needed was to get another convoy through. It was decided to run convoys from Gibraltar (Operation *Harpoon*) and Alexandria (Operation *Vigorous*), timed to arrive at Malta on consecutive days. The *Harpoon* convoy of six merchant ships ran through determined air, mine and surface attacks, losing four cargo ships sunk and several warships damaged. However, the two merchant ships that did reach Malta on 14 June – the day the 8th Army started its pell-mell retreat from Gazala following its defeat by Rommel's Afrika Corps – landed about two months' worth of supplies.

The *Vigorous* convoy of four merchant ships from Alexandria also ran into extremely heavy air attacks and was threatened by an overwhelming surface force. The seven cruisers escorting the convoy were again commanded by Rear Admiral Vian, but unlike the previous *MG1* convoy, *Vigorous* was a failure. The Italians sailed two battleships, four cruisers and 12 destroyers in order to find the convoy and this was duly reported by a British reconnaissance aircraft. Vian was informed of this development at 22:15 on 14 June and that the Italians would probably intercept him around 07:00 on 15 June. Rather than let Vian retire in the face of such a large enemy force, the new Commander in Chief Mediterranean Fleet, Admiral Sir Henry Harwood, ordered it to continue west for Malta until 02:00 on 15 June before reversing course. At 05:25 Harwood then ordered Vian to turn the convoy back towards Malta on the basis that German air attacks between Crete and Cyrenaica would be more dangerous than the Italian fleet. After more air reconnaissance reports came in, Harwood decided to turn the convoys eastwards again, away from Malta. Following an erroneous RAF report that both Italian battleships had been hit by torpedoes from Beaufort torpedo bombers (they had in fact missed), Harwood then ordered Vian to take the convoy west again to try to get to Malta. However, Vian had already received a different report that the Italians were still coming on and he decided, given the damage his ships had received from bomb and E-boat attacks, to continue to the east and see if Harwood would again change his mind. Harwood did, placing the decision to press on to Malta on Vian. Given the damage to his some of his cruisers and the fact that much anti-aircraft ammunition had been expended as the convoy went first west, then east, then west and finally east while under air attack, and that the Germans were still mounting exceptionally heavy air attacks on his force, Vian decided enough was enough. The convoy and Vian's cruisers headed back to Alexandria.

The failure of the two operations was very much down to the Royal Navy's weakness in major units at this time – notwithstanding Harwood's unfortunate habit of trying to control the battle too closely while still in Alexandria and his propensity for having second thoughts once he had made a decision. Only the obsolete and small aircraft carriers *Argus* and *Eagle* could be spared for the *Harpoon* convoy, while none were available for *Vigorous*, and only one battleship, the unmodernized *Malaya*, was available to cover the *Harpoon* convoy and none for *Vigorous*. Airpower and submarines, which the British tried to use as a substitute for surface ships to meet the Italian naval threat, clearly were not as effective as hoped. Indeed the RAF proved itself incapable of stopping a major force of warships. The submarines did slightly better: *P.35* sank the Italian heavy cruiser *Trento* after it had been hit by an air strike. Whatever the reason for the failure, another convoy would soon be needed to re-supply Malta.[21]

In August 1942 a new attempt to break Malta's siege was made, this time from Gibraltar only and with massive surface support. The 14 merchant ships of Operation *Pedestal* were escorted by two battleships, three aircraft carriers, six cruisers and 34 destroyers, plus corvettes and minesweepers. Additionally, the aircraft carrier *Furious* was loaded with Spitfires which were to be flown to Malta, and eight submarines were on patrol to try to intercept any moves by the Italian fleet. Such provision of battleships and above all aircraft carriers meant that the Home Fleet and Eastern Fleet had to be stripped of ships, yet another indication of the follies of the rearmament programme before the war and the inability of Britain's sclerotic shipbuilding industry to build a new Royal Navy in wartime.

On 10 August the convoy passed Gibraltar and the enhanced escort formed round it. The next day *Furious* was launching her Spitfires for Malta when, without warning, HMS *Eagle* was hit by four torpedoes fired from *U-73*, which had slipped past the escorts undetected. The four torpedo hits caused immense damage to the old ship and, having heeled sharply to port, the *Eagle* capsized and sank in about eight minutes. Its loss meant a 25 per cent reduction in the convoy's fighter protection until it came within the range of aircraft operating from Malta. At dusk, the first air attacks occurred, but did not cause any damage. The next day, 12 August, the convoy had to deal with massed air and submarine attacks. By the end of the day the aircraft carrier HMS *Indomitable* had been damaged and the destroyer HMS *Foresight* disabled, but only one of the merchant ships had been damaged and subsequently sunk. However, the weight of attacks had disorganized the convoy as night approached.[22]

With the convoy approaching the narrowest part of the Mediterranean, where the North African coast and first Sardinia and then Sicily squeeze together to limit a fleet's room to manoeuvre, the battleships and surviving aircraft carriers and their close escorts had to turn back to Gibraltar. But now the convoy would be able to draw on the fighters and bombers at Malta for protection – at least during daylight. However, soon after the capital ships and

Fig. 5.11. Operation *Pedestal*. The tanker SS *Ohio* is towed into Grand
Harbour, Valetta, Malta. A destroyer is lashed to the tanker
in order to stop the *Ohio* sinking.

their escorts turned back, leaving the convoy and its close escort
to pass through the narrows between Sicily and North Africa, a
series of explosions damaged the cruisers *Nigeria* and *Cairo* and the
tanker *Ohio*. Then came another air attack which sank the merchant
ships *Empire Hope* and *Clan Ferguson*, while the *Brisbane Star*, which
was damaged in the same attack, eventually reached Malta. Then
the cruiser *Kenya* was torpedoed but was able to keep up with the
convoy despite the damage. The Axis attacks on the convoy continued throughout the night. At 00:40 enemy motor torpedo boats
– E-boats – attacked the convoy from both sides until after 05:00.
HMS *Manchester*, a *Town* class light cruiser, was hit twice and had to
be scuttled while four more of the merchant ships (all stragglers)
were hit and sunk, with one more damaged but still able to keep up
with the convoy. With daylight on 13 August came more air attacks.
The merchant ship *Waimarama* was bombed and sunk in a massive

explosion; later the *Ohio* was repeatedly damaged and disabled, as was *Dorset*, while the already torpedo-damaged *Rochester Castle* was hit by a bomb but continued under way. At 18:00 the three surviving merchant ships still able to move sailed into the Grand Harbour at Malta. The next day *Brisbane Star* reached the harbour, followed on the 15th by *Ohio*, which was towed into port. Five ships out of 14 reached Malta; an aircraft carrier, two cruisers and a destroyer were sunk and two aircraft carriers and two cruisers damaged in order to get the merchant ships through to the beleaguered island. But it was enough to keep Malta going until Allied fortunes in the Mediterranean improved in the late autumn.[23]

In July, while the Navy was still wrestling with the problem of keeping Malta supplied, the Allies decided that as an invasion of Europe in 1942 was impracticable, efforts should be made to launch a combined attack on North Africa – Operation *Torch*. The planners looked at an invasion across five sites: at Casablanca in French Morocco, plus Oran, Algiers, Philippeville and Bône in Algeria to allow a rapid advance into Tunisia before the Axis could react. But there were not enough ships to support five separate landings. Unbelievably the ability of Allied shipping to support Allied plans, made worse by chronic mismanagement of the available shipping, especially in the Pacific, had not been a factor in the Anglo-American discussions between politicians and the chiefs of staff as to what Allied plans for 1942 onwards should be. As a result of the inability to find the ships needed to make five separate landings, the plan had to be reduced to assaults on Casablanca, Oran and Algiers only. The move to invade North Africa did, however, bring Admiral Cunningham back to his old Mediterranean stamping ground as the overall commander of the Allied combined naval task force.

On 8 November the assaults went in. At Casablanca – a USN responsibility – there was resistance from Vichy French forces, but it was eventually overcome by the US army. In the centre, around Oran, unexpected shoals caused problems for the landing craft, but stubborn resistance from the defending Vichy French was overwhelmed by the next day. In Algiers the assault troops were openly welcomed by the French in places and resistance was light. The

Allies' first joint amphibious operation, despite the huge risks and the problems encountered in the planning and execution of the invasion, was a success. Unfortunately the land force was slow to exploit the collapse of the Vichy forces and to capture Tunisia, and the Germans had got there ahead of them. Months of heavy fighting ensued as the Allies slowly pushed back the Germans until on 13 May the surviving German forces in Tunisia surrendered.[24]

Victory in the Mediterranean

Before the Germans had been thrown out of North Africa, the Allies had been considering what the next step in the Mediterranean should be. Sicily was the obvious target, so a deception campaign was mounted which included one of the most unusual intelligence operations ever mounted: Operation *Mincemeat* – 'the man who never was'. This operation saw the Naval Intelligence Division obtain a body, dress it in a Royal Marines uniform, fabricate a cover identity for it, create misleading documents indicating that Sardinia and Greece rather than Sicily were the targets for invasion, and then have a submarine place the body with all the supporting 'evidence' in the sea off Spain where it drifted ashore. The Spanish gave the Germans the documents to copy before returning them to the British naval attaché. The Germans swallowed the story and the deception, moving troops and materiel away from Sicily.[25]

Operation *Husky* – the invasion of Sicily – did not have an easy birth. Admiral Cunningham wanted to exploit the mobility of seapower to strike at different points around the island. The air commanders wanted the airfields in south-western Sicily captured as a priority, something that Cunningham also supported. But when General Bernard Montgomery, commander of the 8th Army, was briefed on the plans he condemned them as being too dispersed and demanded – and got – concentrated landings either side of Syracuse with General George S. Patton's US 7th Army landing just to the east in the Gulf of Gela. Additionally, the timetable for the invasion was driven around the use of airborne forces, which in the end were not deployed as intended, so the seaborne invasion force had to face disadvantageous visibility conditions for no good end. Importantly, the difficult planning process had ensured that the key aspect of planning an amphibious operation was understood at the highest level – that the needs of the landing force's tactical plan dictated how and where the naval force would land them and how the air forces would provide support.

In purely naval terms, however, the assaults on Sicily went well, although the invasion fleet opening fire on the 82nd Airborne Division as it flew overhead was both tragic and avoidable. What was disappointing in the Royal Navy's view was the unwillingness of Montgomery to use small tactical landings to outflank German positions as his forces drove along the coast towards Messina, unlike Patton in the north who was happy to use the mobility of seapower. With Sicily captured, attention turned to the invasion of Italy.

The assault on Italy was another matter. The precursor to the landings at Salerno in the Bay of Naples was the 8th Army's assault crossing on 3 September 1943 of the Straits of Messina, using 300 landing craft to establish a beachhead on the toe of Italy. The planning process for this was as fraught and difficult as that for *Husky*, chiefly owing to Montgomery's abrasive character and his habit of blaming others for problems. On 9 September, as the 8th Army reached the narrow 'instep' of Italy, Cunningham put ashore the British 1st Airborne Division at Taranto. At the same time as Taranto was being seized by Cunningham's coup de main, the Salerno invasion force was nearing its objective.

The greatest problem the landing force faced was lack of air cover – Salerno was beyond the range of single-engine fighters stationed in Sicily. Initially the Allied air forces thought that only nine aircraft could be kept above the invasion areas. As a result the Navy was to provide air cover. However, only two fleet carriers were available, HMS *Formidable* and HMS *Illustrious*, whose aircraft were needed to protect the invasion force on route and indeed the heavy covering force. Such was the shortage of fleet carriers within the Royal Navy that the carrier force to provide air cover over the invasion beaches was created by using HMS *Unicorn* – nominally an aircraft ferry and maintenance carrier – and four escort carriers withdrawn from convoy work in the Atlantic. Eventually the Allied air forces decided that they could keep 36 fighters in the air above the invasion beach, but the hopes for Allied success in the air still effectively rested on the Navy and the army, providing the army could seize an Italian airfield less than two miles from the coast.

The act of getting the assault troops ashore at dawn on 9 September went well, indeed better than during *Torch* and *Husky*. The problems started once the army got ashore. The landing force at Salerno was not well handled by the military commanders and the narrowness of the beachhead meant that there was a great deal of congestion in getting supplies, men and equipment ashore while the Germans reacted most violently. Indeed the Allies had landed on top of 16th Panzer Division. As a result of the rapid and vigorous German response to the landing, the ground troops were unable to get very far inland, leaving them penned in a shallow beachhead under fire from the Germans. The congestion was impossible and the Allies had no room to manoeuvre and did not capture the airfield as intended. Worse, the British and American beachheads had not linked up. The invasion force was heavily attacked from the air too, and the Fleet Air Arm was hard pushed to contain the worst of the German raids.

With the ground attack grinding to a halt and with insufficient depth in the beachhead, the Allied navies' role became one of bombardment and air cover. By 15 September serious consideration was being given to abandoning the American beachhead. General Mark Clark's crisis in confidence passed once the British learned what he was thinking. At the same time, the 8th Army was approaching from the south and on 16 September the Germans started to break off the action and withdraw to a new defensive line in the mountains across Italy. While supporting the troops ashore the Royal Navy was at the receiving end of a new weapon, the German radio-controlled glider bombs, one of which disabled HMS *Warspite* on 16 September, and which were very difficult to defend against while the Allied air defence was so weak. Only days before, *Warspite* had led the Italian fleet into captivity following the Italian capitulation as a result of the invasion of their mainland. On

11 September Admiral Cunningham signalled the Admiralty: 'Be pleased to inform their Lordships that the Italian battlefleet now lies at anchor under the guns of fortress Malta.'[26]

The surrender of Italy did not bring the war at sea in the Mediterranean to an end. The British were anxious to take advantage of the Italian surrender to grab islands in the Aegean which had been garrisoned by Italy – the Americans were less interested, seeing it as yet another British effort to avoid invading France. Again, the main weight fell on the Royal Navy: between 10 and 14 September 1943 the islands of Kos and Leros were seized. However, the Germans had complete air superiority and were determined to eject the British from the region. By mid-October it was all over; it was in many respects a repeat of 1941 – an unmitigated and avoidable disaster.

October also saw important changes in the command and control of the war at sea in the Mediterranean. In the middle of the month Force H was disbanded, its ships desperately needed to strengthen Admiral Somerville's Eastern Fleet. Mid-October also saw Admiral Cunningham hand over as Commander in Chief Mediterranean to Admiral James Cunningham (no relation). 'ABC' Cunningham was bound for London to take over as First Sea Lord from the dying Dudley Pound.

Meanwhile, in central Italy the Allied advance had stalled in front of Monte Cassino – the Gustav Line – and an amphibious assault to unhinge the German position was planned. On 22 January 1944 a joint Anglo-US naval task force attacked either side of the town of Anzio. Within a week 68,886 men plus hundreds of tanks, guns and thousands of tons of supplies had been landed by the Allied navies. Again, German air attacks were damaging and ships were lost to German radio-controlled glider bombs; the cruiser HMS *Spartan* was hit and capsized. Ashore, the Allied ground forces were again badly handled and were stopped dead by the German defences. Rather than being a means of unhinging the German front, Anzio became a besieged enclave, supplied by sea for months until, reinforced, the Allied troops were able to go on the offensive *after* the Gustav Line had been broken in mid-May 1944.[27]

The next major act of the war at sea in the Mediterranean was the invasion of southern France in August 1944. This time the Royal Navy was very much the junior partner to the US Navy and the operation on 15 August was very much an American affair. However, the Royal Navy still remained active along both coasts of Italy, giving support where needed and running supplies. In September 1944 the Germans started evacuating Greece and the Aegean and into this vacuum stepped the Royal Navy – a return that did not have an accompaniment of Stuka dive-bombers unlike 1941 and 1943. On land the Allies continued their slog up Italy until the unconditional surrender of German forces in the region on 2 May. The war in the Mediterranean might now be over, but already, and for months previously, the main weight of the Royal Navy had shifted to the Far East and the war against Japan.[28]

CHAPTER 6

The Far East 1941–45

The Royal Navy in the Far East 1939–41

The signing of the Washington Naval Treaty presented a significant change in the British naval position in the Far East. The treaty
changed the relationship between Britain and Japan – permanently.
Prior to 1922 Japan had been signatory to a bilateral naval treaty
with the British. Indeed Japan had fought on the Allied side in World
War I and had profited accordingly through the division of the post-
war spoils, gaining the German Pacific Ocean islands such as Guam
as League of Nations mandated territories. After Washington, Japan
was in a position of inferiority. Its treaty with Britain had been
replaced with a five-power agreement that enshrined Japanese naval
subservience to Britain and America, while the very fact that the
Anglo-Japanese treaty had been replaced by the Washington Treaty
was also seen as an insult to Japanese pride.

The British also changed their view of Japan, although for far
more practical reasons than pride or even strategy. The Royal
Navy needed an enemy on which to base its plans and procurement programmes. The USA was politically unacceptable as a likely
enemy in the interwar period after the Washington Treaty – which
left Japan as the next largest navy and therefore the next largest
threat.

As a result of this almost bureaucratic approach to who may
or may not pose a threat to Britain in the interwar period, Japan
had been Britain's supposed naval enemy from an early point in the
peace. However, sometimes one is just lucky with one's assump-
tions and the 1930s proved that the Admiralty was indeed right – if

unintentionally, or at least for the wrong reasons – that Japan was a threat. It was Japanese aggression in Manchuria that had persuaded the British government to end its dalliance with disarmament in the early 1930s. But such was the situation that Britain faced in 1939 and 1940 that no ships were available to send to the Far East – quite simply there were more pressing matters for the Royal Navy and British Dominion naval partners to face in the Atlantic and Mediterranean.

Yet what to do about Japan in the interwar period was the back-bone of British naval policy. All the pre-war plans could only work providing everyone kept to the Washington Treaty (and by default the Versailles Treaty too) and did not cheat. The Washington Treaty after all gave the UK a two-power standard against Japan and any other European naval power under the Versailles and Washington treaties. But it did not give Britain enough of a margin against the Japanese and Italian navies if they cheated on the Washington accords and if Germany rebuilt its navy too. Worse, it did not allow for the emergence of such threats at a rate faster than the Royal Navy (and Britain) could rearm to face them. In the interwar period the British assumed a ten-year lead in to a major war; in the end they had at most a seven-year period to prepare. Nor, understandably, did the plans allow for the unimaginable defeat and surrender of France in June 1940.

However, Japan did not join the fighting against Britain in 1939 or 1940. But this does not mean that the area was peaceful. As early as 1939, German surface raiders had operated in the Indian Ocean against Allied merchant vessels, and were in turn hunted by British and Commonwealth cruisers. The *Graf Spee* was the first to pene-trate the Indian Ocean in November 1939 and was followed by the *Admiral Scheer* in February 1940, but between them they only sank three ships in the area. However, the Germans also dispatched a number of disguised merchant raiders – converted merchant ships with their armament hidden away from prying eyes – to the Central and South Atlantic, Antarctic and Southern Oceans, Indian Ocean and the Pacific. Between the start of 1940 and the end of 1941 four disguised merchant raiders operated in the Indian Ocean: *Atlantis*,

Orion, *Pinguin* and *Kormoran*. The *Komet* together with the *Atlantis* and *Orion* operated in the Pacific. In total these five raiders sank 77 merchant ships and whalers – some 451,225 tons of shipping. The Navy's patrolling cruisers had some successes: HMS *Cornwall* found and destroyed the *Pinguin* on 8 May 1941 off the Horn of Africa, the Italian disguised raider *Ramb I* was sunk by HMNZS *Leander* on 27 February in the Arabian Sea and HMS *Devonshire* caught and sank the *Atlantis* on 22 November 1941 in the Atlantic.[1]

However, a disaster had already occurred on 19 November 1941 when the Australian cruiser HMAS *Sydney* found and tried to stop the *Kormoran*, which was pretending to be a Dutch steamer, off the west coast of Australia. For reasons that have never been explained, the *Sydney* closed to within a mile, parallel to the *Kormoran*'s course. Realizing there was no chance of bluffing its way out of trouble, at 16:35 the *Kormoran* unleashed a devastating surprise close-range gun and torpedo attack. The *Sydney* opened fire at almost the same moment as the Germans, and both ships suffered mortal damage in around ten minutes of fighting; the ships then drifted apart blazing furiously. By nightfall they were out of sight of each other. The *Sydney* was never seen again and all 645 of her crew were lost; the *Kormoran* scuttled herself after her engines failed as a result of battle damage and 318 out of the 399 personnel on board were either picked up by Allied ships or reached Australia in lifeboats.

Force Z, Singapore and defeat in the Far East

Patrolling cruisers to deal with German surface raiders were not, however, the answer to the problem of Japan. Fundamentally the British naval problem from 1939 to 1941 was one of how to deter Japan from entering the war rather than to prepare to fight her. Worryingly for the British, although the Japanese did not enter the war, they soon took advantage of the changing situation in Europe in 1940. On 23 September, three months after the fall of France, Japanese forces entered French Indochina. The Vichy regime in the French colony did not resist and the Japanese not only gained access to raw materials but also to bases that were conveniently situated for attacking China from the south-west, where Japan had been fighting for much of the 1930s, and also for launching attacks on British and Dutch colonies in Malaya and the East Indies.[2]

The nub of the issue facing Britain, however, was what would deter Japan? The Admiralty wanted to send a fleet to the Far East, but this was difficult in 1939 given that rearmament could not produce a fleet big enough to face the increasing list of possible enemies the Royal Navy might have to deal with. The fall of France and the entry of Italy into the war ensured that there were no ships to spare for a Far Eastern fleet of the size the Admiralty felt would offer a viable deterrent to Japan. By the middle of 1941, this view was changing, thanks to the increasing level of support coming from the USA. This led the Admiralty to believe in autumn 1941 that it might be possible to establish a Far Eastern fleet by March 1942, consisting of the battleships *Nelson* and *Rodney*, the four unmodernized R class World War I veterans, a battlecruiser, an aircraft carrier, cruisers and destroyers. This was felt by the Navy to be enough to secure the Indian Ocean area against any moves by the Japanese fleet and to secure British and neutral trade from attacks by Japanese cruisers out on commerce-raiding missions. As such the Admiralty was moving beyond deterrence to thinking about what sort of fleet would be needed to protect British interests as well as deter Japan.[3]

However, deterrence was not just a naval problem but also a political one. The politicians, rather unfortunately as it turned out, had a very different view of the situation, of deterrence and what was required of the Navy. For them, naval deterrence in the Far East only came about in August 1941 as the tightening of economic sanctions against Japan following its occupation of French Indochina started to bite. It was Churchill and his foreign secretary, Anthony Eden, who forced the Admiralty to dispatch the new battleship HMS *Prince of Wales* and the veteran battlecruiser HMS *Repulse* – Force Z – in October 1941, under the command of Admiral Sir Tom Phillips, to Singapore to act as the deterrent force they felt was needed. This went against the wishes of the Admiralty who wanted to establish a balanced fleet by March 1942. Force Z arrived in Singapore on 2 December 1941, the day after the Japanese had decided on war. Less than a week of peace remained. Deterrence had failed.[4]

The Admiralty had, however, considered what might happen if Japan refused to be deterred, even before Force Z arrived in Singapore. On 1 December the Admiralty suggested to Phillips that Force Z should be sent away from Singapore. London felt that the ships disappearing would increase the security of the force there and increase its deterrence value by worrying the Japanese – Force Z could pop up anywhere in the region with little or no warning. Phillips did not agree straight away. Instead he attended a series of meetings and conferences with the US and Dutch naval commanders. But events moved faster than the Allies expected, and before the major conference of all Allied and Commonwealth naval commanders could be held in Singapore on 8 December, the Japanese attacked.

In the early hours of 8 December – just after the attack on Pearl Harbor was going in – Japanese aircraft bombed Singapore. Perhaps appropriately, the Navy's first shots in this new war were from its anti-aircraft guns. On the outbreak of fighting, Phillips took command of all HM ships in the Far East area at 08:00 on 8 December. Even before the Japanese had attacked Pearl Harbor, they had started their seaborne landing in northern Malaya. Unfortunately for the British, poor weather, notably low cloud, prevented any air reconnaissance of the southern part of the Gulf of Siam on 7 December. The best information the Allies had on Japanese movements was a sighting at midday on 6 December of a large Japanese convoy and a strong naval escort south-west of French Indochina and heading west into the Gulf. The Japanese could just have been moving to Kohtron on the west coast of French Indochina, but this sighting was enough to make Phillips, then in Manila, recall HMS *Repulse* and her screen which had sailed for Darwin the previous day. It was also enough to persuade the 'ABCD' powers – America, Britain, China and Dutch – to take precautionary measures.

At 00:25 on 8 December – some 80 minutes before the attack on Pearl Harbor – the Japanese attempted to land at Kota Bharu. Despite being initially held by the defenders, by dawn they were ashore and establishing themselves after very heavy fighting. About this time, landings were also taking place on the Siamese coast at Singora, Tepa and Patani to little or no opposition.

Table 6.1. The timings of the Japanese initial attacks across the Pacific and South East Asian Region, 7/8 December 1941.

Local Time/Date	Time Zone	GMT	Event
00:25/8 December	-7½	16:55/7 December	Landing at Kota Bharu (N. Malaya)
08:00/7 December	+10½	18:30/7 December	Attack on Pearl Harbor
04:00/8 December	-7½	21:30/7 December	Air raid on Singapore
05:10/8 December	-8	21:10/7 December	Air raid on Davo (Philippines)
08:00/8 December	-8½	23:30/7 December	Air raid on Hong Kong
09:00/8 December	-8½	00:30/8 December	Air raid on Hong Kong airfield; Japanese troops cross frontier into New Territories

As the Japanese were already ashore, it was imperative that the landing forces were attacked while they were still vulnerable – before they had completed unloading troops, supplies and equipment. In the opening few hours of the war the situation in northern Malaya was 'confused' and Allied intelligence on the numbers and capabilities of the Japanese army and naval air forces was scanty, and what little was known was clouded by racial prejudice. Just as importantly, the British war experience to date indicated that high-level bombing posed little threat, dive-bombing was unlikely beyond 200 miles from an enemy airbase, and that long-range attacks by torpedo-carrying aircraft had not occurred so far. Admiral Phillips felt that with fighter cover and surprise Force Z had a good chance of destroying the Japanese force. At 17:35 on 8 December he sailed with all available ships to attack the Japanese forces at Singora and Kota Bharu, as it was felt that these areas were probably outside the range of Japanese anti-shipping aircraft in southern French Indochina. It was a very small force: the modern battleship *Prince of Wales*, the battlecruiser HMS *Repulse* and four destroyers of various types and antiquity.

Unfortunately, despite the cloudy weather and rain that shielded the ships from Japanese air observation, Force Z was sighted by the Japanese submarine *I-65* at 13:40 on 9 December, which warned of the Royal Navy's approach. Then at 17:40 Japanese reconnaissance aircraft were sighted and it was clear that any chance of surprising the Japanese landing force had been lost; Force Z turned around. At 23:35 that day, a report was received that the Japanese were landing at Kuantan, over 150 miles further south than the then southernmost landing at Kota Bharu. As this was even further from the Japanese airfields in Indochina and close to the return track to Singapore, Admiral Phillips decided to investigate, but did not ask for RAF fighter cover or inform anyone at Singapore of his changed plans. By 08:45 on 10 December reconnaissance by *Prince of Wales*'s Walrus aircraft and the destroyer HMS *Express* proved the report false. At 10:26 a land-based Japanese aircraft found Force Z.[5]

The Japanese had 85 bombers already in the air waiting for information on Force Z and at 11:00 they saw the British ships ahead of them. They launched a devastating and highly disciplined attack that saw first the *Prince of Wales* hit and mortally damaged by a single torpedo hit on her stern at 11:44, and then HMS *Repulse* hit by a single torpedo amidships, which she shrugged off. Both ships kept up the fight, however, the slowly sinking but still moving *Prince of Wales* being hit again by three more torpedoes at 12:23. In the same mass attack *Repulse* was unable to dodge all the torpedoes aimed at her and was hit by up to another four torpedoes just after 12:25; she capsized and sank at 12:33. At 13:10 the order was given to abandon HMS *Prince of Wales* as she listed steeply to port; then at 13:20 she turned turtle and sank. Force Z had been destroyed and with it the

Fig. 6.1. Force Z. HMS *Prince of Wales* arrives at Singapore, December 1941.

Royal Navy's main strike force in the Far East.[6]

The loss of Force Z did not mean the end of the battle, however. From 3 January until 5 February 1942 the Royal Navy escorted seven convoys of supplies and reinforcements for the land forces holding Malaya and Singapore. Indeed these convoys were not attacked by the Japanese until 4 February when BM 12 was bombed by Japanese aircraft in the Banka Straits and then again the next day in the approaches to Singapore, losing two of the transports. However, the success of the Royal Navy in getting reinforcements to Singapore has to be set against the fact that the British 18th Division, two brigades of Indian infantry and 3,500 Australian troops merely swelled the number of soldiers that marched into Japanese prisoner of war camps when Singapore fell.[7]

By 31 January British and Imperial land forces had retreated to Singapore Island, and the causeway linking it to the mainland was demolished. For reasons that are unclear, the army assumed responsibility for the demolition of the naval base on the north side of Singapore Island, despite there being longstanding and detailed plans for the Navy to blow up the dockyard when the time came. Unfortunately the army failed to carry out the demolitions and the

naval base fell almost intact into Japanese hands following their
landings on the island on 8 February. The attempts to evacuate
non-essential personnel from the island once the Japanese landings
started were hampered by the civil authorities. A few ships sailed
after dark on 11 February and the next day the old *D* class cruiser
HMS *Durban*, the destroyers *Jupiter* and *Stronghold*, together with the
gunboat *Kedah* (a converted small passenger ship) escorted a mixed
bag of naval auxiliaries and merchant ships carrying civilians and
non-essential personnel in the face of heavy Japanese air attacks.
The final evacuation attempt occurred overnight on 13/14 February.
Between 35 and 40 ships of various sizes attempted to flee the area
but were destroyed with very heavy loss of life when they managed
to run straight into a Japanese invasion force that was heading for
Sumatra. On 15 February 1942 Britain experienced its worst ever
defeat when Allied forces surrendered at Singapore.[8]

The fall of Singapore did not mean the end of the Royal Navy's
fighting. The Japanese were quick to follow up and pushed south and
south-west from their captured bases in Malaya, French Indochina
and the Philippines, as well as established Japanese outposts in
Taiwan and the Caroline Islands, into Borneo and the Dutch East
Indies. Before the fall of Singapore, in response to the Japanese
thrusts, an American–British–Dutch–Australian (ABDA) command
had been established in early January and the naval component
was a number of cruisers from all four countries, with supporting destroyers – the Royal Navy's contribution was HMS *Exeter* and
some destroyers.

Politically the ABDA area might have made sense, but as a
means of producing an effective fighting force that could successfully intercept the Japanese invasion convoys it was a disaster.
The ABDA naval force under the American Admiral Thomas C.
Hart was compromised from the start. Only the Royal Navy and
Royal Australian Navy had a set of common communication procedures, codes, doctrine and tactics. The lack of common command
and control procedures could not be corrected overnight; indeed
even if such procedures had been in place, the lack of familiarity
between the ships of different nations would have undermined their

usefulness. The provision of engineering support and ammunition to the US ships was a problem after the evacuation of their base in the Philippines and similar problems faced the British after the fall of Singapore. Furthermore, many of the ships were not the most modern or effective in service. For example, the Dutch cruiser *De Ruyter* was under-armed for its size, the US destroyers were flush-deck types based on a World War I design with limited armament, while the only modern USN cruiser, USS *Boise*, was out of action, having run aground. Nor were there any heavy ships – battleships, battlecruisers or aircraft carriers – to strike at the Japanese invasion convoys in overwhelming force; the only capital ships in the region had been HMS *Prince of Wales* and HMS *Repulse*, sunk in December. Then, of course, there was the problem of operating in the face of almost overwhelming Japanese air superiority.

As the Japanese invaded Borneo and the Dutch East Indies, the ABDA naval strike forces tried to intervene. Japanese forces, using newly captured bases in the Philippines, landed on the east coast of Borneo on 11 January and had leapfrogged further south on 23 January. A US destroyer force managed to sink four Japanese trans-port ships, but this was not enough to upset the landings. At the start of February a joint US–Dutch force attempted to stop the Japanese landing in southern Borneo, but were heavily attacked by Japanese aircraft operating from captured airfields further up the Borneo coast and had to turn back after receiving damage. By this stage the Japanese were also moving into the Celebes and Moluccas islands. With the fight for Singapore almost over in mid-February, the Japanese were able to move against the lightly held island of Sumatra to the north-west of Java. On 19/20 February the Japanese started landing at Timor, the only staging post for fighter reinforce-ments on the way to Java from Australia. By 23 February Timor had fallen and Java was effectively cut off from Australian aid.

With the fall of the outlying defences to Java, it was decided to dissolve the ABDA area on 25 February; command of the Allied forces in the region devolved to the Dutch. However, with the fall of Singapore Royal Navy ships were now able to operate as part of the naval strike force and fend off Japanese landings in Java. At the battle of the Java Sea on 27 February the ABDA force tried to sink an invasion convoy heading for Java. HMS *Exeter* was hit in the boiler room by an 8-inch shell from one of the Japanese cruisers and forced to pull out of the battle, while the British destroyer *Electra* and the Dutch *Kortenaer* had been sunk by torpedoes. The ABDA force tried to get at the Japanese force again after dark, but HMS *Jupiter* was sunk by a mine (probably a mislaid Dutch one) and the Dutch cruisers *Java* and *De Ruyter* were torpedoed and lost. The surviving cruisers, HMAS *Perth* and USS *Houston*, broke off the action, but the next night blundered into a Japanese force off Batavia that was in the act of landing and in a vicious close-range battle both ships were destroyed. On 1 March, HMS *Exeter*, hastily patched up and heading for repairs in Trincomalee, was caught and sunk by a force of four Japanese cruisers and three destroyers in the Java Sea. The naval defence of the Dutch East Indies was now gone; Java fell on 9 March. All the Admiralty could do was to try to save what ships and soldiers could be got past the Japanese who were rapidly spreading through the area. The closest British bases from which the war could be fought were now Trincomalee in Ceylon and Fremantle in Western Australia.[9]

The battering the Royal Navy had received in the Far East was not yet over. Although the Admiralty had been attempting to rebuild the Eastern Fleet at Ceylon, many of the ships sent to the Indian Ocean were obsolescent or, in the case of the aircraft carriers, with inexperienced and weak air groups. It was enough to make the commander of this poisoned chalice, Admiral Sir James Somerville, despair. Then the Japanese took steps to keep the British off balance.

Admiral Chūichi Nagumo, who commanded the Japanese aircraft carriers in the attack on Pearl Harbor, took four of his fast carriers and four fast battleships and struck at the Royal Navy in Ceylon. The British received warning that a Japanese attack could be expected on 1 April, and Somerville hoped to use the cover of night to get close enough to launch air attacks to cripple the enemy carriers. However, by 3 April some of Somerville's ships were running short of water and he headed with most of his force for the Navy's new secret refuelling base at Addu Atoll to replenish. On 4

April, while his ships were still being refuelled and taking on water, Nagumo was sighted by an RAF Catalina reconnaissance aircraft 360 miles south-south-east of Dondra Head in Ceylon. On 5 April – Easter Sunday – while the Eastern Fleet was still around 600 miles distant, Nagumo finally struck at Ceylon. Colombo was bombed, but losses were light; the destroyer *Tenedos* and the armed merchant cruiser *Hector* were sunk, while the submarine depot ship HMS *Lucia* and a merchant ship were damaged. At sea the Royal Navy lost the cruisers *Cornwall* and *Dorsetshire*. Somerville again tried to get into a position to launch air attacks from his two modern armoured fleet carriers, but was looking in the wrong place as Nagumo had headed north-east after the sinking of the *Cornwall* and *Dorsetshire* in order to attack Trincomalee.[10]

At Trincomalee was the old and very small aircraft carrier HMS *Hermes* and the destroyer HMS *Vampire*; both were there to prepare for their part in the planned Allied attack on Vichy French Madagascar. In the afternoon of 8 April reconnaissance aircraft sighted a Japanese force in a position that could only mean an attack on Trincomalee or Madras. HMS *Hermes*, with *Vampire* as an escort, was ordered to sea once night fell on 8 April so that they would avoid the expected Japanese dawn air strike. The expected air attack did serious damage to the dockyard and airfield. Unfortunately, as *Hermes* and *Vampire* headed back to Trincomalee in the morning of 9 April they were sighted by enemy aircraft. The Japanese sighting report was intercepted by the Royal Navy and the two ships were ordered back to Trincomalee at full speed while air cover was requested. However, the Japanese attack had done such damage to Trincomalee that the message asking for urgent fighter cover never got through. By mid-morning a heavy Japanese dive-bomber attack had sunk both ships. Again the Eastern Fleet had been unable to close the enemy in time to launch retaliatory air strikes.[11]

Somerville's adroit handling of his ships, keeping the four very vulnerable unmodernized World War I era *R* class battleships out of harm's way, while trying to get close enough to launch air strikes of his own from his two modern armoured fleet carriers, prevented things from being much worse. However, the Admiralty ordered the

Eastern Fleet to shift its main base from Ceylon to Kenya, 3,000
miles to the west.[12]

Despite the strategic retreat to East Africa it was imperative that
the Royal Navy and the local colonial and Dominion navies kept
control of the Indian Ocean, which was a key strategic highway for
the Allies, not just British and Imperial forces. Losing control of the
Indian Ocean would break the supply lines from Australia and New
Zealand to the forces in the Middle East and raise the requests for
the transfer of ANZAC, RAN and RNZN units east for regional
defence to a deafening level. Furthermore, any Japanese move at
sea into the Indian Ocean would threaten supply lines to and from
India, which, as well as providing a significant manpower reserve
for Imperial defence, was also a key supplier of war material and
supplies to the UK as well as Imperial forces in the Middle East.
Thus the Indian Ocean was as crucial for Imperial defence and strategic mobility as the Atlantic was for the forces based in Britain.

The long road back: the Eastern Fleet
and the British Pacific Fleet

From the early summer of 1942 until 1944 the Royal Navy was on
the defensive in the Indian Ocean – distant from the enemy and
without the quality or quantity of ships needed for its safety. The
Navy had enough ships to deny the Indian Ocean to the Japanese
and to safeguard the vital supply route between the Middle East and
Australia, but little else. Nor did it have a fleet train like the US
Navy that would allow it to remain at sea without having to return
to refuel. Instead a secret refuelling base had to be built in the
Maldives.

Only the Navy's submarines could take the fight to the enemy,
but these had been stripped from the Far East in order to reinforce the Mediterranean months before the Japanese attack. With
the Japanese onslaught in South East Asia, submarines leapt to the
top of the Navy's wish list for reinforcements, despite the shallow
water and navigation hazards of the Malay Barrier. Unfortunately all
of its submarines that were still in the UK were either involved in

training new crews or in anti-submarine escorts, or were committed to the close watch being kept on Brest where the breakout of the *Gneisenau* and *Scharnhorst*, as well as the heavy cruiser *Prinz Eugen*, was considered – rightly as it turned out – to be imminent. On 22 December 1941 the Admiralty ordered the Commander in Chief Mediterranean to send two *T* class submarines, *Trusty* and *Truant*, to Singapore. However, Singapore fell before the submarines reached the area, and then Java, the alternative base of Allied submarines, also succumbed. *Trusty* and *Truant* and several Dutch submarines were withdrawn to Colombo.[13]

Two British submarines and a handful of Dutch ones were not going to turn the tide of the war in the Indian Ocean and such was the pressure on the Royal Navy during 1942 and early 1943 that no more submarines could be found to reinforce the Eastern Fleet. Only in July 1943 could the Admiralty start transferring modern submarines from the Mediterranean to the Indian Ocean, a process that was hastened by Italy's surrender in September. Also in that month the Admiralty decided to send all new and refitted *S* and *T* class submarines to the Far East. Finally the Eastern Fleet was getting enough submarines to take the war to the Japanese.

Until the submarines started to arrive in late 1943 and early 1944, the undersea war rested on the 4th Submarine Flotilla based in Ceylon. This combined British and Dutch force not only was tasked with watching the Malacca Straits and carrying out offensive patrols against Japanese shipping and warships in the Bay of Bengal and the closer regions of the Dutch East Indies island chain, but also work with special forces engaged in reconnaissance work and landing agents. The increasing intelligence effort and so few submarines – just three operational ones for the first nine months of 1943 – meant that all too often there were no submarines available to take the war to the Japanese on a systematic basis. Furthermore, Japanese shipping was not plentiful in the Bay of Bengal, although the light cruiser *Kuma* was sunk and the *Kitagami* damaged in January 1944.

As the build-up of British submarines in the Indian Ocean continued into early 1944, it was quickly realized that there would soon be more submarines than possible targets. The answer was to

Fig. 6.2. Many submarine successes were achieved using the boat's deck gun rather than torpedoes. Here the gun crew of the *S* class submarine HMS *Statesman* can be seen, with a number of small dhows burning in the background.

deploy British submarines against Japanese targets in the Java and South China Seas. This meant both an operating base in either northern or western Australia and gaining permission not just from the Australians but also the American navy, whose area the Java and South China Seas were. Happily American and Australian support was forthcoming and the 8th Submarine Flotilla of four *T* class and six *S* class submarines was established at Fremantle in Western Australia during August 1944. With the recapture of the Philippines, Subic Bay became available as a forward base, and from May the 8th Submarine Flotilla, as well as two American flotillas, was based there. However, targets worth a torpedo were scarce even in the Java and South China Seas and most sinkings were by gun action. One notable exception, however, was the sinking of the Japanese heavy cruiser *Ashigara* in the Banka Straits on 8 June 1945 by HMS *Trenchant*. Hit by five torpedoes – demonstrating the value of the *T* class submarine's heavy bow salvo – the *Ashigara* sank in about 30 minutes.[14]

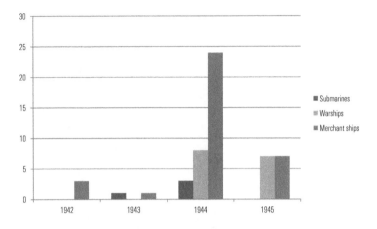

Fig. 6.3. Japanese shipping losses to British submarines,
1 January 1942–15 August 1945.[15]

Midget submarines also played an important part in the closing
stages of the war in the Pacific. At the end of July, the midget submarines *XE1* and *XE3* successfully attacked and severely damaged the
Japanese heavy cruiser *Takao* in Singapore harbour. The mines blew
the *Takao*'s bottom out and she sank upright in the shallow water.
The same day, *XE4* cut the Saigon–Singapore and Saigon–Hong
Kong submarine telegraph cables off Saigon. At Hong Kong *XE5*
spent three days and nights inside the defended harbour attempting
to cut the Hong Kong–Singapore submarine telegraph cable – an
operation that involved making the passage from the open sea into
the heart of the defended harbour and back several times. While
Lieutenant Ian Fraser, commander of *XE3*, and his diver, Leading
Seaman James Magennis, were awarded Victoria Crosses for their
part in the attack on *Takao*, it is likely that the unsung cable-cutting
operations at Saigon and Hong Kong were of greater strategic
importance, for it meant that a completely secure form of communication was now denied to the Japanese which forced them to place
increasing reliance on radio, the traffic from which the Allies could
intercept and decode.[16]

Just as the shortage of submarines in 1942 and 1943 limited
British options in the Far East and Indian Oceans, so too did the

shortage of modern warships and above all carriers with modern strike aircraft. The only real offensive the British could mount at sea was at the start of May 1942 when the Vichy French island of Madagascar was successfully invaded and captured, to forestall any possible Japanese moves. The successful closure of the Mediterranean to Allied shipping meant that the route down the Atlantic, round the Cape of Good Hope and up the east coast of Africa to the Middle East or across the Indian Ocean to India and Australia had become extremely important, especially after Japan entered the war. Madagascar, off the east coast of Africa, stood astride this key supply line. The Allies were worried that the Japanese would attempt to seize it, and after the capitulation of the Vichy regime in French Indochina in 1941 the determination of the French authorities in Madagascar to resist any Axis pressure was clearly doubtful.

In March 1942 the decision to occupy Madagascar, even in the face of Vichy French opposition, was taken. Rear Admiral Syfret, who had taken over command of Force H when Somerville was given the Eastern Fleet, was tasked with coming up with a plan to invade the island and given command of the naval forces allocated to the operation – *Ironclad*. Force H, despite being based in Gibraltar, was effectively the only force that could be spared to form the backbone of the operation. The plan was to land a brigade of infantry and a Royal Marine commando unit, with two more infantry brigade groups in reserve. The landings took place just before dawn on 5 May 1942 and were aided by the fact that the approaches to the invasion anchorage were impassable at night. However, once ashore the army ran into stiff opposition and was still held up on 6 May. It was decided that a party of Royal Marines should be landed in the French rear in order to create a diversion in Diego Suarez, the main French naval base and airfield. The destroyer HMS *Anthony* charged into Diego Suarez harbour at 20:00 on 6 May at a speed of 22 knots, right under the noses of French shore batteries, but they failed to hit her. The *Anthony* went alongside a jetty and the Marines jumped ashore, while the destroyers' close-range guns suppressed the French snipers on the jetty and the woods beyond. The *Anthony* then exited the way she had come and again did so at high speed, and again the French failed to hit her. The Marines made their way to the French naval depot and swiftly overwhelmed the rather feeble resistance, forcing the French commandant and then the artillery commander to surrender. When the army attack started at 20:30 French resistance started to collapse and by 03:00 the battle was over; Diego Suarez – and effectively Madagascar – was now in Allied hands.

With the winding up of the naval campaign in the Mediterranean, as well as the sinking of the *Scharnhorst* and crippling of the *Tirpitz* in northern waters, the Admiralty now could send modern warships to the Eastern Fleet in early 1944. Just as importantly more modern aircraft were reaching the carrier air groups – Barracuda torpedo/dive-bombers and Firefly strike fighter/reconnaissance aircraft, as well as Lend-Lease American naval aircraft such as the Hellcat and Corsair fighters and Avenger torpedo/dive-bombers. However, these modern aircraft were not always problem-free. The Fairey Barracuda, which had been introduced into squadron service from January 1943 onwards as the Navy's new torpedo, dive-bomber and reconnaissance aircraft, was found to be rather underpowered for the hot and humid conditions of the Far East. This meant that the effective range of the Barracuda with a full bomb load was little more than 100 miles. It also had manually folded wings, making rapid ranging and removal of aircraft from flight decks difficult. Replacing the Barracuda with the American equivalent, the Avenger, was not a straightforward matter either. While the Avenger had power-folded wings, it was not a dive-bomber, so accurate bombing was harder to achieve. Moreover, it could not drop the British Mark XIIB 18-inch torpedo, using instead the inferior and unreliable US Bliss-Leavitt Mark VIII (not to be confused with the British Mark VIII 21-inch torpedo used by submarines and surface ships). The Corsair, on the other hand, had not been an initial success with US carriers and had been offered to the US Marine Corps and the Royal Navy. The British, however, found the Corsair superior to any British fighter available to the Navy and adopted it with enthusiasm and success. There were problems with the supply of US Hellcats, too: the USN's initial rejection of the Corsair meant that the

Americans were reluctant to send any Hellcats to the British until the Corsair was improved enough to be acceptable to them.[17]

Table 6.2. Royal Navy (including Imperial forces) strength
in the Far East and Indian Ocean, 1941–45.[18]

	Dec 1941	Dec 1942	Dec 1943	Dec 1944	Aug 1945
Battleships and battlecruisers	2	4	2	5	5
Aircraft carriers	1	2	0	4	9
Cruisers	21	20	18	17	22
Destroyers	13	20	20	33	59
Submarines	1	7	14	38	47
Armed merchant cruisers	12	13	3	0	0
Escort carriers	0	0	1	5	22
Fleet support	0	0	0	5	
Amphibious ships	0	0	2	10	3

The additional resources in ships and aircraft that started to arrive in the Indian Ocean from late 1943 came at just the right time. No sooner had the first fleet carrier to be transferred to the Eastern Fleet, HMS *Illustrious*, arrived in the theatre in January 1944, than the Royal Navy had to face a significant increase in Japanese warships at Singapore. The British feared that this increase in enemy strength might be a prelude to sorties into the Indian Ocean which the Eastern Fleet was too weak to repel. The successful US Navy air attacks on the main Japanese fleet base at Truk in the Caroline Islands had forced the Japanese Combined Fleet of four modern battleships, three aircraft carriers and numerous cruisers to move to Singapore, which had excellent docking facilities as well as being closer to fuel supplies from Borneo and the Dutch East Indies.[19]

The flow of ships, supplies and aircraft to the Indian Ocean from late 1943 allowed a rejuvenated Eastern Fleet under Somerville to

Fig. 6.4. The Eastern Fleet at sea. HMS *Valiant* can be seen, with the
Free French battleship *Richelieu* beyond and astern of her.
On the horizon can be seen a *Colony* class cruiser.

start attacking Japanese bases and economic facilities in Sumatra
and Java. But in early 1944 Somerville was still critically short
of aircraft carriers, having only one fleet carrier, HMS *Illustrious*,
available to him. As a result, the US Navy lent the Eastern Fleet
the large fleet carrier USS *Saratoga* and an escort of three destroyers
(another area of temporary British weakness in the Indian Ocean).
The expanded Eastern Fleet was asked by the Americans to carry
out diversionary attacks on the north-western end of the Dutch East
Indies in April. It was hoped that the British force, reinforced as it
was by the USS *Saratoga*, would hold Japanese warships and aircraft
in the west while the Allies launched a major attack on Dutch New
Guinea at the eastern end of that long island chain stretching from
west of Malaya to the Pacific. The naval base on the island of Sabang
off Sumatra was selected as the Eastern Fleet's first major operation.
    At 05:30 on 19 April 1944 the carrier force of HMS *Illustrious*

Fig. 6.5. Operating aircraft from carriers was a dangerous business, and aircrew losses from accidents often exceeded losses from enemy action. Here a long-range fuel tank explodes underneath a Corsair fighter as it lands on HMS *Victorious* in October 1944.

and USS *Saratoga* started launching their aircraft from a point some 180 miles south-west of Sabang. The plan was for the bulk of the force – some 17 Barracudas and 13 Corsairs from *Illustrious* and 11 Avengers, 18 Dauntless dive-bombers and 16 Hellcats from *Saratoga* – to attack Sabang's naval base and airfield, with the brunt of the attack falling on the harbour installations, oil tanks and naval base. Additionally, another eight of *Saratoga*'s Hellcats were to attack the airfield at nearby Lho Nga. The American planes arrived over Sabang at 06:57, with the British arriving one minute later, completely surprising the Japanese. Three out of four oil tanks were destroyed and heavy damage done to the port facilities, but unfortunately there was little Japanese shipping in the harbour – only one small freighter was sunk and another damaged and driven ashore. The attacks on the airfields destroyed 24 Japanese aircraft and only one Allied plane was shot down, but the pilot was picked up by the

submarine HMS *Tactician* which had been positioned off the coast on
search-and-rescue duties.[20]

Then in May the Eastern Fleet launched successful air strikes
against an oil refinery at Surabaya in Java. The impetus for this
strike was the *Saratoga*'s imminent departure for a refit in Australia.
By accompanying the American carrier part of the way the Eastern
Fleet and the *Saratoga* could launch an effective strike at Surabaya
from a different direction than normally used by air attacks launched
from Australia. At Surabaya the oil refinery at Wonokromo was set
on fire and eventually burned out while the harbour area was also
damaged and one merchant ship sunk, but unfortunately several
Japanese submarines survived the strike. July saw the Eastern Fleet,
which had been strengthened by the arrival of the fleet carriers HMS
Victorious and HMS *Indomitable*, attack Sabang for a second time. This
time the Eastern Fleet's four battleships and battlecruisers joined the
fray, bombarding the harbour while the aircraft carriers attacked
local airfields and provided the fleet with air cover. The Japanese
reconnaissance aircraft that tried to find the British were shot
down and a group of nine or ten Zero fighters intercepted by FAA
Corsairs. The weakness of the Japanese response and the ability of
the battleships HMS *Valiant*, HMS *Queen Elizabeth*, the battlecruiser
Renown and the French battlecruiser *Richelieu* to close the coast for
a shore bombardment without interference shows how things had
changed off the Dutch East Indies since the desperate days of early
1942. All in all, eight such attacks on Japanese possessions along the
Malay barrier were mounted between March and October 1944.[21]

More significantly, it was accepted, grudgingly by Churchill, and
in the face of outright opposition from the highest echelons of the
US Navy who did not wish to share the coming battle with anyone,
that the Royal Navy would send a British Pacific fleet to fight alongside the Americans in the assaults to clear away the final obstacles to
an invasion of the Japanese home islands. On 22 November Admiral
Sir Bruce Fraser hoisted his flag as the Commander in Chief, British
Pacific Fleet (BPF), and much of the resources of the Eastern Fleet
were transferred across to his command. Such was Fraser's seniority
that he outranked the US sea-going commanders. To avoid awkward

command issues, he decided, once in the Pacific, to direct the fleet from onshore, while day-to-day command at sea was carried out by his deputy, Vice Admiral Sir Bernard Rawlings. Fraser had actually been in command of the Eastern Fleet since August 1944 – Somerville had been sent to Washington to take on Fleet Admiral Ernest King who was the professional head of the US Navy and the chief cause of US opposition to the BPF. King is often character-ized as anti-British, although perhaps this is unfair. He was irascible and bullying, but above all extremely pro-US Navy rather than anti-British. Through intense British pressure, however, King's opposi-tion to the BPF was overcome, and the Royal Navy would share in the forthcoming victory over Japan.

In March 1945 the British Pacific Fleet joined the US Navy's Central Pacific Command. On its way from Ceylon, first to Australia and then ultimately to a new forward operating base in the Admiralty Islands chain, the BPF carried out two massive raids on the oil refinery at Palembang, Sumatra. Away to the north, the Eastern Fleet's successor, the East Indies Fleet, commanded by Vice Admiral Sir Arthur Power, was also carrying the fight to the Japanese. Indeed 1945 began well when five destroyers found and sank the Japanese heavy cruiser *Haguro* in the Malacca Straits in a brilliantly executed torpedo attack that scored eight hits on the Japanese ship which went down in a matter of minutes.[22]

Before the main attacks on Palembang, the BPF had launched two smaller raids, one in December and one in early January on targets in Sumatra. The BPF's first attack on Palembang targeted the Pladjoe oil refinery and four nearby Japanese airfields on 24 January 1945. Forty-three Avengers were to attack the Pladjoe refinery, with 27 Corsairs, 11 Fireflies and 16 Hellcats as escorts; four Avengers and four Hellcats were tasked with attacking Mana airfield, while 24 Corsairs were to strafe Lembak, Palembang and Talangbetoetoe airfields. The attack left the refinery burning and sending up clouds of thick black smoke, while on the ground at least 34 Japanese aircraft were destroyed and 11 in the air – all for the loss of six Avengers, two Corsairs and one Hellcat. At the end of January came the second attack, this time with the Soengei Gerong refinery as its main target. The strike on 29 January by 46 Avengers and their escorts was more accurate than the previous attack on the Palembang refineries – production was stopped until the end of March and from then both refineries were only working at a third of their normal output. However, the Japanese response was more determined and a few enemy bombers managed to find and attack the fleet, but they were destroyed before they could cause any damage. In all, the BPF lost 16 aircraft to Japanese fire and another 25 from other causes, while the Japanese lost at least 30 aircraft in the air and another 38 were destroyed on the ground by BPF attacks on local Japanese airfields. Above all, the BPF had gained desperately needed experience in delivering major, set-piece air attacks prior to it entering the Pacific and facing the main weight of Japan's forces.[23]

The BPF's first operation in the Pacific was as part of US Admiral Raymond Spruance's Fifth Fleet. Operating as Task Force 57, the BPF was part of the Okinawa invasion force – Operation *Iceberg* – but the Americans never allowed the BPF into the forefront of operations against the Japanese homeland. Task Force 57 was given the job of suppressing airfields on Sakashima Gunto, an island group between Okinawa and Formosa, thus preventing the Japanese from moving aircraft to the invasion site from bases further west. However, the BPF was two days late getting into position because of King's refusal to commit the British force to the Okinawa operation, preferring to have had it stand by to provide cover for the Australian invasion of Borneo. In the end the damage received by some US aircraft carriers from Japanese air attacks during warmup operations prior to the launching of the main invasion ensured that the Royal Navy's aircraft carriers were needed for the invasion of Okinawa. From 26 March until 20 April the BPF attacked the Japanese airfields and fended off retaliatory strikes, usually spending two days attacking Japanese airfields and then a couple of days refuelling at sea before moving back towards the islands to resume operations. While the BPF was refuelling at sea, US carriers maintained the pressure on the Japanese in the BPF's operating area. On 11 and 12 April the BPF attacked airfields on Formosa in

Fig. 6.6. HMS *Victorious* moments after being hit, but
only slightly damaged, by a kamikaze aircraft.

order to further disrupt Japanese efforts to get aircraft into position for attacks on the US Okinawa invasion fleet. This move had
been prompted by Admiral Spruance, the commander of the US
Fifth Fleet, of which the BPF was a part, who felt that the armoured
flight decks of the British carriers would better absorb damage from
kamikaze suicide attacks than the unarmoured American ones. In
all, the BPF had spent 12 out of 26 days in action. It is a telling
comment on the combat power of the BPF that it was replaced not
by a task group from the US fast carrier task force, TF 58, but the
escort carriers of the US Fifth Fleet's carrier support group.[24]

On 4 May Task Force 57 was back on station off the Sakashima
Gunto islands and launching attacks against airfields. This time,
however, the battleships and cruisers got into the action as well as the
aircraft carriers, closing the coast to bombard the Japanese airfields
on 4 May. Unfortunately, the detaching of the battleships and others
for bombardment tasks reduced the anti-aircraft screen and one

kamikaze managed to hit the recently joined HMS *Formidable*; the damage was heavy and resulted in the centre boiler room being put out of action, but the armoured deck, although penetrated, took most of the punishment, allowing the ship to remain under control. By the early hours of 5 May the *Formidable* was steaming at full power again. The bombardment of the airfields was found to have a very positive impact the next day when the air strikes experienced much less anti-aircraft fire from Japanese units. *Formidable* was not the only carrier to be hit by kamikazes: HMS *Indomitable* and HMS *Victorious* were also hit but not put out of action, and *Formidable* was hit for a second time on 9 May. By the time the BPF withdrew, of the four armoured fleet carriers with the force, only HMS *Indefatigable* had escaped damage from kamikaze attacks. Despite this, the BPF kept up the attacks on the Japanese for three weeks until, on 25 May, it again withdrew to Manus for a refit.[25]

However well the BPF performed in combat, it faced many problems. First, by its own admission, the standard of anti-aircraft gunnery was poor in the Royal Navy. Quite simply there was not enough time or facilities available to the Navy for this vital area of training during the war. Thankfully the BPF did not experience the same ferocity of suicide attacks that beset the American fast carrier groups during the invasion of Okinawa. Second, the BPF's logistics situation was fragile and always close to collapse, relying as it did on a fleet train that had been cobbled together rather than designed for the purpose. Indeed the BPF's stores organization was still being developed in Australia when the fleet arrived and needed to re-supply its ships. In many respects the BPF's fleet train was the result of the Navy's pre-war and wartime reliance on operating from shore bases rather than replenishing at sea. Third, the BPF had to service no fewer than six different types of aircraft within the carrier force, and the differences between various carriers meant that certain aircraft types could or could not be operated from certain ships, making flexibility in air operations extremely difficult, especially when ships had been damaged. Worse still, the US-supplied aircraft in the BPF had been modified to British standards, which meant that aircraft stocks could not be replenished from local US sources. Fourth, even in something as fundamental to long-range operations as refuelling at sea, the Royal Navy's usual technique of refuelling from astern of tankers was inferior to that of the US Navy's alongside method. It also suffered from shortages of refuelling equipment, of suitable tankers, even of refuelling hoses. The Royal Navy was, one way or another, making life difficult for itself. That it waged war against Japan so successfully is a testament to the determination of its officers and men.[26]

The BPF returned to the fray on 16 July, this time as Task Force 37 attached to Admiral William Halsey's Third Fleet, which was ranging up and down the Japanese coast at will as the enemy's ability to continue the war evaporated. Yet Japan fought on against the Allied onslaught. At this stage of the campaign, not only was the BPF launching aircraft against the Japanese mainland but also engaging in shore bombardment using the battleship *King George V* and its cruiser force. On 15 August, following the triple hammer blows of the nuclear bombs dropped on Hiroshima and Nagasaki, the destruction of the 'Kwantung' Army in Korea and Manchuria by the Soviet Red Army after it entered the war on 9 August, and the often overlooked near starvation of the Japanese people as a result of the Allied submarine campaign, the Japanese surrendered unconditionally. At sea, the BPF's logistics situation, always fragile thanks to its small *ad hoc* fleet train, was becoming desperate; it was running low on fuel and was due to return to Sydney to re-supply and refit. It was decided that only a small squadron could be supported in Japanese waters to witness the formal surrender. In the end only the battleships *Duke of York* (with Admiral Fraser) and *King George V*, the aircraft carrier *Indefatigable*, the cruisers HMS *Newfoundland* and HMNZS *Gambia* plus ten destroyers (two of them Australian) remained off Japan and were allotted berths in Tokyo Bay to watch the ceremony. On 2 September the Japanese formally surrendered to the representatives of the Allied powers on the USS *Missouri*. Admiral Sir Bruce Fraser signed on behalf of Great Britain. The Royal Navy's World War II was over.[27]

Epilogue

World War II was above all else a maritime war, and therefore the Royal Navy's war. The navy that emerged triumphant at the end of the conflict was the largest Britain had ever produced. It had endured heavy losses and seen many lives lost, yet in the end it had not only kept Britain in the war but had prevented a German invasion, carried the fight back into Europe and even as far as the shores of Japan.

The Royal Navy also felt, quite rightly, that it had had a better war than it had had during World War I. Some of this improvement was down to the service itself – there had been significant efforts to correct the perceived failings of the 1914–18 navy and Grand Fleet during the interwar period. The navy that fought World War II was more confident in its fleet commanders and in its tactics; it had also assimilated new weapons and new technologies. However, some of the improvements in the Navy's performance during 1939–45 were also due to factors outside the narrow scope of this book – especially the often neglected fact that the British government was immeasurably better organized by 1939 to control and resource a global war than it had been in 1914.

The ability to use and control the sea – and to prevent enemies from doing so – was fundamental to British and Allied strategy. Even before Britain and France had been ejected from Norway and then defeated on land in France and the Low Countries, the Royal Navy was crucial to the war-making potential of Britain, protecting imports of vital equipment and resources as well as allowing the Allies to contemplate different means of tightening the economic blockade of Germany. Once Britain, her empire and Dominions continued the fight after the defeat of France the Royal Navy became the service on which all hopes rested. If the Navy was defeated Britain would face invasion or starvation; if Britain were not just to survive but emerge victorious the Navy would have to supply enough petrol from abroad to keep the RAF's untried and untested strategic bomber force in the air, or it would have to control the oceans sufficiently to allow armies to take the fight to the enemy, from Africa through to the liberation of France and occupied Europe and finally to the defeat of Japan. In the end it did both.

In short, every offensive action taken by Britain and her Allies depended on seapower, and it was the Royal Navy that almost single-handedly provided that power in the Mediterranean, the Atlantic and the Indian Ocean. Only when the war reached the Pacific did the Royal Navy have to take a supporting role to another navy, held back by the demands being made on its limited resources in other areas of the global war.

Despite the vital role the Royal Navy played in winning World War II, if Britons nowadays reflect on the war, they are likely to think about the 'little ships of Dunkirk' rather than the role the Navy's ships played in rescuing most of the British Expeditionary Force and French army trapped on the coast. Or they might think about the RAF's role in saving Britain from a seaborne invasion and be unaware of the Navy's very likely destruction of the German invasion barges if they ever set sail. Or they might remember D-Day and the liberation of Europe but inexplicably not remember that the Allied armies did not miraculously appear on the Normandy beaches, but were transported and sustained by seapower. The World War II history that people remember is about myths and half-truths; these myths have now become our history – a history that seems to have little place for cold facts and little place for the Royal Navy.

But despite its hard-fought victories, by 1945 the Royal Navy was no longer the largest navy in the world – that accolade now belonged to the US Navy. Nor would the peace remain for long. Soon the world would face a new war – a cold war – where power competed and postured but drew back from direct confrontation. For the Royal Navy, however, the Cold War was as inadequate a description of its activities as the 'Phoney War' had been during the last conflict. From the outset the Navy was deeply involved in a violent peace.

The Royal Navy and seapower won the war by allowing a small island to exploit the use of the sea, and in the process adding more garlands to an already proud history. But the Cold War that followed the hot war against Germany and Japan would place new trials and inflict new stresses on the Navy. Huge technological and social changes would confront the Royal Navy as it struggled to deal with global responsibilities, superpower confrontation and 'limited' wars that seemed anything but limited to those who fought in them, all in the face of a steadily reducing fleet. And while the Navy's story in World War II may be forgotten and neglected, rather like today's navy, a navy – the Royal Navy – is still a vital part of Britain's national toolkit for survival, and we forget its history – and ours – at our peril.

Notes

Introduction

1. C. Kitching, *Britain and the Problem of International Disarmament* (London, 1999), pp. 9, 10, 20; see also H. Strachan, *The Outbreak of the First World War* (Oxford, 2004), p. 4, quoted in J. Hinton, *Protests and Visions* (London, 1989), p. 76.

2. K. Middlemas and J. Barnes, *Baldwin: A Biography* (London, 1969), p. 736; P. Williamson, *Stanley Baldwin* (Cambridge, 1999), pp. 47, 305–6. See also G.C. Peden, *Arms, Economics and British Strategy: From Dreadnoughts to Hydrogen Bombs* (Cambridge, 2007), pp. 108–17; D. Redford, *Submarine: A Cultural History from the Great War to Nuclear Combat* (London, 2010), pp. 136–40.

3. O. Babji, 'The Royal Navy and the defence of the British Empire', in K. Neilson and G. Kennedy (eds), *Far Flung Lines* (London, 1997), pp. 173–6, 184–5; C. Bell, *The Royal Navy, Seapower and Strategy*, pp. 22, 24, 101–3; G.A.H. Gordon, *British Seapower and Procurement between the Wars*, pp. 124–6; Peden, *Arms, Economics and British Strategy*, pp. 102–3.

4. TNA, ADM 1/9081, Board Memo on a new standard of naval strength, dated 26 April 1937; TNA, CAB 16/112, DRC 37. Spending on the Royal Navy in 1935 was £56.6 million: B. Mitchell, *British Historical Statistics* (Cambridge, 2011), p. 591. S.W. Roskill, *Naval Policy between the Wars*, vol. 2 (London, 1976) , pp. 358–9.

Chapter 1. A 'Phoney' War?

1. TNA, ADM 116/140, intercept by Malin Head radio, 3 September 1939.

2. TNA, ADM 1/10033, sinking of SS *Athenia* by German submarine, 3 September 1939; ADM, 199/2130, interviews with survivors from 3 September to 30 November 1939.

3. TNA, ADM 156/95, loss of HMS *Courageous*, Board of Enquiry, 4 October 1939, p. 4, recommendation 26.

4. NHB, CB3301(1), Naval Staff History, *Home Waters and the Atlantic*, vol. 1 (1954), pp. 90–1.

5. CB 3304(1A), Naval Staff History, *The Defeat of the Enemy Attack on Shipping*, p. 217; C. Barnett, *Engage the Enemy More Closely* (London, 1991), pp. 78–81; S.W. Roskill, *The War at Sea* (London, 1954), vol. 1, pp. 70, 113–16.

6. NHB, CB3301(1), Naval Staff History, *Home Waters and the Atlantic*, vol. 1 (1954), p. 42.

7. TNA, ADM 1/19900, sinking of the *Rawalpindi*.

8. NHB, CB3301(1), Naval Staff History, *Home Waters and the Atlantic*, vol. 1 (1954), pp. 45–6.

9. *Daily Express*, 13 December 1939, pp. 1, 5; *Daily Mirror*, 13 December 1939, p. 1; *Manchester Guardian*, 13 December 1939, p. 6; *The Times*, 13 December 1939, p. 8; *The Times*, 14 December 1939, p. 8; *Daily Mail*, 16 December 1939, p. 6; *The Times*, 19 December 1939, p. 8.

10. TNA, CAB 65/6, War Cabinet Minutes 86/40.

11. Barnett, *Engage the Enemy More Closely*, pp. 140–1; Roskill, *The War at Sea*, vol. 1, pp. 207–11.

12. BBC news, 'Ceremony marks 70th anniversary of Dunkirk evacuation', http://news.bbc.co.uk/1/hi/uk/10188650.stm (accessed 8 July 2010).

13. W.S. Churchill, 'The war situation', *Hansard*, House of Commons Debates, 4 June 1940, vol. 361, col. 791.

14. Roskill, *The War at Sea*, vol. 1, pp. 224–5, 227; see also A. Calder, *The Myth of the Blitz* (London, 1991), pp. 26–8; M. Smith, *Britain and 1940: History, Myth and Popular Memory* (Abingdon, 2000), pp. 44–5.

15. NMRN, BR 1736(48)(2), Naval Staff History, *Home Waters and the Atlantic*, vol. 2 (1961), p. 127.

Chapter 2. The War Against the U-boat: The Battle of the Atlantic from the Fall of France to America Entering the War

1. G. Hessler, *The U-Boat War in the Atlantic 1939–1945* (London, 1989), p. 48; J. Terraine, *Business in Great Waters: The U-boat Wars 1916–1945* (London, 1989), p. 256.

2. NHB, *Monthly Anti-submarine Reports*, November 1940, pp. 20–5; A. Hague, *The Allied Convoy System 1939–1946* (St Catherines, Ontario, 2000), p. 131.

3. CB 3304(B), *Defeat of the Enemy Attack on Shipping*, p. 60.

4. *Ibid.*, pp. 304–5

5. TNA, ADM 205/56, Letter from AOC Coastal Command to 1SL, 17 November 1941; TNA, CAB 66(20), WP(41) 308, 29 December 1941; J. Buckley, *The RAF and Trade Defence 1919–1945* (Keele, 1995), pp. 105–6, 107, 109–14.

6.   D.K. Brown, *Nelson to Vanguard* (London, 2006), pp. 103–7.

7.   *Ibid.*, p. 129.

8.   B. Lavery, *Churchill's Navy* (London, 2006), p. 139.

9.   B. Lavery, *In Which They Served* (London, 2008), p. 35, see also chapters 3, 5 and 7; D.A. Rayner, *Escort*, 2nd ed. (London, 1955), pp. 64, 74.

10. CB 3304(B), *Defeat of the Enemy Attack on Shipping*, table 13; Roskill, *The War at Sea*, vol. 1, p. 616.

11. Barnett, *Engage the Enemy More Closely*, p. 262.

12. Roskill, *The War at Sea*, vol. 1, p. 616.

13. *Ibid.*, p. 609.

14. Barnett, *Engage the Enemy More Closely*, p. 262; W.J.R. Gardner, *Decoding History* (London, 1999), p. 46; Roskill, *The War at Sea*, vol. 1, pp. 364, 497–8, 609–11.

15. Sir C. Webster and N. Frankland, *The Strategic Air Offensive Against Germany 1939–1945*, vol. IV (London, 1961), p. 133, note 15; TNA, CAB 86/1, BA (42)7, The Part Played by the Royal Air Force in the Battle of the Atlantic during 1941, 23 February 1942; TNA, CAB 86/1, BA (42) 7, Attacks on submarine bases 1941.

16. Barnett, *Engage the Enemy More Closely*, p. 262; Roskill, *The War at Sea*, vol. 1, pp.364–5; Terraine, *Business in Great Waters*, p. 314.

17. J. Terraine, *The Right of the Line* (London, 1985), pp. 240–4.

18. Gardner, *Decoding History*, pp. 120–45.

19. P. Beesly, *Very Special Intelligence* (London, 2000), pp. 70–2, 94–6; F. Hinsley, *British Intelligence in the Second World War*, vol. II (London, 1981), pp. 170–9; J. Winton, *Ultra at Sea* (London, 1988), pp. 94–6; cf. Terraine, *Business in Great Waters*, pp. 325–6 where it is implied that 'Hydra' and *Heimisch* are different codes when they are the same thing. Hydra was the name given to the code after 1943.

20. D. Syrett, 'The Battle for Convoy HX133, 23–29 June 1941', *Northern Mariner*, vol. 12 (2002), no 3, p, 44; CB 4050/41(8), Monthly Anti-Submarine Report, August 1941, p. 19.

21. Syrett, 'The Battle for Convoy HX133', pp. 44–6; CB 4050/41(8), Monthly Anti-Submarine Report, August 1941, pp. 20–2.

22. Syrett, 'The Battle for Convoy HX133', pp. 47–50; CB 4050/41(8), Monthly Anti-Submarine Report, August 1941, pp. 22–32.

23. CB 3304(B), *Defeat of the Enemy Attack on Shipping*, pp. 304–5; Hinsley, *British Intelligence*, vol. II, p. 169.

24. J. Goldrick, 'Work Up', in S. Howarth and D. Law (eds), *The Battle of the Atlantic 1939–1945* (Annapolis, MA, 1994), pp. 220–5; D. Macintyre, *U-boat Killer* (London, 1999), p. 20; Roskill, *The War at Sea*, vol. I, pp. 358–9.

25. D. Howse, *Radar at Sea: The Royal Navy in World War 2* (London, 1993), pp. 57–8, 79, 84–8, 100; cf. Terraine, *Business in Great Waters*, pp. 315–16, which states that *Vanoc* had a Type 271.

26. A. Price, *Aircraft Versus Submarine* (London, 1980), pp. 53, 54–8; Terraine, *Business in Great Waters*, pp. 248–9.

27. TNA, ADM 205/56, CC/PBJ/709/41, Letter from C in C Coastal Command to First Sea Lord, 2 November 1941; Buckley, *The RAF and Trade Defence,* p. 170; Price, *Aircraft Versus Submarine*, pp. 75–6; Terraine, *Business in Great Waters*, pp. 371–2.

28. TNA, ADM 205/56, Letter from AOC Coastal Command to 1SL, 17 November 1941; TNA, CAB 66(20), WP (41) 308, 29 December 1941; TNA, CAB 86/2, 18 November 1942; Peden, *Arms, Economics and British Strategy*, p. 177.

29. TNA, ADM 205/15, Minute on the operational data of Coastal Command aircraft; TNA, ADM 205/10, Admiralty reply to Prime Minister's minute, 8 October 1941; see also D. Redford, 'Inter and Intra-Service Rivalries and the Battle of the Atlantic', *Journal of Strategic Studies*, vol. 32 (2009), pp. 906–12.

Chapter 3. The War Against the U-boat: The Battle of the Atlantic 1942–45

1. Hinsley, *British Intelligence in the Second World War*, vol. II, p. 179; Terraine, *Business in Great Waters*, pp. 424–5.

2. CB 33049(1A), *Defeat of the Enemy Attack on Shipping*, p. 302.

3. TNA, ADM 1/12062, Battle of the Atlantic General Review February–May 1942, 18 May 1942.

4. Hinsley, *British Intelligence in the Second World War*, vol. II, pp. 177–9.

5. J. Rowher, *The Critical Convoy Battles of March 1943* (London, 1977), p. 36.

6. M. Williams, *Captain Gilbert Roberts and the Anti-U-Boat School* (London, 1979), pp. 85–123

7. Rowher, *The Critical Convoy Battles of March 1943*, pp. 36–7

8. PRO, ADM 205/56 (note 37).

9. Peden, *Arms, Economics and British Strategy*, p. 177; PRO, CAB 86/2, 18 November 1942; NHB, D/NHB 2-2-15, R.H.R. MacKay, *An Account of Seventeen Convoys Conducted by Capt R. H. R. MacKay*, p. 10; Barnett, *Engage The Enemy More Closely*, pp. 380, 583–4, 600–1; N. Friedman, *British Carrier Aviation* (London, 1988), p. 186.

10. CB 3304(1A), Naval Staff History: Defeat of the Enemy Attack on Shipping 1939–1945: A Study of Policy and Operations, pp. 293–4; Barnett, *Engage the Enemy More Closely*, p. 583, 600–1; Friedman, *British Carrier*

Aviation, pp. 186–7, 188; Terraine, *Business in Great Waters*, p. 552.

11. PRO, AIR 14/1454, Note on H2S and U-Boat Detection, Memorandum by AOC-in-C Bomber Command, 26 March 1943; PRO, CAB 86/2, AU Committee minutes, 3rd meeting, 18 November 1942; PRO, CAB 86/2, AU Committee, 8th meeting, 23 December 1942; COS (42), 204th meeting, 22 December 1942.

12. Barnett, *Engage the Enemy More Closely*, pp. 458–76; R. Goette, 'Britain and the Delay in Closing the Mid-Atlantic "Air Gap" During the Battle of the Atlantic', *The Northern Mariner* (2005), pp. 19–41; Redford, 'Inter and Intra-Service Rivalries and the Battle of the Atlantic', pp. 906–12.

13. TNA AIR 8/405, Harris to Churchill, 17 June 1942; Redford, 'Inter and Intra-Service Rivalries and the Battle of the Atlantic', pp. 899–928.

14. PRO, ADM 205/23, 30th meeting of the Battle of the Atlantic Committee, 10 February 1942; PRO, ADM 205/30, AU (42) 5, 2nd meeting of the AU Committee, 13 November 1942; PRO, ADM 205/15, Undated memo to 1SL; PRO, AIR 41/47, The RAF in the Maritime War, p. 357.

15. PRO, ADM 205/14, Minute from Prime Minister to 1SL, 21 October 1942; C. Ashworth, *RAF Coastal Command 1936–1969* (Yeovil, 1992), p. 236; PRO, ADM 205/23, AU (42) 3rd meeting.

16. Redford, 'Inter and Intra-Service Rivalries and the Battle of the Atlantic', pp. 899–928.

17. Barnett, *Engage the Enemy More Closely*, pp. 597–600; Roskill, *The War at Sea*, vol. 2, p. 486; Rowher, *The Critical Convoy Battles of March 1943*, pp. 210–13; Terraine, *Business in Great Waters*, pp. 558–69.

18. TNA, ADM 199/2060, Monthly Anti-Submarine Report, March 1943, 15 April 1943, p. 3; TNA CAB 86/3, AU (43) 97, 31 March 1943, tables 1 and 2; D. Redford, 'The March 1943 Crisis in the battle of the Atlantic: Myth and Reality', *History* (2007), p. 67. The global shipping shortage is covered by the excellent C. Behrens, *Merchant Shipping and the Demands of War* (London, 1955) and the equally good K. Smith, *Conflict over Convoys* (Cambridge, 1996).

19. Barnett, *Engage the Enemy More Closely*, pp. 602–3; D. Syrett, *The Defeat of the German U-Boats* (Columbia, SC, 1994), pp. 25–62; Terraine, *Business in Great Waters*, pp. 588–93.

20. Barnett, *Engage the Enemy More Closely*, pp. 606–9; Syrett, *The Defeat of the German U-Boats*, pp. 63–95; Terraine, *Business in Great Waters*, p. 594.

21. A. Price, *Aircraft Versus Submarine* (London, 1980), pp. 105–10, 138; D. Syrett, 'The Safe and Timely Arrival of SC130, 15–25 May 1943', *American Neptune* (1990), pp. 219–27; Syrett, *The Defeat of the German U-Boats*, pp. 96–144.

22. Syrett, *The Defeat of the German U-Boats*, pp. 181–229.

23. Price, *Aircraft Versus Submarine*, pp. 105–10, 138.

24. A. Burn, *The Fighting Captain* (Barnsley, 1993), pp. 124–38, 171–2; Terraine, *Business in Great Waters*, p. 624.

25. M. Llewellyn-Jones, *The Royal Navy and Anti-Submarine Warfare, 1917–49* (London, 2006), pp. 51–2; M. Milner, *The U-boat Hunters* (Annapolis, MA, 1994), pp. 171–2, 172–3.

26. Barnett, *Engage the Enemy More Closely*, p. 858.

Chapter 4. Home Waters and the Home Fleet 1940–45

1. Roskill, *The War at Sea* vol. 1, p. 242.

2. H.R. Allen, *Who Won the Battle of Britain?* (St Albans, 1974), pp. 173–5; J. Ray, *The Battle of Britain: New Perspectives* (London 1996), pp. 80–2. Even the official history was unable to disguise the decline of the air defence system in late August and early September. For the definition of air superiority see http://www.raf.mod.uk/rafcms/mediafiles/374F7380_1143_EC82_2E436D317C547F5B.pdf (accessed 21 February 2013).

3. K. Larew, 'The Royal Navy in the Battle of Britain', *The Historian*, vol. 54 (1992), pp. 243–5; J. Levy, *The Royal Navy's Home Fleet in World War II* (Basingstoke, 2003), chapters 4 and 5.

4. Levy, *The Royal Navy's Home Fleet*, chapter 5.

5. BR 1736(48)(2), *Home Waters and the Atlantic*, vol. II, p. 209; see also Roskill, *The War at Sea*, vol. 1, p. 288.

6. BR 1736(48)(2), *Home Waters and the Atlantic*, vol. II, p. 211; Barnett, *Engage the Enemy More Closely*, pp. 196–7; Roskill, *The War at Sea*, vol. 1, pp. 287–9.

7. NHB, *Monthly Anti-submarine Reports*, November 1940, p. 19.

8. *Ibid.*

9. NHB, *Monthly Anti-submarine Reports*, December 1940, p. 11; BR 1736(48)(2), *Home Waters and the Atlantic*, vol. II, pp. 218–23; Roskill, *The War At Sea*, vol. 1, pp. 291–2.

10. Roskill, *The War At Sea*, vol. 1, pp. 373–8; Hinsley, *British Intelligence in the Second World War*, vol. 1, p. 331.

11. NHB, BR 1736(7)(48), The Passage of the Scharnhorst, Gneisenau and Prinz Eugen through the England Channel, 12 February 1942, pp. 1–5.

12. *Ibid.*, p. 13; Redford, 'Inter and Intra-Service Rivalries and the Battle of the Atlantic', pp. 913–16, 923–4. In August 1941 the Butt Report, which analysed over 600 photographs taken at the moment bombers released their bombs, concluded that only one in five Bomber Command aircraft were dropping their bombs within five miles of a target in Germany, falling to one in ten if the target was in the Ruhr. The Air

Staff and Bomber Command refused to accept the findings of this independent report. Post-war analysis suggests that not fewer than 49 per cent of British bombs dropped on south-west Germany between May 1940 and May 1941 fell on open countryside: see R. Davis, *Bombing the European Axis Powers* (Maxwell, Al, 2006) pp. 29–30; D. Richards, *The Royal Air Force 1939–1945*, vol. 1 (London, 1953), p. 239; C. Webster and N. Frankland, *The Strategic Air Offensive Against Germany 1939–1945*, vol. 1 (London, 1961), pp. 178–80.

13. NHB, BR 1736(7)(48), The Passage of the Scharnhorst, Gneisenau and Prinz Eugen through the England Channel, 12 February 1942, pp. 14–17; *The Times,* 14 February 1942, p. 5.

14. NHB, BR 1736(34)(48), The Attack on St Nazaire.

15. B. Ruegg and A. Hague, *Convoys to Russia* (Kendal, 1993), pp. 20–5, 84; A. Hague, *The Allied Convoy System 1939–1945* (St Catherines, Ontario, 2000), pp. 187–91; R. Woodman, *Arctic Convoys* (London, 1995), pp. 33–51.

16. Barnett, *Engage the Enemy More Closely,* p. 703; Woodman, *Arctic Convoys,* pp. 92–9.

17. Woodman, *Arctic Convoys,* pp. 213–57.

18. D. Pope, *73 North: The Battle of the Barents Sea 1942* (London, 1988).

19. Cf. Roskill, *The War at Sea,* vol. 2, p. 401. K. Poolman, *Escort Carrier 1941–1945: An Account of British Escort Carriers in Trade Protection* (Littlehampton, 1972), pp. 38–50, 123.

20. M. Howard, *Grand Strategy,* vol. 4 (London, 1970), p. 331; Roskill, *The War at Sea,* vol. 2, pp. 400, 402; TNA, ADM 205/27, minute, 10 March 1943.

21. J.D. Brown (ed. D. Hobbs), *Carrier Operations in World War II* (Barnsley, 2009), pp. 23–8.

22. Barnett, *Engage the Enemy More Closely,* pp. 739–44.

23. *Ibid.,* p. 748; Hague, *The Allied Convoy System,* pp. 188–91; Woodman, *Arctic Convoys,* pp. 441–5.

24. Roskill, *The War at Sea,* vol. 2, pp. 240–4; NHB, BR1736(26), *Raid on Dieppe (Naval Operations),* pp. 1–8.

25. NHB, BR1736(26) *Raid on Dieppe (Naval Operations),* pp. 15–16, 19, 20–30, 33–9, 50.

26. NMRN, BR1736(42)(1), Operation Neptune: landings in Normandy, June 1944, pp. 14–17; J. Ehrman, *Grand Strategy,* vol. V (London,1956), pp. 279–86, 332–5; Howard, *Grand Strategy,* vol. IV, pp. 191–275.

27. See NMRN, BR1736(42)(1), Operation Neptune.

28. NMRN, BR1736(42)(1), Battle Summary No. 39, Operation Neptune, pp. 90–107; Ehrman, *Grand Strategy,* vol. V, pp. 337–43; Roskill, *The War at Sea,* vol. 3, part 2 (London, 1994), pp. 36–53.

29. Barnett, *Engage the Enemy More Closely*, pp. 829, 835.

30. *Ibid.*, pp. 845–9; R. Neillands, *The Battle for the Rhine 1944. Arnhem and the Ardennes: The Campaign in Europe* (London, 2005), pp. 77–85, 155–7; Roskill, *The War at Sea*, vol. 3, part 2, pp. 145–6.

31. NMRN, BR1736(37), The Campaign in North-West Europe, June 1944–May 1945, pp. 47–54; Barnett, *Engage the Enemy More Closely*, pp. 850–1; Neillands, *The Battle for the Rhine 1944*, pp. 167–73; Roskill, *The War at Sea*, vol. 3, part 2, pp. 147–54.

32. NMRN, BR1736(37), The Campaign in North-West Europe, June 1944–May 1945, pp. 68–9.

Chapter 5. The War in the Mediterranean

1. CB 3302(1), Naval Staff History, *The Mediterranean*, vol. 1, p. 22.

2. D.K. Brown, *Nelson to Vanguard* (London, 2000), pp. 49–51, 55–6.

3. BR 1736(6), Naval Staff History, *Selected Operations (Mediterranean), 1940*, pp. 3–24; CB 3302(1), Naval Staff History, *The Mediterranean*, vol. 1, pp. 45–9.

4. D. Howse, *Radar at Sea* (London, 1993), p. 63.

5. BR 1736(11), Naval Staff History, *Selected Convoys (Mediterranean), 1941–1942*, pp. 9–10, 110–11; CB 3302(1), Naval Staff History, *The Mediterranean*, vol. 1, p. 45; Barnett, *Engage the Enemy More Closely*, p. 321; Roskill, *The War at Sea*, vol. 1, pp. 421–2; D.K. Brown, *Carrier Operations in World War II* (Barnsley, 2009), p. 48; BR 1736(11), Naval Staff History, *Selected Convoys (Mediterranean), 1941–1942*, pp. 9–10.

6. BR 1736(11), Naval Staff History, *Selected Convoys (Mediterranean), 1941–1942*, p. 13.

7. CB 3302(2), Naval Staff History, *The Mediterranean*, vol. 2, p. 48.

8. J.R.M. Butler, *Grand Strategy*, vol. 2 (London, 1957), pp. 439–46; M. Howard, *The Mediterranean Strategy in the Second World War* (New York, 1968), pp. 11–12.

9. CB 3302(2), Naval Staff History, *The Mediterranean*, vol. 2, pp. 68–71.

10. BR 1736(35), Naval Staff History, *The Battle of Cape Matapan*, p. 63; Hinsley, *British Intelligence in the Second World War*, vol. 1, p. 403; cf J. Greene and A. Massignani, *The Naval War in the Mediterranean 1940–1943* (Rochester, 1998), pp. 146, 148.

11. Greene and Massignani, *The Naval War in the Mediterranean 1940–1943*, pp. 146–8; Hinsley, *British Intelligence in the Second World War*, vol. 1, pp. 403–5.

12. A. Cunningham, *A Sailor's Odyssey* (London, 1951), p. 326; Hinsley, *British Intelligence in the Second World War*, vol. 1, p. 405.

13. Cunningham, *A Sailor's Odyssey*, p. 327; see also BR 1736(35), *The Battle*

of Cape Matapan, p. 8.

14. M. Simpson (ed.), *The Cunningham Papers*, vol. 1 (Aldershot, 1999), pp. 451–2, 454.

15. M. Simpson, *A Life of Admiral of the Fleet Andrew Cunningham* (London, 2004), p. 106.

16. Cunningham, *A Sailor's Odyssey*, p. 395; Simpson, *A Life of Cunningham*, pp. 106; 113BL Add MSS.

17. G. Simpson, *Periscope View* (London, 1972), pp. 101–2.

18. Barnett, *Engage the Enemy More Closely*, p. 220; Roskill, *The War at Sea*, vol. 1, p. 307; M. Van Creveld, *Supplying War: Logistics from Wallenstein to Patton,* 2nd ed. (Cambridge, 2004), pp. 184–92, 199–200; E. Grove, *The Royal Navy Since 1815* (Basingstoke, 2005), p. 195; R. Hammond, *The British Anti-Shipping Campaign in the Mediterranean 1940–1944: Comparing Methods of Attack* (Unpublished University of Exeter PhD thesis, 2011), pp. 51–2.

19. BR 1736 (52)(2), Naval Staff History, *Submarines*, vol. II, p. 277.

20. NMRN, BR1736(11), Battle Summaries 18 & 32, Selected Convoys (Mediterranean), 1941–1942, pp. 34–53.

21. NMRN, BR 1736(11), Selected Convoys (Mediterranean), pp. 55–79.

22. *Ibid.*, pp. 87–90.

23. *Ibid.*, pp. 90–7, 133–4.

24. NMRN, BR1736(31), Operation Torch: Invasion of North Africa.

25. E. Montagu, *The Man Who Never Was* (London, 1968), M. Howard, *British Intelligence in the Second World War*, vol. 5 (London, 1990), pp. 88–93.

26. BR 1736(27), The Invasion of Sicily: 'Operation Husky'; Barnett, *Engage the Enemy More Closely*, pp. 627–56.

27. Barnett, *Engage the Enemy More Closely*, pp. 686–90.

28. NMRN, BR1736(36), Battle Summary 43, The Invasion of the South of France.

Chapter 6. The Far East 1941–45

1. NMRN, CB 3303(1), Naval Staff History, War with Japan, vol. 1, pp. 33–4; E. Grove (ed.), *Defeat of the Enemy Attack on Shipping* (Aldershot, 1997), table 27.

2. NMRN, BR 1736(8)/1955, Loss of HM Ships Prince of Wales and Repulse, p. 1.

3. C. Bell, 'The "Singapore Strategy" and the Deterrence of Japan: Winston Churchill, the Admiralty and the Dispatch of Force Z', *English Historical Review*, vol. 116 (2001), pp. 614–15.

4. Barnett, *Engage the Enemy More Closely*, pp. 394–406; C. Bell, 'The "Singapore Strategy" and the Deterrence of Japan', pp. 604–34.

5. NMRN, BR 1736(8)/1955, Loss of HM Ships Prince of Wales and Repulse, pp. 9–12; BR 1736(50)(2), Naval Staff History, War with Japan, vol. 2, p. 48.

6. NMRN, BR 1736(8)/1955, Loss of HM Ships Prince of Wales and Repulse, pp. 12–17. The number of torpedoes that hit the *Prince of Wales* appears to have been overestimated. Subsequent surveys of the wreck show that there were only four torpedo hits in total and that the first hit was the fatal one. See http://www.rina.org.uk/hres/Death%20 of%20a%20Battleship%20-%202012%20update.pdf (accessed 9 January 2013).

7. NMRN, BR 1736(50)(2), Naval Staff History, War with Japan, vol. 2, p. 68.

8. *Ibid.*, pp. 70–2.

9. *Ibid.*, pp. 94–9.

10. *Ibid.*, pp. 124–6.

11. *Ibid.*, pp. 127–8.

12. Barnett, *Engage the Enemy More Closely*, p. 863.

13. NMRN, BR 1736(52)(3), Naval Staff History, Submarines vol. 3, pp. 6–8.

14. *Ibid.*, pp. 11–17.

15. *Ibid.*, pp. 114–16.

16. *Ibid.*, pp. 16–17; Barnett, *Engage the Enemy More Closely*, pp. 893–4; W. Jameson, *Submariners VC* (Penzance, 2004), pp. 188–204.

17. N. Friedman, *British Carrier Aviation* (London, 1988), pp. 211, 213–17; D. Hobbs, *The British Pacific Fleet* (Barnsley, 2011), pp. 37, 40.

18. Figures from NHB 'Pink lists' for December 1941, 1942, 1943, 1944 and August 1945 include all warships listed as operating or refitting in/ around the Indian Ocean and Far East; that is, at various times: China Fleet, East Indies Command, Eastern Fleet, RAN, RNZN, British Pacific Fleet, as well as attached Allied 'Free' navies.

19. NHB, BR 1736(50)(4), Naval Staff History, War with Japan, vol. 4, pp. 181–2; Brown (ed. Hobbs), *Carrier Operations in World War II*, p. 79.

20. NHB, BR 1736(50)(4), Naval Staff History, War with Japan, vol. 4, pp. 209–10; Barnett, *Engage the Enemy More Closely*, p. 871; Brown, *Carrier Operations in World War II*, pp. 80–1; Hobbs, *The British Pacific Fleet*, pp. 39–41.

21. NHB, BR 1736(50)(4), Naval Staff History, War with Japan, vol. 4, pp. 214–22; Barnett, *Engage the Enemy More Closely*, pp. 871–3; Grove, *The Royal Navy since 1815*, pp. 209–10; Hobbs, *The British Pacific Fleet*, pp. 41–54.

22. NHB, BR 1737(50)(6), Naval Staff History, War with Japan vol. 6, pp. 38–42.

23. NHB, BR 1736(50)(6), Naval Staff History, War with Japan, vol. 4, pp. 24–6; Hobbs, *The British Pacific Fleet*, pp. 63–107.

24. NHB, BR 1737(50)(6), Naval Staff History, War with Japan, vol. 6, pp. 199–203, 209; Grove, *The Royal Navy since 1815*, p. 211, Hobbs, *The British Pacific Fleet*, p. 145.

25. Hobbs, *The British Pacific Fleet*, chapter 8.

26. NHB, BR 1737(50)(6), Naval Staff History, War with Japan, vol. 6, pp. 196–9, 202–5.

27. Barnett, *Engage the Enemy More Closely*, pp. 890–2; Hobbs, *The British Pacific Fleet*, pp. 126–58, 175–99, 252–93.

Bibliography

Unpublished material
The National Archives
Admiralty papers
Cabinet Office papers
Air Ministry and Air Staff papers

Naval Historical Branch
An Account of Seventeen Convoys Conducted by Capt R. H. R. MacKay
Monthly Anti-Submarine Reports
Naval Staff Histories
Naval Staff Battle Summaries
Pink Lists

National Museum of the Royal Navy
Naval Staff Histories
Naval Staff Battle Summaries

Newspapers and periodicals
Daily Express
Daily Mail
Daily Mirror
Hansard
Manchester Guardian
The Times

Books and articles
Allen, H.R., *Who Won the Battle of Britain?* (St Albans, 1974)
Ashworth, C., *RAF Coastal Command 1936–1969* (Yeovil, 1992)
Barnett, C., *Engage the Enemy More Closely* (London, 1991)
Beesly, P., *Very Special Intelligence* (London, 2000)
Behrens, C., *Merchant Shipping and the Demands of War* (London, 1955)

Bell, C., 'The "Singapore Strategy" and the Deterrence of Japan: Winston Churchill, the Admiralty and the Dispatch of Force Z', *English Historical Review*, vol. 116 (2001)

Brown, D.K., *Nelson to Vanguard* (London, 2006)

Brown, J.D. (ed. D. Hobbs), *Carrier Operations in World War II* (Barnsley, 2009)

Buckley, J. *The RAF and Trade Defence 1919–1945* (Keele, 1995)

Burn, A., *The Fighting Captain* (Barnsley, 1993)

Butler, J.R.M., *Grand Strategy*, 6 vols. (London, 1957–76)

Calder, A., *The Myth of the Blitz* (London, 1991)

Cunningham, A., *A Sailor's Odyssey* (London, 1951)

Davis, R., *Bombing the European Axis Powers* (Maxwell, Al, 2006)

Friedman, N., *British Carrier Aviation* (London, 1988)

Gardner, W.J.R., *Decoding History* (London, 1999)

Goette, R., 'Britain and the Delay in Closing the Mid-Atlantic "Air Gap" during the Battle of the Atlantic', *The Northern Mariner*, vol. 15 (2005)

Goldrick, J., 'Work Up', in S. Howarth and D. Law (eds), *The Battle of the Atlantic 1939–1945* (Annapolis, MA, 1994)

Greene, J. and A. Massignani, *The Naval War in the Mediterranean 1940–1943* (Rochester, 1998)

Grove, E., *The Royal Navy since 1815* (Basingstoke, 2005)

Hague, A., *The Allied Convoy System 1939–1946* (St Catherines, Ontario, 2000)

Hammond, R., *The British Anti-Shipping Campaign in the Mediterranean 1940–1944: Comparing Methods of Attack* (Unpublished University of Exeter PhD thesis, 2011)

Hessler, G., *The U-Boat War in the Atlantic 1939–1945* (London, 1989)

Hinsley, F., E. Thomas, C. Ransom, R. Knight, M. Howard, *British Intelligence in the Second World War*, 5 vols. (London, 1979–90)

Hobbs, D., *The British Pacific Fleet* (Barnsley, 2011)

Howard, M., *The Mediterranean Strategy in the Second World War* (New York, 1968)

Howse, D., *Radar at Sea: The Royal Navy in World War 2* (London, 1993)

Jameson, W., *Submariners VC* (Penzance, 2004)

Larew, K., 'The Royal Navy in the Battle of Britain', *The Historian*, vol. 54 (1992)

Lavery, B., *Churchill's Navy* (London, 2006)

——, *In Which They Served* (London, 2008)

Levy, J., *The Royal Navy's Home Fleet in World War II* (Basingstoke, 2003)

Llewellyn-Jones, M., *The Royal Navy and Anti-Submarine Warfare, 1917–49* (London, 2006)

Macintyre, D., *U-boat Killer* (London, 1999)

Milner, M., *The U-Boat Hunters* (Annapolis, MA, 1994)

Montagu, E., *The Man Who Never Was* (London, 1968)

Neillands, R., *The Battle for the Rhine 1944. Arnhem and the Ardennes: The Campaign in Europe* (London, 2005)

Peden, G.C., *Arms, Economics and British Strategy* (Cambridge, 2007)

Poolman, K., *Escort Carrier 1941–1945: An Account of British Escort Carriers in Trade Protection* (Littlehampton, 1972)

Pope, D., *73 North: The Battle of the Barents Sea 1942* (London, 1988)

Price, A., *Aircraft Versus Submarine* (London, 1980)

Ray, J., *The Battle of Britain: New Perspectives* (London, 1996)

Rayner, D.A., *Escort*, 2nd ed. (London, 1955)

Redford, D., 'The March 1943 Crisis in the Battle of the Atlantic: Myth and Reality', *History*, vol. 92 (2007)

——, 'Inter and Intra-Service Rivalries and the Battle of the Atlantic', *Journal of Strategic Studies*, vol. 32 (2009)

Richards, D., *The Royal Air Force 1939–1945*, 3 vols. (London, 1953–54)

Roskill, S.W., *The War at Sea*, 3 vols. (London, 1954–61)

Rowher, J., *The Critical Convoy Battles of March 1943* (London, 1977)

Ruegg, B. and A. Hague, *Convoys to Russia* (Kendal, 1993)

Simpson, G., *Periscope View* (London, 1972)

Simpson, M., *A Life of Admiral of the Fleet Andrew Cunningham* (London, 2004)

—— (ed.), *The Cunningham Papers*, 2 vols. (Aldershot, 1999–2006)

Smith, K., *Conflict over Convoys* (Cambridge, 1996)

Smith, M., *Britain and 1940* (Abingdon, 2000)

Speller, I. (ed.), *The Royal Navy and Maritime Power in the Twentieth Century* (London, 2005)

Syrett, D., 'The Safe and Timely Arrival of SC130, 15–25 May 1943', *American Neptune* (1990)

——, *The Defeat of the German U-Boats* (Columbia, SC, 1994)

——, 'The Battle for Convoy HX133, 23–29 June 1941', *Northern Mariner*, vol. 12 (2002)

Terraine, J., *The Right of the Line* (London, 1985)

——, *Business in Great Waters: The U-boat Wars 1916–1945* (London, 1989)

Van Creveld, M., *Supplying War: Logistics from Wallenstein to Patton*, 2nd ed. (Cambridge, 2004)

Webster, Sir C., and N. Frankland, *The Strategic Air Offensive Against Germany 1939–1945*, 4 vols. (London, 1961)

Williams, M., *Captain Gilbert Roberts and the Anti-U-Boat School* (London, 1979)

Winton, J., *Ultra at Sea* (London, 1988)

Woodman, R., *Arctic Convoys* (London, 1995)

——, *Malta Convoys* (London, 2000)

Index